# By the Book

## A One Year Devotional Through the Bible

# DAVID GORDEUK

GoLive
Publications

A Publishing Ministry of Hobe Sound Bible Church
PO Box 1065
11295 SE Gomez Avenue
Hobe Sound, FL 33475
www.hobesoundbiblechurch.com

Written by Dr. David A. Gordeuk
davidgordeuk@hobesoundbiblechurch.com

Cover design by Mark Going
Interior design by Mark Going and Jonathan Slagenweit
Proofed by Janice Gordeuk, Janene Fiala, and Louise Crouse

ISBN 978-0-9845192-0-0

Printed in the United States of America

Second Printing: May 2012
05-12-500-JO

# A One Year Devotional Study Through the Bible — from Genesis to Revelation

It is not always easy for families to keep up a consistent devotional life. The fast pace of living, conflicting schedules, competing media, and unexpected interruptions make doing devotions an exercise in discipline. In addition, some families struggle with what to do to make devotions meaningful. This devotional book can be of help. Here's how.

These studies are designed to aid families or individuals to go through the story line of the Bible in one year. It can be used as part of family devotions or personal quiet time. The study covers the high points of the Biblical story presented chronologically so that basic doctrines of the faith emerge as the story develops. Though each day has a devotional format, theology has not been omitted. The basic Wesleyan themes of God, man, sin, salvation, sanctification, and holiness are presented along the way. There are two tracks in the studies. One is the basic discussion of the question presented at a level that most children over the age of six can understand. This is followed by "Thinking Deeper," a more in-depth discussion of the subject. In addition to theological issues, subjects discussed touch on world view, apologetics, creationism, and practical Christian living.

One goal of these devotionals is to encourage regular devotions for at least five days each week. This devotional guide is a companion for your Bible. Included in each lesson is a reference from the Bible. The Bible passage should be read first. The question that follows is intended to stimulate reflection on the passage read. The comments written each day are explanations and illustrations of the truths that have been asserted. So each day there is a Bible passage, question and answer to memorize, and a basic commentary. Every Friday is review day, so all four questions of the week can be reviewed.

If you will spend several minutes each day with the Bible and this devotional book, by the end of a year you will have been exposed to the high points of the Biblical record in chronological order, and you will also have considered basic Christian doctrines. In addition, you will establish a pattern for your devotions that will bless your spiritual life in the future.

CREATION

**Bible Reading:** Genesis 1:1; Psalm 102:24-27

# Q1. Who was in the beginning?

### A. God was in the beginning.

God was in the beginning. We read in the Bible that "Before the mountains were brought forth, or ever thou hadst formed the earth and the world, even from everlasting to everlasting, thou art God" (Psa 90:2 KJV). We can't really understand it, but God had no beginning and no ending. You were once a little baby. There was a time before you were born that you did not exist. But God always was. He never had a beginning.

A young boy and his friends were exploring on a college campus. They walked to the basement of a large building. The floor was made of old bricks. "This floor is a hundred years old," said one of the older boys who had studied about the building. "Wow," thought the boy, "I'm standing on something a hundred years old!" He thought about that for a long time. A hundred years is a long time. But the world was created thousands of years ago. Yet, before that, God was there. He always was and He always will be.

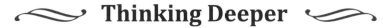

## Thinking Deeper

Christians begin with the eternal God. On the other hand, atheists begin with eternal matter. If matter is eternal, then there is no creator of matter. That means we have no God to whom we are accountable. God is not necessary, nor real. Karl Marx and Vladimir Lenin were materialists who promoted communism. They saw religion as their great enemy, because it placed material things beneath God. For them the only thing that mattered was materialism. So they killed people who believed in God. Why not? Since there is no God and only material things, then it is not wrong to kill people who get in the way. Who would they answer to? Not God, since God is a Spirit and they only believed in material things. According to those who have studied communism's effect on mankind, more than 100 million people were killed by communists in the Twentieth Century. Contrast that with the accomplishments of Christians who believe God tells them to love people. They have built hospitals and schools in nations around the world, dug wells for people in drought, helped with food, clothing, and shelter in natural disasters, and were involved in other efforts to alleviate pain and suffering in the world. What we believe is extremely important.

*We can't really understand it, but God had no beginning and no ending.*

**Bible Reading:** Isaiah 42:5-11

# Q2. What did God do in the beginning?

## A. In the beginning, God created the heavens and the earth.

When did it all begin? Some people believe that what makes up the world has always existed, but that is not true. There was a beginning. There was a time when all things started. Back then, whenever that was, God created the heavens and the earth. That was the beginning. Everything we see, hear, or touch came from the time that the Bible calls the beginning. God had no beginning and will have no ending. But the heavens and the earth were created in the beginning. God is the One who created it all. "Thou, even thou, art LORD alone; thou hast made heaven, the heaven of heavens, with all their host, the earth, and all things that are therein, the seas, and all that is therein, and thou preservest them all; and the host of heaven worshippeth thee" (Nehemiah 9:6 KJV).

## ∽ Thinking Deeper ∽

There are people who believe that matter evolved from nothing. Somehow a radiant energy field began vibrating, and bang! the energy transformed itself into matter. The matter then organized itself into complex arrangements of protons, neutrons, and electrons which organized themselves into molecules and then into all the complex arrangements of the elements that make up matter as we know it. All this was guided by the evolutionary principle of increasing complexity and organization. At the beginning of all this was supposedly a vibrating energy field. But where did that come from, and what was the guiding mechanism that organized all the complexity? There is no answer. We are to take by faith their assumptions that it all happened by a great accident of empty space. (Who created the space?) The Bible declares that in the beginning was God, who out of nothing (ex nihilo) created the universe according to His laws and ordered everything according to His decrees. Believers have their faith in the eternal God, instead of having faith in nothing.

> *There was a beginning. There was a time when all things started.*

---

# TABLE OF CONTENTS

**Bible Reading:** Job 38:1-7

# Q3. Was God created?

### A. No. God was before all things and He created all things.

God has always been. He existed before anything was ever created. There is no one who came before God. No one could have created God, because there was nothing before Him. God had no mother or father. He is the first that ever was, and He was always there.

If you went to the moon, you wouldn't find any roads or sidewalks or paths or trails. Years ago astronauts landed there and walked around. But they didn't find any footprints, because no one had ever been there before except God. He created it in the beginning when He created everything. "Before the mountains were brought forth, or ever thou hadst formed the earth and the world, even from everlasting to everlasting, thou art God" (Psalm 90:2 KJV).

## Thinking Deeper

Before He created anything, was God lonely? We know from the Bible that God is One God in three Persons. There is God the Father, God the Son, and God the Holy Spirit – Three in One. From eternity past God has existed in perfection, part of which is His perfection in love. God is love. The Trinity, one God in three Persons, has always existed in perfect love. Francis Schaeffer in *The God Who is There* said , "Within the Trinity, before the creation of anything, there was real love." Although God is greater than we can imagine, yet we can identify with this aspect of God. We can experience love. That helps us understand that although God is Creator, He is also Person. He is not merely a Star Wars type "force." He is not merely the totality of all things, as pantheists claim. He is a divine person who loves. We can know Him and experience His love.

> *No one could have created God, because there was nothing before Him.*

**Bible Reading:** John 1:1-3

# Q4. Was anything made without God?

## A. No. God made all things.

Who made the sky? Who made the sun, or the stars, or the moon? Who made the earth and the trees and the grass and the flowers? Who made the oceans and the lakes and the streams? God made it all. God is the Creator. He made everything. A preacher named Jonah said, "the God of heaven...hath made the sea and the dry land" (Jonah 1:9). There is nothing anywhere that God didn't make.

What about a cake? Did God make that? When a boy's mother bakes a cake, she takes flour that came from wheat that God made. Then she takes sugar that grew in sugar cane that God made. She takes other things that God made and stirs them together and then puts it in a pan and bakes it in the oven. The mother made the cake, but she did it using things God had already created. So it is really true that God made everything.

### ⤳ Thinking Deeper ⤸

Materialists believe that matter is what matters. They see the universe as self-existing. Yet, they have no adequate explanation for the existence of matter. What mechanism sustains it? Evolutionists explain things on the basis of natural processes, but they have no explanation for the existence of those processes.

A teacher in Cuba was making fun of the existence of God. She told the students that they would have a test. They were to close their eyes and ask God for ice cream. When they opened their eyes, there was no ice cream. "See," she said, "God didn't answer your prayers. Now close your eyes and ask Castro for ice cream." While their eyes were closed, the teacher had some helpers place small cartons of ice cream on each student's desk. When they opened their eyes, there was ice cream on their desks. "See, Castro answered your prayers, but God didn't." One student in the class objected. "I want to thank Castro for bringing the ice cream to class, but I also want to thank God for making the grass for the cow to eat so it could give Castro milk to make the ice cream from." Nothing was made without God.

> *There is nothing anywhere that God didn't make.*

**Bible Reading:** Colossians 1:12-17

**Questions in Review**

Q1. Who was in the beginning?
> A. God was in the beginning.

Q2. What did God do in the beginning?
> A. In the beginning, God created the heavens and the earth.

Q3. Was God created?
> A. No. God was before all things, and He created all things.

Q4. Was anything made without God?
> A. No. God made all things.

Have you ever been afraid? A little boy named David was home alone in a thunderstorm. He was so afraid that he crawled under a bed, waiting for the storm to end, and wishing his parents would come home. Finally, the storm ended, and he crawled out from under the bed. It's not wrong to be afraid of things like thunder and lightning, tornados or hurricanes. But it is always good to remember that God is bigger than any of those things and He can help us. He made everything and He knows how to protect us. The Bible says, "The eternal God is thy refuge, and underneath are the everlasting arms" (Deuteronomy 33:27 KJV). A refuge is a safe place. God is our safe place when we trust Him. The shepherd boy David wrote, "What time I am afraid, I will trust in thee" (Ps. 56:3). Next time you are afraid, remember to trust in the Lord.

*He made everything and He knows how to protect us.*

## ∼ Thinking Deeper ∼

The Mormon belief system says that God has evolved into what He is from being like we are. They state it like this: "As we are, God once was. As God is, we can become." But the Bible says that God was in the beginning, and at that time created the world, as well as the stars, planets and galaxies. The eternal, unchangeable God did not evolve from man. And no man is going to be another God over his own universe. God has made it clear that from the beginning He created all things, and that nothing has ever been created that He didn't create. There never has been another God, and there never will be another. God created all things apart from Himself. He is not in the flowers or rocks or trees, but He made them all. We live in a special place, created by God, and we are responsible to Him as we live in His world.

CREATION II

**Bible Reading:** Genesis 1:1-8

# Q5. How many days did God take to make things?

### A. God made things in six days.

Have you ever wondered why we have seven days in a week? It is because that is how God started it. When He created things, He took six days. Then He rested for a day. That was the first week. That was the beginning. After creation, time has been measured by days and weeks and months and years. God has created things so that the stars and sun and moon all move together perfectly. Everything is in order because God has made it that way.

On October 17, 2007, in Key West, Florida, the sun rose at 7:26 AM. Did you know that in ten years from that date, October 1̶ Key West at 7:26 AM? God keeps perfect time! He seven days. The first six days He worked, and the s̶ then on the sun has been rising and setting right on

## ∿ **Thinking Deep**

During the French Revolution, the lead government decided to experiment with a ten day get rid of the old ideas that were influenced by the a week was seven days, they wanted to change it. ten day week, wrote, "No creation of the republic hold of the priests over their superstitious dupes." T into twelve months of thirty days, but then they ha they designated as holidays! It didn't take long fo experiment was a failure. The government could c failed to re-do the time that God had already put int

Atheists have a major problem. They act as own laws, yet they live in a world that God created. of Paul's day knew better, for they understood that and have our being" (Acts 17:28).

**Bible Reading:** Genesis 1:9-13

# Q6. What did God make in six days?

## A. God made heaven and earth, the sea and everything in them in six days.

How could God make everything in six days? It is because with God nothing is impossible. For God, time is not a problem. He can make things in an instant. Of course it seems impossible for us to understand how God could have created so much in six days. But God can speak and make things happen just by His words. That's how He made everything. He spoke and it happened. "Through faith we understand that the worlds were framed by the word of God" (Hebrews 11:3).

Jesus showed how God can do what seems impossible by speaking. He was with his disciples in a boat in a storm. The waves were about to sink them when Jesus spoke to the storm. Immediately it was calm. Because He is so great, he can do anything.

## ᭺ Thinking Deeper ᭺

There is a theory that things came into being by what is called the Big Bang. It all supposedly started with the explosion of a "primeval atom." We are not told where that atom came from, and no one really knows anything about it. We are told that the Big Bang happened anywhere from ten to twenty billion years ago. After that, the universe began evolving into what it is today. All this supposedly happened by natural processes, without any designer, and without any mechanism in place to channel the energy into any organized form.

Faith concepts have been criticized for explaining things that ignorant people don't understand. Yet this so-called scientific theory of the origin of the universe is based on speculation without any real understanding. It is built on guesses upon guesses. The Bible is clear that our understanding about how the world came into being is by faith. Our faith is in the eternal God, who is capable of doing anything.

*For God, time is not a problem.*

**Bible Reading:** Genesis 1:14-23

# Q7. What did God make in the first three days of creation?

**A. On day 1, He separated light from darkness.
On day 2, He separated water above the sky
from water below the sky.
On day 3, He separated land from water and
made plants.**

Does your room look better if it is a mess, or if it is in order? When you pick up your clothes and toys and put them in their right place, your room looks neat and attractive. You actually feel better when you walk into a neat room than when you walk into a messy room. If things are scattered around, your room looks messy, and you probably don't feel good about it. When God made the world, He put things in order. He put the sky in its place, the water in its place, the land in its place, and the plants where they belonged. He separated things and put them where they belonged, "and God saw that it was good."

## ∼ Thinking Deeper ∼

The Biblical record shows that the order found in the universe came about because of God's power and direct creative activity. What began "without form and void" took on order and fullness because God made it that way. It continues to have order because God continues to keep it orderly. The second law of thermodynamics indicates that things tend to become more disorderly. Left to themselves, things fall apart. A major problem with the theory of evolution is that it must explain how things became more complex and more orderly without a controlling force. The standard answer is that "natural selection" is that force. But that really explains nothing. It gives no means by which chaos is directed into order, and then kept in order. On the other hand, the Bible declares that God created and is sustaining the worlds and life. Jesus "is before all things, and by him all things consist [are held together] " (Colossians 1:17). If Jesus were not holding things together, everything would immediately and completely fall apart. He who created order is sustaining that order.

> *He put the sky in its place, the water in its place, the land in its place, and the plants where they belonged.*

*THE FALL OF MAN*

**Bible Reading:** Job 38:4-7

## Q9. What was all of creation like when God made it?

### A. All of creation was very good, including man.

Alex drew a picture on a piece of paper. While he was drawing, he made a hole in the paper with his pencil. His picture was ruined. He threw it away. He threw several pictures away because he ruined them. He kept trying, though, until he drew one he thought was pretty good. He saved that one and his mother put it on the refrigerator. The waste basket was half full of rumpled papers that Alex had ruined. He took it out to the trash can.

When God created things, He didn't have to take out the trash. In the Bible we read, "Good and upright is the Lord" (Psalm 25:8). Because God is good, everything He made was good. He made a good world. He made good trees and good flowers and good animals. After He made man, He looked at everything He made and "saw that it was very good." Nothing that God made was bad. He didn't have a trash can for things that He ruined. Everything was just right the first time God made it.

## Thinking Deeper

One of the chief objections to Christianity is that there is pain and suffering in the world. If God is good, how can He allow such misery? How could a good God create a world that is so full of violence and suffering? On its face, this seems like a reasonable argument, but it misses something important. It assumes that the world that now is reflects the world as God originally created it. Those who argue this assume "uniformitarianism," that is, that the world's processes now in place have always been this way. As the inspired Peter wrote, they presume that "all things continue as they were from the beginning of the creation" (2 Peter 3:4). But that is not true. Things now are not as they were. God created everything in such a way that when He finished, He concluded that it was very good. What is now is different than what was then. Major changes have happened. It is a misrepresentation of reality to conclude that God created a world full of pain, suffering, and death. Those were absent from God's perfect creation. Someone else must take the blame for evil in the world. What God made was very good.

> *When God created things, He didn't have to take out the trash.*

**Bible Reading:** Gen. 2:15-17

# Q10. What rule did God make for Adam and Eve in the Garden of Eden?

## A. They were not to eat of the tree of knowledge of good and evil.

A seven year old boy was praying at the altar. He wanted to be right with God, but as he prayed he remembered some raspberries he had eaten. It's not wrong to eat raspberries, but it is wrong to take what doesn't belong to you. He had eaten them in his neighbor's garden without permission. That was wrong. So as he prayed, he realized that he needed forgiveness. He also needed to make restitution by going and offering to pay for the raspberries. When he did, he felt a great burden leave him.

When Adam and Eve were in the garden, they were free to eat whatever was there – except for the fruit of that one tree. That didn't belong to them. It belonged to God, and He told them not to eat it. Since God created all things, He could decide what to give to man. He gave man all the fruit except from that one tree. God was very good to man to give him so much.

## Thinking Deeper

Couldn't God have created man in an environment where man had no opportunity to disobey? Think about it. If there were no opportunity to obey, there would be no concept of obedience. If there were no obedience there would be no concept of Lordship. Man with no laws at all would not have the ability to obey God. When Jesus said to his disciples, "If ye love me, keep my commandments," he was connecting love and obedience. God is love, and God wanted man to love Him. In the Garden of Eden there was one place where man could very clearly show love for God. He could be obedient about the tree of knowledge of good and evil. He had the opportunity to obey God's command and in doing so he had the opportunity to show his love for God. God's command was in place to encourage man to love Him.

Man was created on a distinctly different level than the animals. God never gave the animals such a prohibition as He gave man. Animals were not capable of an obedient, willful love to God in the same way that man was. In fact, after creation, animals were to relate to man. They came before Adam who gave them names.

*God was very good to man to give him so much.*

WEDNESDAY

**Bible Reading:** Romans 6:23

# Q11. What did God say would happen if they ate the forbidden fruit?

## A. They would die the same day.

Joey's father told him not to let their dog, Sport, out of his pen. "He could get run over if he runs to the road." But Joey wanted to play fetch with the dog, so when his father wasn't looking, he opened the gate. The dog seemed happy to run after the ball and bring it back. Joey threw the ball high. It bounced out on the road. "Stop!" yelled Joey. But Sport was too excited to listen. He ran onto the road, right in front of a car. The driver tried to stop, but couldn't. The car ran over Sport. He was dead. Joey was frightened. He ran to his room, crying. How sad he was that his dog died. He wished he had listened to his father.

When God placed man in the Garden of Eden, He didn't make many rules. The only rule we know about was that God told man not to eat of the fruit from one tree. That was only one rule. But God told Adam that if he broke that rule he would die. God gave the rule to Adam to spare him from the trouble and sadness that sin brings. God wanted Adam and Eve to be happy in the Garden of Eden, so he gave them instructions not to eat from the tree of knowledge of good and evil. God didn't want man to die.

## Thinking Deeper

Why did God give rules? Did He do it to make man miserable? Is God a killjoy who doesn't want man to have any fun? That is what many people think about God's laws. He makes restrictions so that man can only live an austere life. But think about what God did. He placed Adam and Eve in a beautiful garden. He gave them everything they needed. There were many, many kinds of plants and trees. The Garden of Eden was full of wonderful colors, delightful odors, and a whole array of delicious fruit to enjoy. They were in paradise. There was only one restriction, don't eat of the fruit of the tree of knowledge of good and evil. The rule was made for man's benefit. God's law was to protect man from that which was harmful. There was pleasure in eating the forbidden fruit, but it would only last for a moment. The knowledge of good and evil would bring death. God gave the law to protect man. God gives rules for our benefit. "O that there were such an heart in them, that they would fear me, and keep all my commandments always, that it might be well with them, and with their children for ever" (Deuteronomy 5:29). It is out of love for us that God gives laws to protect us from that which is harmful.

> *God gave the rule to Adam to spare him from the trouble and sadness that sin brings.*

# Q12. Who tempted Eve to doubt God's word?

### A. The serpent tempted Eve to doubt God's word.

Nicholas was a good ice skater and a great help to his hockey team. He got into some trouble at home, and his father told him he could not play hockey for several weeks. But just that week his team was to play against another team that was really good. One of his friends persuaded Nicholas to play. "You can come over to my house and use my skates. Tell your dad that you're coming over to study. He'll never find out." Nicholas listened to his friend and played the game. However, his father sensed something was not right and went to the hockey rink during the game. He saw his son playing. When Nicholas got home, his father was waiting for him. He didn't get away with his disobedience.

Eve was in the Garden of Eden when the serpent came to her and tempted her to disobey God's word. In fact, the serpent contradicted God's word. "Ye shall not surely die." Eve listened to Satan's lies instead of God's truth. She ate it and then gave it to Adam. They both disobeyed God. But they didn't get away with their disobedience. God knew what they did. Nobody can ever hide what they do from God.

*Eve listened to Satan's lies instead of God's truth.*

## ∼ Thinking Deeper ∼

Aldous Huxley was an atheist who believed in naturalism. He believed that all phenomena have natural causes and there is nothing supernatural. He admitted that his belief system of meaninglessness liberated him from any restraints. His was a philosophy of lawlessness. No one had any right or standing to tell him anything was wrong. If you erase God from your thinking, you end up like Huxley with no restraints, except death. Satan's lie that there is no death as a result of sin does not change the fact of death. Huxley died. He suffered the result of sin, even though he didn't believe in it. Satan's lies are no refuge from the truth of God.

Satan came to Eve in the form of a serpent. He can also assume other forms in his efforts to cause us to doubt God's word. He can come "as a roaring lion," or "as an angel of light." He can come as a whisper in our ear, or through the words of a friend who asks us to compromise God's ways, or through an author of a book that questions God's word. He may ride into your thinking on the words of a teacher that questions the Bible, or through a program that promotes evolution, or through philosophies that tell us that only natural processes can explain creation and existence. When God's word is questioned, you can look behind the question and somewhere find Satan's influence.

**Bible Reading:** 2 Corinthians 11:1-3

## Questions in Review

**Q9  What was all of creation like when God made it?**
>   **A. All of creation was very good, including man.**

**Q10 What rule did God make for Adam and Eve in the Garden of Eden?**
>   **A. They were not to eat of the tree of knowledge of good and evil.**

**Q11 What did God say would happen if they ate the forbidden fruit?**
>   **A. They would die the same day.**

**Q12 Who tempted Eve to doubt God's word?**
>   **A. The serpent tempted Eve to doubt God's word.**

Jacob was happily playing with one of his Christmas presents when he saw an advertisement for a new game for his Play Station. "Mom," he begged, I need that new game!" She thought a moment, then said, "You have plenty of games already and you don't have time to play all of them. I don't think you need a new one." Now Jacob was not happy. He wanted that game. Other kids had it. Why couldn't he have it? Jacob was grumpy all day because he kept thinking about the game he couldn't have.

Eve was in a perfect garden with more than enough fruit of all kinds. Yet when she was tempted by the forbidden fruit, she gave in to the temptation. Satan tempted her by making her think she didn't have everything that she needed. When we forget how good God is and how He gives us everything we really need, we can become unhappy. Then Satan has a great chance to tempt us to do wrong. We should be thankful for the things we have. That will help us avoid Satan's lies.

> *Satan tempted her by making her think she didn't have everything that she needed.*

## ∼ Thinking Deeper ∼

One of the great methods in advertising is to create discontent, and then promise that the product will fill that void and bring contentment. Analyze the ads you see or hear and note how many of them use this technique. They start by pointing out something in which you are supposedly deficient. You're not as handsome or beautiful as you could be. You don't have as good of a car as you could have. You have the wrong credit card. Your complexion is in need of some help. Your razor is wrong. You have the wrong cologne. You don't go to the right places for vacation. Your job is less than it could be. You don't make nearly enough money. You use the wrong paper towels. Your kitchen floor is not as clean as it should be. The answer to all these flaws is to buy their product. Instantly, you will be beautiful and have just what you've always wanted. Eden is only a purchase away. That is until you see the next ad. Proverbs says that "the eyes of man are never satisfied" (Proverbs 27:20). Satan used that technique on Eve and it worked.

THE FALL OF MAN II

**Bible Reading:** Genesis 3:6, 1 Timothy 2:14

# Q13. What did Adam do when he ate the fruit Eve offered him?

## A. Adam disobeyed God when he ate the fruit.

God intended Adam and Eve to have a wonderful life in the Garden of Eden. But Eve was tricked by the serpent. Satan, who was actually speaking through the serpent, told Eve that she would become wise if she ate the fruit God told them not to eat. So Eve ignored God's word and ate the fruit. Adam was not tricked. He knew it was wrong but ate it anyway.

A story is told about a bear and a fox who went fishing. When they came to the pond, they read a sign which said, "No Trespassing!" While they were thinking about what to do, an osprey called to them from the pond and told them that the fish were really biting. However, the bear and fox decided to obey the sign. They went over the hill to fish in a stream where it was okay to fish. While they were fishing, Mr. Crow came flying overhead with some news. He had seen the sheriff arrest the osprey for trespassing. The end of the story has the bear and the fox eating fish, while the osprey is sitting in jail. Adam and Eve could have continued living in paradise if only they had obeyed God. Instead, they disobeyed and brought great trouble upon the world.

## ～ Thinking Deeper ～

Why is it that a woman is prohibited in the church from taking an authoritative position over the man? According to Paul's inspired first letter to Timothy, the reason has to do with what happened in the Garden of Eden. Although Eve ate the forbidden fruit first, Adam carries the blame for bringing sin on the world. Eve was deceived by the serpent when she ate the fruit. We can only speculate about what would have happened had Adam refused to follow her lead. Adam was not deceived by the smooth talking serpent. He knew what he was doing was wrong. But he did it anyway. The onus of sin being brought into the world rests on him. When Paul wrote that a woman is not to take authority over a man, he refers to Eve's predilection to deception. It has nothing to do with ability or intelligence. Adam, as the head of the human race (the first Adam), bore a great responsibility as the authoritative leader of the home. Although he tragically failed that test, the position of leadership has not been taken from him. Adam bore a great responsibility of leadership, and fathers and husbands bear that same responsibility. It is God-given.

*God intended Adam and Eve to have a wonderful life in the Garden of Eden.*

**Bible Reading:** Genesis 3:6-11

## Q14. Why did Adam and Eve hide from God?

### A. They hid from God because they had sinned.

Why do we wear clothes? Have you ever thought about it? Whose idea was it for people to need to cover up? All over the world, whether it is hot or cold, people sense the need to cover themselves up. This all started in the Garden of Eden after Adam and Eve disobeyed God. Suddenly they felt ashamed. They needed clothes, but they didn't have any. Before they sinned they didn't need clothes. Some people think they were covered in a holy light. Even though they didn't have clothes at first, they didn't feel shame. After they sinned they knew they were naked, and they were ashamed. They tried to cover up with leaves. When God found them hiding, He saw their shame and provided clothes for them. "Unto Adam also and to his wife did the LORD God make coats of skins, and clothed them" (Gen. 3:21).

## Thinking Deeper

Having a sense of modesty is natural. As children develop, the awareness of their need to cover their bodies also develops. In Christian homes, that sense is to be encouraged. The Bible has quite a bit to say about modesty as a guide to how Christians dress themselves. (The priests who ascended stairs in O.T. worship were to cover themselves for decency purposes; men and women were directed to wear clothing that distinguished the sexes; 1 Timothy requires "modest apparel.") Every day most people in the world rise and get dressed. In more affluent societies many people spend significant time deciding on what outfit to wear for what occasion. It is a part of life that we take for granted. It is also a part of life that does not go unnoticed by the tempter. The same liar that told Eve she wouldn't die if she ate the forbidden fruit, now tells her descendents that it is not shameful to uncover their bodies. Adam and Eve both knew they should cover themselves, lest they be ashamed. When people lose their natural shame, they are accepting the falsehood that the innocence of Eden can be recovered by pretending. This present world accepts immodesty because of the deception of Satan. This is in spite of the natural awareness, which has been part of the human experience since Eden, that modest clothes are necessary. Immodesty is not only uncouth. It is also un-Christian.

*When God found them hiding, He saw their shame and provided clothes for them.*

**Bible Reading:** Genesis 3:12-15

# Q15. What hope did God give to Adam and Eve even though they sinned?

## A. God promised that one day the seed of the woman would bruise the serpent's head.

A big part of feeling guilty after doing wrong is wondering if anyone will still like you after what you did. Adam and Eve hid from God because they were guilty. They had disobeyed. When God spoke to them, He didn't ignore their sin. A lot of bad was coming because of what they had done. It was quite clear that Satan used trickery and deception to start the process that led to all the evil. He had lied. The Bible calls him the "father of all liars" (John 8:44). But even though they did wrong by listening to Satan's lies, God told them that something good was going to come. Somehow, through "the seed of the woman" the head of the serpent would be bruised. Jesus would be the seed of the woman, and through Him God was planning to destroy Satan's power. He was giving hope for mankind.

## ～ Thinking Deeper ～

The belief system referred to as Deism states a belief in God as Creator, but doesn't believe that God intervenes in the world He created. It contends that God put all the physical laws in place, and since then has essentially abandoned the world. That is certainly not the description of God that we find in the Bible. God came to walk with man in the cool of the day. God was involved in bringing man to account for eating the forbidden fruit. God changed the arrangements of the world from its beginning state of paradise in the Garden, to its present condition of being under the curse. And along the way God made prophecies that He was intimately involved in fulfilling. This first recorded prophecy is one of hope in the midst of the curse. Here is the beginning revelation of the plan that God had to redeem humanity. If God used the "seed of the woman" to bruise the serpent's head, then Deism must be rejected. When Jesus died on the cross and cried, "It is finished," he fulfilled this prophecy. He destroyed the power of Satan. The serpent's head was bruised. Hope for man is accomplished. The vilest sinner can be delivered from sin and the power of Satan because God through Jesus intervened on our behalf. Thank the Lord!

*God was planning to destroy Satan's power.*

**Bible Reading:** Genesis 3:16-19

## Q16. What did God do because Adam disobeyed Him?

### A. God brought a curse on the world because Adam disobeyed Him.

There's an old story about a king who brought a farmer and his wife into his palace for a night. He gave them a wonderful room with a magnificent bed, fine chairs, and fruit to eat. On a stand was a pot with a lid on it. The king told the couple to enjoy the room and make themselves comfortable. "Just don't open the lid of that pot." They did enjoy the room, but kept looking at the pot. After a time, the farmer's wife became very curious. "I wonder what is in that pot," she said. "We're not to look in it," said her husband. But her curiosity overcame her. Finally, she persuaded her husband to help her lift the lid and peek into the pot. When they did, two mice jumped out and ran out of the room. When the king returned, he saw that the mice were no longer in the pot. "You must return to your farm," said the king. He had intended to give them great gifts, but their disobedience instead caused the king to send them home in disgrace. They lost an opportunity to enjoy great blessings.

When Adam and Eve sinned, they lost their place in the Garden of Eden. Their sin caused a curse to be brought on the world.

*Their sin caused a curse to be brought on the world*

## ～ Thinking Deeper ～

Atheists denounce the existence of God, because they say a loving God would not have made a world filled with imperfection and suffering. They miss the point that the world God made was a perfect environment, without suffering, but was marred because of man's sin. Instead of blaming man for his responsibility for the trouble in the world, skeptics blame God for making an imperfect world, and then deny that there is a God because the world is not perfect. The fact is that the earth was cursed as a direct consequence of man's disobedience. God didn't create an imperfect world. It became imperfect because when man sinned he brought the curse upon himself and all of creation. Therefore, "The whole creation groaneth and travaileth in pain together until now." (Romans 8:22) Paul's inspired writing reveals that the suffering in the world can be traced back to the sin of the first Adam. "In Adam all die" (1 Cor. 15:23). But because of the "second Adam," the Lord Jesus Christ, all things will one day be restored.

**Bible Reading:** Isaiah 43:25-27

**Questions in Review**

**Q13. What did Adam do when Eve offered him the fruit?**
  **A. Adam disobeyed God when he ate the fruit.**
**Q14. Why did Adam and Eve hide from God?**
  **A. They hid from God because they had sinned.**
**Q15. What hope did God give to Adam and Eve even though they sinned?**
  **A. God promised that one day the seed of the woman would bruise the serpent's head.**
**Q16. What did God do because Adam disobeyed Him?**
  **A. God brought a curse on the world because Adam disobeyed Him.**

Davy threw the baseball hard at the spot he had marked out as a strike zone on the cinder block wall. Crash! The ball missed the target and broke a window. He retrieved his ball and went back to the pitching spot. Surely he could do better. He wound up and let the ball fly. Double crash! He hit the frame right between two windows and broke them both. Now he was in trouble. He had broken three windows on two pitches. He couldn't believe it. His dad would find out when he came home from work. Slowly Davy picked up the broken glass. He dreaded the thought of his dad coming home. But when he did come home, Davy had a bit of a surprise. His dad forgave him! He still had to fix the windows, but his dad showed him love.

> *God showed his mercy by promising a savior.*

After Adam and Eve sinned, they knew that they had done an awful thing. The beautiful life they had been given was ruined. The world would never be the same. The beauty of that perfect garden would be marred by the curse. But all was not hopeless. God showed his mercy by promising a savior.

## ❧ Thinking Deeper ❧

Someone wondered why Noah didn't squash those two mosquitoes that were on the ark. Behind that question is the question of why did God make mosquitoes and other such pests in the first place? Was it for food for bats and birds? Before the fall of man we have no record of a predator/prey dynamic. Something significant must have happened to all of the creatures following the curse. Henry Morris in *The Genesis Record* suggests that after the curse harmful mutations changed the nature of many of the created beings. It appears that the relationship of the creatures to one another also changed for the worse. This world of stalking, killing, and eating other living creatures, with the accompanying suffering and death, is not God's original creation. Blame sin.

# MAN'S WICKEDNESS

**Bible Reading:** Romans 5:12, 17-19

# Q17. What came into the world because of Adam's sin?

## A. Death came into the world because of Adam's sin.

"Mommy, hug me. Mommy, hug me!" The little boy had been in the hospital for weeks, and couldn't understand why his mother wouldn't hug him. What he didn't know was that the doctor had told his mother that if she touched him, she would get the disease from him. There was no cure. If she hugged him, she would die, too. But her heart was too full of love for him to keep ignoring his pleas. She hugged him. The smile on his face was worth a million dollars. His mother loved him and was with him, even though he was sick. A few days later he died. And then, just as the doctor had warned, she got the same awful disease. Yet, she was glad she had hugged her son. It was a mother's love.

When Adam sinned, death came into the world. We who are descended from Adam face death. Even though man had fallen into sin, God loved the world. He wanted to save the world, so He sent Jesus, His Son, into the world. But coming into the world as a human being meant Jesus would have to die. He would face the result of sin. He would die on a cross. God sent Jesus into the world even though He knew Jesus would die. It was the Father's love.

## Thinking Deeper

Some skeptics object to Christianity because they blame God for not caring about man. If God is love, why does he allow suffering in the world? Why is there disease and deformity? If He is powerful, why doesn't He do something about injustice?

These questions stem from the view of God promoted by the Deists, who believe God created the world and then became uninvolved. There are no miracles, no salvation, no divine intervention. If Jesus existed, he certainly wasn't God, because God does not interfere with man. We are on our own. Practically, this is the same as atheism.

But this is not the Christian view of God. God is involved in the world, and has been since creation. God was involved with man in the Garden and after the Fall. He showed His care by giving them clothes when they were naked, and by driving them out of the Garden so they wouldn't eat of the tree of life and live forever in their state of sin (Genesis 3:22). God was involved when He prophesied that a redeemer would come to save the world, and He was involved when He sent His Son to die for the sins of mankind. He is involved now in extending His love to "whosoever will...take the water of life" (Revelation 22:17).

*When Adam sinned, death came into the world.*

**Bible Reading:** Genesis 4:1-8

# Q18. Who was the first murderer?

### A. The first murderer was Adam's son Cain, who killed his brother Abel.

Danny and David were having an argument when David became so angry that he grabbed a hammer and started after his brother. Fortunately, Danny was quick enough to get away before something terrible happened. When their mother learned what had happened, she took David into her bedroom. "What is in your heart is what makes people murderers," she said with a concerned tone in her voice. "You need to ask God to take that out of your heart." David went to his knees, realizing that she was right.

Cain was so angry with his brother that he killed him. That was the first of many murders. Because of Adam's sin, people are born with a sinful nature. It is important for even children to seek God's cleansing in their hearts. Without God's grace, all people are capable of doing evil things. King David, the Psalm writer, understood that. He wrote, "Create in me a clean heart, O, God, and renew a right spirit within me" (Ps. 51:10).

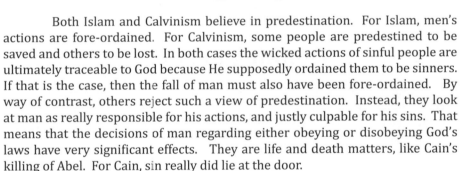

## ❧ Thinking Deeper ❧

*Without God's grace, all people are capable of doing evil things.*

Both Islam and Calvinism believe in predestination. For Islam, men's actions are fore-ordained. For Calvinism, some people are predestined to be saved and others to be lost. In both cases the wicked actions of sinful people are ultimately traceable to God because He supposedly ordained them to be sinners. If that is the case, then the fall of man must also have been fore-ordained. By way of contrast, others reject such a view of predestination. Instead, they look at man as really responsible for his actions, and justly culpable for his sins. That means that the decisions of man regarding either obeying or disobeying God's laws have very significant effects. They are life and death matters, like Cain's killing of Abel. For Cain, sin really did lie at the door.

Sin in a person's heart is something that he was born with, but that he is responsible for seeking God to remedy. Each one of us is born in sin and incapable of escaping its clutches and deception on our own. But there is good news. We are not condemned by some kind of predestination to continue living in sin. There is an open invitation for all men to come to Christ. Jesus said, "Come unto me, all ye that labour and are heavy laden, and I will give you rest" (Matthew 11:28). When we trust in Jesus Christ, we no longer live by our own strength, but by God's power, "But now being made free from sin, and become servants to God, ye have your fruit unto holiness, and the end everlasting life" (Romans 6:22).

**Bible Reading:** Genesis 6:1-5

# Q19. How wicked did man become after Adam's sin?

## A. Man became so wicked that he always did evil.

After God made man in the Garden of Eden, God said that all of His creation was very good. That means that man was also very good. God was pleased. But after Adam sinned and left the Garden, he was no longer good. In fact, man became so bad that by Noah's day man thought only evil thoughts and did evil things.

One reason that some big cities are dangerous is that gangs of bad people do nothing but cause trouble and break the laws. It is not safe to go into some neighborhoods in the daytime or at night. There are too many bad people around. Some of them are on drugs or alcoholic drinks. Many of them steal from others. Some of them are very violent. The parents of children who love them are careful to keep away from these evil people. But in Noah's day it was dangerous everywhere. Man was very wicked. Sin causes people to keep getting worse and worse.

## ∽ Thinking Deeper ∾

Margaret Mead was an anthropologist who studied a primitive tribe in the South Pacific in the first part of the Twentieth Century. She reported that she had found a people that were happy and free in their unspoiled environment. They lived without many restraints and got along very well. Her reported research fueled the idea of the "happy savage," and gave an anthropological argument for throwing off traditional moral restraints. The idea of original sin was discarded. After all, people should not be shackled by an outmoded code of morality which stifled creativity, sensitivity, and indulgence in personal pleasure.

*In fact, man became so bad that by Noah's day man thought only evil thoughts and did evil things.*

Late in the twentieth century her research was called into question. It was determined that her methods were flawed, and her conclusions were not valid. The way she described tribal life on that South Pacific Island was far from accurate. But she had succeeded in helping to push several generations of easily led academics into a false worldview. They condemned missionaries for "spoiling" the pristine lives of those who had never been influenced by the Christian view of morals.

Missionaries had been telling a different story all along. These tribal people were laden with occultism and fear. The Gospel, instead of spoiling them, actually set free those who accepted Jesus Christ. Margaret Mead's substandard research has been rightfully rejected. The concept of original sin has been substantiated, and the need for the Gospel of Jesus Christ has been confirmed all over the world.

**Bible Reading:** Genesis 6:5-7

# Q20. How did God feel about man's wickedness?

### A. God felt so sorry He had made man that He decided to destroy mankind.

A gardener planted a patch of black raspberries. The first few years the raspberries did very well. But then, some wild blackberries began growing among the raspberries. The blackberry bushes were very prickly. In fact, they became so prickly and thick that the gardener could not get into the patch to pick the raspberries. Soon, the raspberry patch was completely ruined. The raspberry patch had become too overgrown to be any good at all.

Mankind became so wicked during the days of Noah that there was nothing good left. What had been so good and pure in the Garden of Eden was now evil and wicked. God saw nothing left to keep, so He decided to destroy mankind.

*God saw nothing left to keep, so He decided to destroy mankind.*

## ⌑ Thinking Deeper ⌑

Did God predetermine that man would sin and fall into wickedness? If He had determined that man would sin, God would not have been "grieved at his heart" when man did sin. We read that God was pained in his heart by the wicked imagination of man's heart. No, it was not God's plan for man to do evil. The sin of man made it necessary for God to step in with the plan of redemption. At the same time, we must realize that God knew beforehand that man would sin. God knows all things, even before they happen. However, just because God knew beforehand that man would sin does not mean that God planned for man to sin. That is the difference between determinism and foreknowledge. Because of His foreknowledge, God had a plan in place to save man even before man sinned. We read in the Bible that Jesus is the "Lamb slain from the foundation of the world." God was not taken by surprise by what happened. He had already planned what He would do. Yet God was not unmoved by the wickedness of man. He was grieved at man's sin and decided to destroy mankind with a flood.

On a personal level, God is not surprised when we sin. He knows everything that will happen ahead of time. God has an eternal perspective which includes foreknowledge of our sins. There is also a present view of happenings that God is experiencing. He is not uninvolved. The Bible says that God is angry at the wicked every day. That is why we need to repent of our sins. We can "flee from the wrath to come" and find safety in God's Grace.

**Bible Reading:** I John 3:9-12

**Questions in Review**

**Q17. What came into the world because of Adam's sin?**
        A. Death came into the world because of Adam's sin.
**Q18. Who was the first murderer?**
        A. The first murderer was Adam's son Cain, who killed his brother Abel.
**Q19. How wicked did man become after Adam's sin?**
        A. Man became so wicked that he always did evil.
**Q20. How did God feel about man's wickedness?**
        A. He felt so sorry He had made man that He decided to destroy mankind.

"I found another one!" squealed Sarah, as she picked up a small rock from the gravel parking lot. She and her friend Julie were looking for fossils. They each had a small pile of stones that had the fossilized remains of small animals that had died many years before in a flood. The girls found those fossils in Kansas, which is in the center of the United States.

Fossils can be found in many places all over the world. With a little diligence, you can sort through gravel or rocks, and find fossils where you live. Each fossil is a record of something that has been alive. Each fossil also reminds us that something died. Before Adam and Eve, there were no fossils, because nothing had died until they sinned. When you find a fossil, remember that it was because of Adam that "sin entered into the world, and death by sin" (Romans 5:12).

*Before Adam and Eve, there were no fossils, because nothing had died until they sinned.*

## ～ Thinking Deeper ～

One of the necessary elements in evolutionary theory is gradual change in species. That means that animals must live and die. Eventually, through many generations, a new life form emerges. Charles Darwin believed that as archaeologists did more work, this important evidence for evolution would be found in the fossil record. He predicted that multitudes of transitional forms (animals that are between one kind and another, for example, part dinosaur, part bird) would be found in the fossils. But they are not there. It is one of the unexplainable aspects of evolution. Where are the fossils of intermediate forms? This concept also requires death.

Before man ever existed, according to evolutionists (including theistic evolutionists), there were millions of life forms that lived and died during the evolutionary process. But the Bible clearly says that death came into the world by sin. Before the fall of man, God said everything He made was very good. Theistic evolutionists must believe that God was calling suffering, violence, and death very good, because that is what the fossils have recorded. They must also reinterpret the relationship of sin and death. For them, death came before sin. But that contradicts the record of the scriptures. It is better to accept the presupposition that the Bible is true, than to reinterpret it to fit the very questionable and unscientific presuppositions of evolution.

*THE FLOOD*

**Bible Reading:** Genesis 6:8-9; 7:1

# Q21. Why did God save Noah during the flood?

## A. God saved Noah because he was righteous.

When Uncle Ted was a teen-ager, some of his friends climbed into a car and asked him to go along for a ride. They were off to have fun! He looked inside the car and saw that there were already too many for the car to handle safely. "Come, on," they said. "Don't miss out." But he decided not to risk going along. "No," he said. "I'd rather stay behind." Leaving him behind, they drove off, looking for fun. What they didn't count on was having a wreck, but before the night was over, most of them had died in a horrible accident. Uncle Ted was spared because he didn't go along with the crowd.

In his day, Noah was the only one in the world who kept his family from the ungodly influence of the crowd. Everyone else went along with the evil people who were out to "eat, drink and be merry." They all died. Noah stood alone in a very wicked day. Because he did, he saved himself and also his family. God saw that Noah was righteous and spared him. "Noah found grace in the eyes of the Lord" (Genesis 6:8). God gives grace to those who follow Him.

## Thinking Deeper

Every person who lives on earth is a descendent of Noah and his three sons, Shem, Ham, and Japheth. Genetically, every trait from skin color, to shape of eyes, to composition of hair of people living now can be traced back to Noah's family. All the diversity we see now came from their genetic makeup. We all come from the same family line, though that line has taken several distinct branches. If a person is human, Noah is in his family tree. You are one of Noah's descendents, just as is someone from Mongolia or Afric, or Indonesia or Taiwan. The Bible says that God "hath made of one blood all nations of men for to dwell on all the face of the earth, and hath determined the times before appointed, and the bounds of their habitation" (Acts 17:26).

To discriminate against other people based on their distinctive physical characteristics is wrong and is often based on ignorance. It is the evolutionists who have popularized the concept that man has emerged from less than human forms. Hitler was convinced that some races" were more developed than others and should be preferred, while lower races, which could pollute the gene pool, should be eliminated. Margaret Sanger, founder of Planned Parenthood, had very similar beliefs. She favored forced sterilization of inner city black people because of her desire to manipulate human genetics (a policy called "eugenics"). These leaders of evil were willingly ignorant of the fact that all people, regardless of race or station, are valuable as God's creations and all of one blood.

> *In his day, Noah was the only one in the world who kept his family from the ungodly influence of the crowd.*

**Bible Reading:** Genesis 20:11-16

## Q22. Where was the place of safety during the flood?

### A. The ark was the place God provided for safety during the flood.

Harry was an eighty-three year old man who lived on the side of Mt. St. Helens in Oregon. When the mountain began to become active as a volcano, officials from the area warned Harry to leave the mountain. They told him it was unsafe to stay. But Harry had a lot of money tied up in his lodge, and he wanted to protect it. Whatever his reason was for staying, he refused to come off of the mountain. On May 18, 1980, Mt. St. Helens erupted with such force that it sent a blast of fiery air down the mountain at 300 miles per hour, followed by a major portion of the mountain itself actually blowing up. Harry was never found. He had refused to listen to the warnings.

Unlike Harry, Noah listened to God's warning about a coming flood. He built the ark according to the instructions God gave him. Because he obeyed God, Noah, his family, and the animals with them were all safe on the ark.

### ∽ Thinking Deeper ∽

A white scrap of paper caught Japheth's eye as he was exploring the top of the mountain. It had been caught on some tree branches. He read the shaky handwriting with great interest. "As I write this, I am ankle deep in water in my sailboat galley. The pumps can't keep up with the water that keeps pouring in because of the incredible rain, which is most unprecedented in that it has never rained in the history of the world until the last few days. I have radioed some of my few remaining friends, and all them are having the same trouble. The only captain I haven't heard from is Noah, but none of us like him anyway. He's so exclusive. 'No one can be saved except on the ark.' How intolerant! We never even considered it. Our boats are modern and tested. Plus, why the ark? There are many ways to float on water. Scientists have demonstrated to everyone's satisfaction that any buoyant vessel will be sufficient for flotation on the waters. We just didn't understand rain. But still, who's to say which boat is best? If it would just quit raining! Anyway, I've got to do something fast. The water's up to my waist, and this boat can't float much longer. My plan is figure out how to get rid of all this water and to find land."

Japheth carefully folded the note and put it in his pocket. "Poor guy," he muttered to himself. "He never had a chance after he rejected the ark."

> *Because he obeyed God, Noah, his family, and the animals with them were all safe on the ark.*

**Bible Reading:** Genesis 7:17-20

## Q23. How much of the earth was covered by the flood?

### A. The whole earth was covered by more than twenty feet of water.

The highest mountain in the world is called Mt. Everest. It is part of the Himalayas, a mountain range on the continent of Asia. Mt. Everest is 29,035 feet, or 5.5 miles, high. It is about 500 miles from the Indian Ocean. If you would climb to the top of Mt. Everest and begin digging around in the rocks, you could find fossils! How did they ever get way up there? Some of them would be fossils of animals that had lived in the ocean. When did the ocean cover Mt. Everest? The answer is the flood of Noah's day. The Bible tells us that the water covered the mountains by over twenty feet of water. That's when those fossils got to the top of the mountains. The Bible has the answers for a lot of questions we have about our world.

### ❧ Thinking Deeper ❧

Did you know that many cultures in the world have a legend about man being saved from the destruction of a worldwide flood on an ark? These legends are so diverse as to have been found among peoples in Hawaii, Syria, Canada, and ancient Babylonia. At least a dozen legends include the idea of an ark being provided, and more than that have a legend of a worldwide flood.* Where did these ideas come from? It is unlikely that so many different people groups so widely separated geographically would have come up with such a story if there is not some truth behind it. When legends among primitive tribal people emerge which parallel the Biblical account of the flood, it indicates that such an event is in the collective memory of man the world over.

God has not left us without evidence of the truth of His Word. When we read in the Bible that the whole world was covered by water, we would expect to find evidence for such a claim in the world we live in. Sure enough, when we climb a mountain we find evidence that even the top had once been under water. There is rock strata laid down by water. Embedded in the rocks are fossils, many of them marine. How did that happen? The Biblical account of the universal, world-wide flood is the answer.

*(For documentation, or more details, see www.nwcreation.net/noahlegends. html )

> *The Bible has the answers for a lot of questions we have about our world.*

**Bible Reading:** Genesis 7:21-24

# Q24. What was destroyed in the flood?

### A. All living creatures on land were destroyed, except for those on the ark.

What ever happened to the dinosaurs?  The Bible tells us that all the creatures that lived on the earth died in the flood, except for the animals that were on the ark.  So the fossils of dinosaurs that are found are a reminder of how God destroyed the earth.  Remember why God destroyed the whole earth?  It was because of man's sin.  When boys and girls and moms and dads sin, they do a lot of harm.  They not only harm themselves but also those who are close to them.  In Noah's day, man became so wicked that God decided to send a flood and destroy all living things.  When man sinned, he not only harmed himself but also all the rest of the world.   Everyone in the world was destroyed because of their sin.  Except for Noah.  When Noah got on the ark, he saved his family.  He also saved the animals that were close to him.  It is important that each one of us follows Jesus.  He is the place of safety not only for us but also for those we love.

## ∼ Thinking Deeper ∼

Could there have been dinosaurs on the ark?  Yes.  There is no reason they would have had to have been full grown.  Young, small dinosaurs would have done as well as young, small crocodiles. After the flood their populations could have grown.  But something obviously happened to them.  They are considered to be extinct since none have been seen for hundreds of years.  There are stories that "dragons" were living with men in times past.  One story, which in the literature of that time was considered true, is the story of St. George and the dragon.  There are also stories from China of an emperor who had dragons as pets. These dragons may have been what we call dinosaurs.  The word "dinosaur" (meaning "terrible lizard") was not even in existence until 1841.  Since the King James version of the Bible was written in 1611, it could not have used the word.  However, the Bible does speak of creatures which fit the description of dinosaurs. (Job 40:15-24; Job 41).

Evolutionists claim that dinosaurs went extinct millions of years ago, but they are using their presuppositions of uniformitarianism and an old earth.  The presuppositions of creationists are different.  The fact of dinosaurs' extinction does not harm the story of the ark any more than does the fact that the dodo bird has become extinct.  In fact, it is a continuing reminder of the "bondage to decay" brought by the fall of man.

> *"The Bible tells us that all the creatures that lived on the earth died in the flood, except for the animals that were on the ark."*

**Bible Reading:** Hebrews 11:6-7

Questions in Review

**Q21. Why did God save Noah during the flood?**
    **A. God saved Noah because he was righteous.**
**Q22. Where was the place of safety during the flood?**
        **A. The ark was the place God provided for safety du**
        **the flood.**
**Q23. How much of the earth was covered by the flood?**
        **A. The whole earth was covered by more than twenty**
        **feet of water.**
**Q24 What was destroyed in the flood?**
        **A. All living creatures on land were destroyed except**
        **for those on the ark.**

A boy had a new pair of shoes that he had to wear to school. His other pair was at the shoemaker's. His mother said, "Don't play kickball at school. You have new shoes, so I don't want you to play." When recess came, he took off his shoes. Even though she told him not to play, he thought it would be all right since his shoes were off. When he kicked the ball with his bare foot, he felt something snap in his toe. For weeks he suffered with a very sore foot. He should have listened to his mother.

It is easy to put our own meaning into words and make them say what we want them to say so we can do what we want to do. Some put their own meaning into what God has said. Some big people are embarrassed that the Bible speaks of a flood that destroyed the whole world. They think that couldn't have happened. So they change the meaning of the story and say it didn't really mean what it says. But that is a dangerous thing to do. God says that when we change His Word, we can get very serious punishment (Revelation 22:18,19). It is important to listen to what God says, learn to understand it, and then live by it.

*It is important to listen to what God says, learn to understand it, and then live by it.*

## ❧ Thinking Deeper ☙

People who hold to the theory of theistic evolution happening over millions of years also have a very difficult time believing in the worldwide flood described in Genesis. One writer claimed to believe in inerrancy but still did not take Noah's writing at face value. He said you must see things through the eyes of the writer of the time. Noah, being surrounded by a local flood, must have felt that the whole world was under water. But Noah's view is not what is in question. It is Moses who was writing under the inspiration of the Holy Spirit. Just as Moses' writings reflects the knowledge of God when he wrote about the order of the days of creation, so too it reflects God's understanding of what happened at the flood.

The plain reading of Genesis is a major stumbling block to old earth theistic evolutionists who don't believe in a worldwide flood. Based on a straightforward reading of Genesis, the local flood theory "doesn't hold water."

# THE WORLD AFTER THE FLOOD

**Bible Reading:** Genesis 9:1-3

## Q25. How do man and animals relate after the flood?

### A. Man can eat animals, and animals are afraid of man.

Wild animals are shy creatures when it comes to man. Have you ever gone outside and seen a wild animal that didn't see you? Do you remember what it did when it finally spotted you? It probably ran. Rabbits and squirrels and birds and fish and butterflies and deer and coyotes and chipmunks and weasels and beavers: all of them are afraid of people. They hide or run or swim away when they see a person come too close.

A hunter was walking in the woods when he heard something coming his way. He paused and waited. Soon a black bear lumbered into sight. It came straight toward the hunter. When it came so close that he could have hit it with a rock, the hunter stomped his foot. That big black bear took one look and then ran off, fast. What made it run? The Bible tells us that after the flood, God told Noah that the fear and dread of man would be in the animals.

## Thinking Deeper

The first place the Bible speaks about eating meat is after the flood. That's when God told Noah that the animals were food for man. Until then, man was apparently a vegetarian. After that, God gave man instructions for eating meat. There was the instruction about not eating blood. There were later instructions about how animals should be brought to an altar of sacrifice, ceremonially offered, and then used for food. Numerous times the Bible describes how animals were used for food. Abraham had a calf killed to offer his angelic visitors. Isaac loved the venison his son Esau brought him. On one occasion, the Lord fed the Israelites in the wilderness with quail. The Lord gave detailed instructions to Moses about clean and unclean animals, and which were to be eaten and which were not. Solomon's court enjoyed different varieties of meat daily. Jesus spoke about "killing the fatted calf" in celebration of the prodigal son's return. Peter saw a vision of all kinds of animals and the Lord told him, "Rise, Peter, kill and eat." These are but a few of the times eating meat is mentioned in the Bible.

It all started after Noah left the ark. God put the fear of man in the animals and gave man permission to use animals for food. But man is not to misuse animals, for we read that "the slothful roasteth not that which he took in hunting: but the substance of a diligent man is precious" (Proverbs 12:27). As a steward of God's creation, man is to be responsible in his use of natural resources, including the animals.

> *The Bible tells us that after the flood, God told Noah that the fear and dread of man would be in the animals.*

**Bible Reading:** Genesis 9:4-7

## Q26. What rule did God give to protect man from murder?

### A. Man has authority to punish a murderer by death.

When the western part of the United States was still wild, there were a lot of stories about men who would shoot each other. It wasn't all just cowboys and Indians. One man was killed while sitting in a saloon and playing cards. His name was Wild Bill Hickok. He was a lawman who had been involved with shoot-outs with quite a few desperados. He was so quick with his pistols that no one could ever out draw him. One day, however, he was playing cards at a saloon in Deadwood, South Dakota, with his back to the door, when a man named Jack McCall stepped behind him. "Take that," he said, and shot him. Wild Bill died instantly. It was later learned that McCall had been paid to kill Wild Bill Hickok by a man who held a grudge. Jack McCall was tried and found guilty of murder. He was hanged at Yankton, South Dakota, on March 1, 1877.

The first law about murder was given to Noah after the flood. God told him that if a man killed another man, then the people who are in authority are to sentence the killer to death.

### ⚭ Thinking Deeper ⚭

God's instructions to Noah after he left the ark are sometimes referred to as the Noahic Covenant. These instructions went further than the instructions God gave man in the Garden of Eden. Man now had a societal/governmental responsibility that Adam never had. Before sin entered the world, man's relationship to other humans was without problems. There was no need for societal laws. But after the fall, sin ravaged human relationships. The evil started with Cain killing Abel, and expanded until by Noah's day "the earth was filled with violence" (Genesis 6:11). After the flood, God gave Noah instructions that confirmed what He had told Adam (be fruitful, multiply, replenish the earth), but now dealt with the need for the death penalty. Here was the beginning of the principle that the penalty must fit the crime. After Noah, Moses' writings, under the inspiration of the Holy Spirit, expanded the principle by the phrase "an eye for an eye, and a tooth for a tooth." If a man put out another's eye, his punishment was to lose an eye of his own. If he broke another's tooth, his punishment was to lose a tooth. It would not have been appropriate to merely require a tooth of someone who destroyed an eye. The eye is much more important. The punishment must fit the crime.

Later, Jesus gave instructions for individuals to use the law of love instead of relying on the legal requirements of "an eye for an eye." But for government, the law of fitting the punishment to the crime is still valid, as evidenced by Paul's inspired warning in Romans 13:4 that the authority "beareth not the sword in vain." It is the legitimate responsibility of government to protect the lives of citizens in implementing penalties for crimes that fit the crimes committed, including "whoso sheddeth man's blood, by man shall his blood be shed."

*Before sin entered the world, man's relationship to other humans was without problems.*

**Bible Reading:** Genesis 9:8-17

# Q27. What is the rainbow?

### A. The rainbow is the token of God's promise not to ever again destroy the earth by flood.

A songwriter wrote a song about rainbows that helps remind us of the rainbow colors. The first line goes like this: "Rainbows Over You, God's Blessed Vow." The first letters in those words are the first letters of the colors red, orange, yellow, green, blue and violet, which are the colors of the rainbow. If you memorize that line, you can remember the right order of colors when you draw a rainbow. The next time you see a rainbow, check to see if that is the order that the colors appear against the sky.

Rainbows are so beautiful that most people stop and look when one appears. Rainbows are in the sky for a reason. God said he put the rainbow in the sky as a reminder that he would never again destroy the earth with a flood. That didn't mean there would never be floods in various places in the world. It did mean God would never again use a flood to destroy the whole world with all the people in it like he did in Noah's day. Whenever you see a rainbow, thank the Lord for his promise to us.

## ❧ Thinking Deeper ❧

The Bible records two major changes in the earth's atmosphere after the flood. One is that before the flood, it did not rain on the earth (Genesis 2:4-6). Instead, the earth was watered by a mist that rose up from the ground. When the rains came during Noah's Flood, the whole atmosphere changed in major ways. Rain was a new thing. The second change is the creation of rainbows. God set a rainbow in the clouds, and told Noah that the rainbow was a sign of God's covenant with Noah and all mankind. This was new. Both rain and rainbows were changes on the earth after the flood. These are not incidental changes. The Bible gives descriptions of both in clear words. New things happened. This poses a challenge for evolutionists. Either they discount the Bible as pure myth, as the atheists do, or (if they are theistic evolutionists) they must somehow use a new method of interpretation of the Bible (a new hermeneutic). They would say something like this: since science has proven that rain must have occurred for millions of years, and rain and rainbows have really always been on earth, we must find the meaning behind the story of rain and rainbows. This method of interpreting the Bible would fit well with either classical liberalism (which denied the truth of the Bible), or with neo-orthodoxy (which set man's interpretation of the Bible as primary). In both cases the truth and authority of the Bible is denied. It is dangerous to give up on the historicity of the Biblical record. That is the first step to unbelief and apostasy.

> *God set rainbows in the clouds, and told Noah that the rainbow was a sign of God's covenant with Noah, and with all mankind.*

# Q28. How did God populate the earth after the Tower of Babel?

## A. God confused the language of man and scattered man over the earth.

It was the first day of first grade and Stephan had a problem. He didn't know how to speak English. His parents were both from Russia, and they spoke Russian in the home, even though they lived in America. Now Stephen went to school where they spoke only English. It was hard at first because he couldn't understand the teacher. She would say, "No school tomorrow. It's a vacation day." The next morning Stephen walked to school. No one was there. The door was locked. After he waited around for about half an hour, Stephen decided there was no school and went home. Yet Stephen didn't give up. He kept going to school until he learned to understand English. Because he liked to learn, he became a good student.

There are many different languages in the world. Some of them are very different from others. If you ever go to a foreign country, you will probably hear a language you don't understand. The Bible tells us that God confused the languages at the Tower of Babel so people would spread out over the world.

## ∽ Thinking Deeper ∽

The instructor in the college language class made fun of the Biblical account of the Tower of Babel. "We know that all of the languages on earth do not have one origin. They are too dissimilar. Therefore, they couldn't have come from Babel." But the instructor's theory of language development was not at all convincing. If, as she intimated, language evolved, then we would expect that languages have a common origin. Or the various languages would have had to have evolved simultaneously among various people groups who themselves were evolving. That is too fantastic to be believable.

Actually, the account of Babel fits the worldwide language condition the best. The Bible describes the confusion of languages in a moment, not a gradual evolving of various languages as people drifted away from Babel to populate the earth. Actually, the languages were confused at first, and then people drifted away. Language didn't change because people became separated from each other as evolutionists would predict. Rather, they divided into groups and then drifted away from each other because they couldn't understand one another's languages at all.

Contemporary linguists who hold to evolutionary theory are frustrated because they have no good clues to the evolution of language. There are no "primitive" or "simple" languages among apes or even among so called "primitive peoples," just as there are no transitional forms of evolving animals in the fossil record. The Bible's description of what we find in the world is much more believable than the theories accompanying the mythology of evolution. "The Lord did there confound the language of all the earth: and from thence did the LORD scatter them abroad upon the face of all the earth."

*The Bible tells us that God confused the languages at the Tower of Babel so people would spread out over the world.*

**Bible Reading:** Psalm 24:1-10

**Questions in Review**

**Q25. How do man and animals relate after the flood?**
   A. Man can eat animals, and animals are afraid of man.
**Q26. What rule did God give to protect man from murder?**
   A. Man has authority to punish a murderer by death.
**Q27. What is the rainbow?**
   A. The rainbow is the token of God's promise not to
      ever again destroy the earth by flood.
**Q28. How did God populate the earth after the Tower of Babel?**
   A. God confused the language of man and scattered
      man over the earth.

Have you ever heard the story of Santa Claus coming down the chimney with a sack of presents? Have you ever heard the story of how Jesus was born in a stable in Bethlehem? Both these stories are told at Christmastime. One of them is a fairy tale, and one of them is true. At Easter, there are also two stories. One is the fairy tale of a bunny who stops at the homes of good children and leaves colored eggs or candy in their baskets. The other is the true story about how Jesus was crucified on a cross and buried, and then in three days he arose from the grave. There are also two stories told about how the world became like it is. The Bible tells the true story of the sin of man, the flood, and how God confused the languages at the Tower of Babel. People who don't believe in God tell a story of how man and the world just happened over millions and millions of years, with no God. Make sure you know the Bible so you can know what is true and what is a fairy tale.

*Make sure you know the Bible, so you can know what is true and what is a fairy tale.*

## ⌒⌐ Thinking Deeper ⌐⌒

Postmodernists have basically given up on the ability of anyone to really know what is true, or even if there is something that is really true. But they don't live their lives like postmodernists when it comes to some things. They can't just decide that Kansas City is twenty miles from New York. Even a postmodernist puts more than one gallon of gas in his car to make that trip. He doesn't decide half way that New York doesn't exist, either. It's in the areas of morals and education and social interaction that people want to be post-modernists. Unless he is on a drug trip or has completely lost contact with reality, a postmodernist doesn't depend on the Easter bunny to bring him his breakfast. Even though a postmodernist decides to have an abortion, believing that what she has done is just fine, she can't deny the tears of sorrow that flow unbidden in the dark of her sleepless night.

The truth is, we live our real lives in the world that God created. His Word, the Bible, describes how things are, how they got this way, and the consequences that come for choices we make. Real truth is found in Jesus Christ.

GOD'S CHOSEN PEOPLE

**Bible Reading:** Genesis12:1; Hebrews11:8-11

## Q29. What did God ask Abraham to do?

### A. God asked Abraham to leave his country for a new country.

Jenny was excited to be going on the trip. She and her father and mother and her sisters and brothers had all left their home in Russia. They were on their way to America. After a trip on the train, they were now getting on a ship that would cross the big Atlantic Ocean. When they came to New York Harbor, they would see the Statue of Liberty. The adventure of a new country with a new language and new ways was ahead of her and her family. Best of all, the family would be free to worship God. They were leaving a communist country that taught against God, to go to a free country where people could freely obey the Bible.

When God called Abraham to go to a new country, He was giving Abraham a chance to start a new life. Abraham didn't know everything that was ahead, but he believed God would guide him. Abraham obeyed God because he believed.

## Thinking Deeper

Using Abraham as an example, Dr. Allan Brown has described faith as having three characteristics: 1) believing what God says, 2) obeying what God commands, and 3) trusting what God promises. Abraham somehow knew that God was speaking to him when he left Haran to go to the promised land. We, "having a more sure word of prophecy" in the inspired scriptures, are blessed with the clear written record of what God has said.

Some attacks on the Christian belief system attempt to undermine the truth of the Bible by claiming it has been changed over time to fit with prejudice of church leaders and their hunger for power (as in Dan Brown's *The Da Vinci Code.*) These attacks are based on a basic misunderstanding of how we got the Bible and how it has been preserved (or, as in Dan Brown's case, a not so hidden agenda to promote the ancient heresy of Gnosticism). The writings of the church fathers show that from the beginnings of the church the books included in our Bible now were the ones they considered to be inspired in the early days of the church. As far as the Bible being changed by some unscrupulous church leaders, the mountains of manuscript evidence in existence are testimony to the reliability of the Bible. The evidence shows that the Bible is remarkably unchanged.

Our enemy knows that if we doubt the truth of the Bible, then we have little reason to trust the Bible's promises or to obey its commands. On the other hand, since we have good reason to trust the Bible's reliability, our foundation of faith is strong. We can, like Abraham, believe what God says.

> *Abraham didn't know everything that was ahead, but he believed God would guide him.*

**Bible Reading:** Genesis 12:2-3

# Q30. What did God promise to Abraham?

## A. God promised Abraham a land, a nation, a name, and a blessing.

The phone rang and Colin answered. It was his dad. "When I come home, we're going fishing. Get your things ready." Colin hung up the phone. He was excited. He loved to fish. He got the poles and fishing box and took them to where the boat was tied. Then he got his hat and some sunscreen. He wanted to be ready when his father came home. It wasn't long until his father came home, and in just a few minutes they were in the boat. Colin was happy that he had everything ready. Going fishing with his dad was one of his favorite things to do. Because he believed what his father promised him, he had gotten everything ready, and they were on their way.

Abraham heard the voice of the Lord. God made him some promises. Because Abraham believed God, he was ready to do what God told him to do. If we really believe God like Abraham did, we will do what He tells us to do.

## ∼ Thinking Deeper ∼

*God said it. I believe it. That settles it.*

"God said it. I believe it. That settles it for me." This piece from a song provoked a response from someone who slightly reworded the concept. "God said it. That settles it." From the first statement, one can infer that the issue is based on one's belief. From the second, one can infer that the issue is based on the word of God. What is important in either statement is the context.

There is often a problem with songs, in that a phrase without a context becomes part of the thinking in the minds of people. If truth is based on my belief (as in the first phrase), then I am falling into the trap of existentialism, which holds that truth is authenticated by my experience. On the other hand, if the meaning is that God's truth is appropriated to me by faith, then that is a different matter.

Some things God has said are true and will come to pass regardless of my belief or my unbelief. Since He said it, that settles it. God's covenant of the rainbow is such a truth. No one's belief or unbelief affects that promise of God. But some things God has said will not come to pass unless there is faith. The conditional promises of God are dependent upon belief. In Abraham's case, God's promise was conditional. If Abraham would go to the country God showed him, God would give him the blessings He promised.

God's truth is not based on our belief or unbelief. It stands because it is true. But the benefits of God's truth to us as individuals only come as we appropriate God's promises by faith

---

**Bible Reading:** Genesis 15:1-6

## Q31. How was God going to bless Abraham's family?

### A. God promised he would have too many descendents to count.

Grandpa's favorite pictures were of family reunions when the whole family was together. He had large pictures of different reunions in various rooms of his house. He liked to take visitors to these pictures and point out his children and grandchildren. He could tell you how many there were in the family, and he knew them all by name. He was thankful for every one of them, and when he prayed he would often say, "Don't let a one of them miss Heaven."

Grandpa was like Abraham in this way. One of his best blessings was his large family. At first, Abraham was afraid he would not have children. He was old and only had servants in his house. But God promised him a blessing. His family was going to be really big!

## Thinking Deeper

For some time in America it has been assumed that the ideal family has a father, a mother, and two children. Families with four or more children are certainly not mainstream. This attitude has permeated much of American life. Children are to be planned at the convenience of the parents. The organization, Planned Parenthood, has enjoyed favorable public opinion because its very name has ridden the wave of the popularization of small and planned families. The slogan, "Every child a wanted child," also part of the equation, gives cover to the abortion complex of the culture. If a child is going to be an inconvenience, then it should be aborted. Otherwise, it could be born into a family where it might be abused. (Isn't the irony overwhelming: kill the baby so it won't be abused!) The underlying reason for this whole way of thinking is that the needs and wants of parents should be primary. Children are not to be on the scene if it inconveniences the adults. Their value is in how much they make the parents look or feel good. What a contrast to God's view of children.

When God told Abraham he was going to bless him, he told him he would have children. Children, in God's eyes were not a curse or an inconvenience, but a blessing. The Bible makes that case over and over again. "Children are an heritage of the Lord." "The fruit of the womb is his reward." "Happy is the man that hath his quiver full of them."

God calls children a blessing. When the culture sees them as a curse, then the culture is wrong. Christians' love, care, and nurture of children is a strong testimony to the culture that we reject their world view, and that we agree with God.

> *Children, in God's eyes were not a curse or an inconvenience, but a blessing.*

**Bible Reading:** Genesis 17:15-21

# Q32. Through which son of Abraham did God make a covenant?

## A. God's covenant would come through Isaac.

An elderly widow woman in Mississippi looked out her window after Hurricane Katrina. Many trees had been blown over leaving her land in a big mess. One very large tree was leaning on her roof. She had no idea what she was going to do. That afternoon, something happened that she didn't expect. Some Christian men who had heard about her need came with large equipment and began moving the trees. Another group of Christian volunteers arrived with chain saws and rakes and helped remove the brush and smaller trees. The widow stood outside her house and wept with joy. She had received an unexpected blessing.

Abraham and Sarah thought they were too old to be parents. One day they received a great surprise from God. He told them they would have a son and they were to name him Isaac. God promised them an unexpected blessing.

*The Bible has blessed people the world over for multiplied generations.*

## ∾ Thinking Deeper ∾

The Bible makes it clear that God's blessing on the world would come through Isaac. Abraham had a son to Hagar, his wife's servant, and they named him Ishmael. When God gave Abraham the promise for a son with his wife, Abraham wanted God to consider Ishmael. "O that Ishmael might live before thee!" God remembered Ishmael and promised that he would be blessed and have many descendents. However, God's plan for blessing the world was to be through Isaac. "But my covenant will I establish with Isaac."

God had promised Abraham that "in thee shall all families of the earth be blessed." That special covenant blessing was to come through Isaac. How was it to happen? One way was that God used the descendents of Isaac to be the ones who received the inspired Word of God. The Bible, both Old and New Testaments, was written almost exclusively by the descendents of Isaac, and more specifically, by the descendents of Isaac's second son Jacob, later called Israel. The Bible has blessed people the world over for multiplied generations.

Another way that all families are blessed is that "the seed of Abraham," the Lord Jesus Christ, is the savior of all who will believe in Him. Jesus, the promised Messiah, is as descendent of Isaac through his son Jacob, and more specifically, through Jacob's son Judah. So we have this definite line of blessing: Abraham, Isaac, Jacob and Judah. Through that line would come the Lord Jesus, the gift of God, who "so loved the world that he gave his only begotten son, that whosoever believeth on him should not perish but have everlasting life."

**Bible Reading:** Deuteronomy 7:1-8

**Questions in Review**

**Q29. What did God ask Abraham to do?**
    **A. God asked Abraham to leave his country for a new country.**
**Q30. What did God promise to Abraham?**
    **A. God promised Abraham a land, a nation, a name, and a blessing.**
**Q31. How was God going to bless Abraham's family?**
    **A. God promised he would have too many descendents to count.**
**Q32. Through which son of Abraham did God make a covenant?**
    **A. God's covenant would come through Isaac.**

When he was a little boy, Stephen heard about a neighbor man who died. He looked up into the big sky and made a wish. "I wish I would never have to die, and could live forever." When he grew older, he still had a desire in his heart to live forever. But he didn't know anything about the Bible or about Jesus. After he grew up, he went to a Bible conference. He heard about Jesus and how on the cross Jesus died for his sins. He decided he very much wanted Jesus to be his savior. Would Jesus save someone like him? Yes! When he opened his heart, Jesus came in. Now Stephen had the hope of eternal life, because Jesus promised "whosoever liveth and believeth in me shall never die."

The Bible says, "Whosoever shall call upon the name of the Lord shall be saved." When you believe God like Abraham did, God will count you righteous just like he counted Abraham righteous.

 **Thinking Deeper**

John Calvin was a theologian in the 16th Century who considered the issue of predestination. St. Augustine dealt with this issue in the fourth century but did not develop it in the same detail or with quite the same emphasis as Calvin did many years later. Calvin came to the conclusion that God chose some to be saved and some to be lost. The person had no real choice in the matter. Hence the Calvinist term "unconditional election."

The concept of God's foreknowledge is a difficult concept because we, as humans, see things from our time-bound perspective. God has no such limitations. He "sees the end from the beginning." John Wesley considered this in his message "On Predestination," where he said, "We must not think they are because he knows them. No: he knows them because they are." God's knowledge of past, present, and future does not cause them, any more than our knowledge that the sun will rise tomorrow causes it. Therefore, your decision to accept Jesus as savior is not forced on you by God's foreknowledge. His invitation is open: "Look unto me, and be ye saved, all the ends of the earth" (Isaiah 45:22).

> *When you believe God like Abraham did, God will count you righteous just like he counted Abraham righteous.*

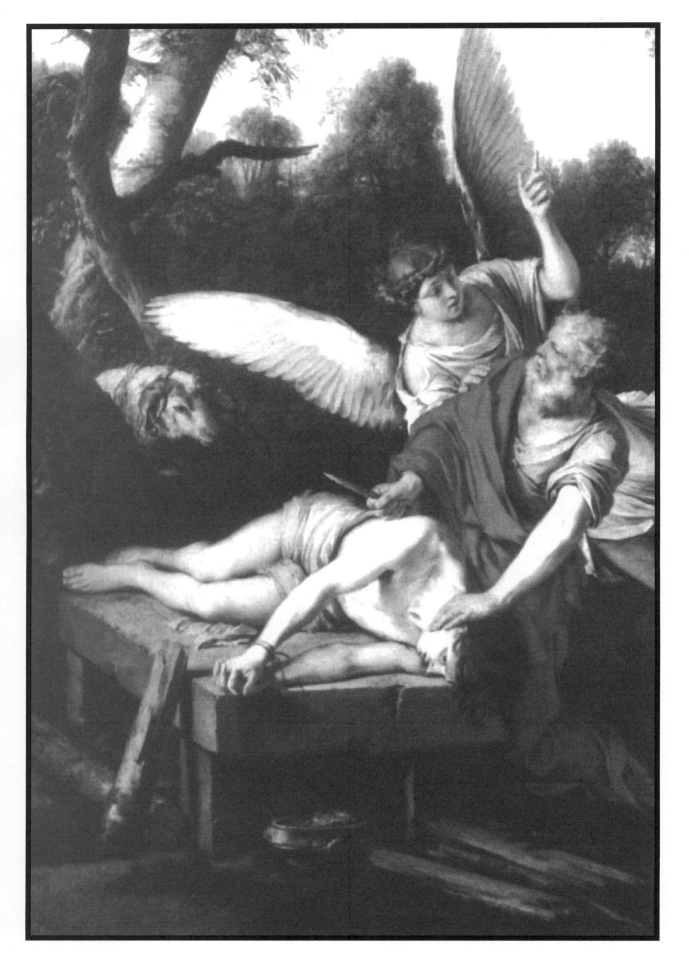

*ABRAHAM'S FAITH*

**Bible Reading:** Genesis. 21:1-6

# Q33. How old was Abraham when Isaac was born?

### A. Abraham was a hundred years old when Isaac was born.

Do you know any lady who is ninety years old? What would you think if someone told you that a ninety year old woman was going to have a baby? You would probably think they were joking. You would probably laugh. We don't think of ninety year old ladies having babies. We think of them having great-great-grandchildren. We don't see women in their nineties going around pushing baby strollers. That's for younger women.

When Sarah, Abraham's wife, was ninety years old, God told her she was going to have a baby. When she heard from the Lord that she was going to have a baby, she laughed. She may have thought it was impossible. Even though she was old, Sarah did have that baby. They named him Isaac. God sometimes does impossible things to show His power. With God, nothing is impossible.

## Thinking Deeper

According to Guinness World Records, the oldest mother to give birth is a Spanish woman who had twins at age 67. That's pretty old to start raising a baby! Despite the interest we have in world records, we need to be a bit cautious about the supposed validity of some of the records reported. According to their literature, "A fact may only become a Guinness World Record™ when it's tested, verified and elevated above all suspicion." Their reported fact about the world record age of a woman giving birth is 67. In contrast, the Bible tells us that people used to live longer than they do now, and some people had children when they were hundreds of years old. Abraham was one hundred and Sarah was ninety when Isaac came along. But the Guinness records ignore these and many other facts. It could be inferred that, according to them, Biblical accounts and details are not "above suspicion." The Bible is not a category that fits with their way of thinking. The trouble with this is that as far as the modern world is concerned, the Bible has become marginalized. It is not worthy to consult in matters of factual investigation. It has about the same legitimacy as a fairy tale. Given this view of the Bible, it is no wonder that much of the world leaves it on the shelf, collecting dust.

The contrasting Christian worldview sees the Bible as very relevant to daily life. It is God's revealed word, profitable for "profitable for doctrine, for reproof, for correction, for instruction in righteousness: that the man of God may be perfect, thoroughly furnished unto all good works" (2 Timothy 3:16).

*God sometimes does impossible things to show His power.*

**Bible Reading:** Genesis 22:1-2

## Q34. What did God ask Abraham to do with Isaac?

### A. God asked Abraham to offer Isaac as a sacrifice to the Lord.

A little boy had a teddy bear that he loved very much. He played with it, took it with him, and even slept with it. Although he hadn't noticed, it had become quite dirty. Its seams were coming apart. An eye was missing. One day his mother said she wanted his teddy bear. He didn't want to give it to her. But he obeyed and gave her his teddy bear. Then how he missed it! What he didn't know was that his mother had a plan for the teddy bear. In a few days she had a surprise for him. She gave his teddy bear back. It had both eyes. Its seams were sewn together. Instead of a dirty grey color, it was clean and white. She had washed it and cleaned it and then gave it back to him. How glad the boy was that he had given his teddy bear to his mother!

By faith Abraham was willing to sacrifice his son Isaac to God. But God didn't let Abraham take his son's life. God had a plan for Isaac and had a ram caught in a bush to take Isaac's place as a sacrifice. Abraham was thankful that he had been willing to obey God. God blesses those who obey Him.

*Abraham came away from the mountain with his son alive and with a new view of God.*

## ～ Thinking Deeper ～

In Abraham's day, religious devotion was often marked by the sacrifice of children. The gods would be pleased by great sacrifice. Abraham was devoted to God. Was he as devoted as the worshipers of false gods? When he took Isaac to the mountain he was proving that he was as devout as any other worshipper. He had heard the voice of the true and living God. He could do no less than offer his son. Yet Abraham believed God's promise that through Isaac many nations would be blessed. How could that happen if he sacrificed him? Abraham believed that God would raise Isaac from the dead. So Abraham took the knife to slay his son. At that moment God intervened. He had a substitute sacrifice, a ram caught in the thicket. It was the ram that served in Isaac's place. This was also a picture of how God would provide His Son as a substitute sacrifice for man, when Jesus would go to the cross.

Abraham came away from the mountain with his son alive and with a new view of God. Human sacrifice was not the demand of God. While the worshipers of false gods like Baal and Molech continued to sacrifice children, God instructed His people to offer substitute sacrifices. The value of human life, the value of children, and the value of family was preserved and protected by Abraham's experience on that mountain in the land of Moriah.

**Bible Reading:** Genesis. 22:3-14

# Q35. How did God provide a substitute for Isaac on the altar?

### A. God provided a ram caught in a thicket to take Isaac's place.

A poor old widow lady ran out of food one day. She knelt by her window and, as was her custom, prayed out loud. "Lord, please send me some food." A man happened by right at that time and heard her prayer. "That woman is foolish," he thought to himself. "She thinks God hears her prayer. I'll play a trick on her." He went to a store, bought a loaf of bread, then came back and threw it through her window. "She thinks God sent her that bread," he thought as he ran off laughing. The woman took the bread and again knelt to pray. "Lord, I don't know who it was that You sent to get me this bread, but bless him, and thank You for answering my prayer."

God provides for us in various ways. Abraham probably didn't expect to find a substitute sacrifice for his son on top of the mountain, but God had the ram there just at the right time. God will do great things for us as we have faith in Him.

 **Thinking Deeper**

God's ways are often a surprise. Abraham was likely surprised to find the ram in the thicket. Ina Ogden would probably be surprised at how widely her influence has been a blessing. She had been selected to travel a circuit where she would be able to reach thousands of people. Not long before her tour, her father was in an accident. He needed care, and she was the logical caregiver, but it meant cancelling her travel plans. Her hopes for being a blessing were dashed. After a time of adjustment, she made a conscious effort to be a cheerful Christian despite her disappointing circumstances. She never did that extensive travel tour that would have allowed her to bless thousands. But while she was doing her quiet duties, she wrote some words that were eventually put to music. Along with millions of others, you have probably been blessed with her song "Brighten the Corner Where You Are."

*God provides for us in various ways.*

God's substitutes for our plans are always better than our plans. It is because Abraham trusted God that God worked in ways Abraham didn't anticipate. Disappointments, as has been said, are opportunities for God's appointments. God loves us and plans good for us and not evil. He does work all things for the good of those who love Him. It is our place to follow Abraham's example and believe God.

**Bible Reading:** Genesis 22:15-18

## Q36. From where did a blessing come to Abraham after he offered his son?

### A. An angel came from heaven with a blessing for Abraham.

Do you know that angels are real? The Bible tells us about many times when angels visited people. Often the ones who were visited fell on their faces when they realized it was an angel. Angels are holy beings who sometimes brought messages to people from God. It was usually a very important message. Abraham had a special visit from an angel after he obeyed God. He must have been surprised and also felt very special. God blessed Abraham in a special way because Abraham believed God.

## Thinking Deeper

English literary critic and one time atheist C.S. Lewis experienced something unexpected after he became a Christian. He had been considering the claims of Christ, and the force of the truth that Jesus really was the Son of God brought him, as he said, "kicking and screaming" into the faith. What he hadn't considered was that he would find something in his life that he hadn't had before. Several years before he died, Lewis wrote about his journey to faith. He titled the book *Surprised by Joy* (1956). Lewis found that there was more to the Christian experience than bare faith. God is there, and God reveals Himself to those who come to Him in humble faith. Experiencing "the transcendent," that which is beyond ourselves, or rather He who is beyond ourselves, makes an impression that is like no other. He didn't expect it, but C. S. was surprised by joy when he believed God.

Abraham probably didn't expect the blessing he received after he had offered his son. The angel of the Lord confirmed the blessing Abraham was to receive. Abraham's faith opened a great door of blessing.

*God is there, and God reveals Himself to those who come to Him in humble faith.*

**Bible Reading:** Romans 4:1-8

**Questions in Review**

**Q33. How old was Abraham when Isaac was born?**
   **A. Abraham was a hundred years old when Isaac was born.**
**Q34. What did God ask Abraham to do with Isaac?**
   **A. God asked Abraham to offer Isaac as a sacrifice to the Lord.**
**Q35. How did God provide a substitute for Isaac on the altar?**
   **A. God provided a ram caught in a thicket to take Isaac's place.**
**Q36. From where did a blessing come to Abraham after he offered his son?**
   **A. An angel came from heaven with a blessing for Abraham.**

Misha was a young Russian boy who was dying, but Misha wasn't afraid. Before he got sick, his tutor told him about Jesus and how he could be saved. Misha knew he needed to be saved because something inside convicted him of sin. So Misha asked Jesus to wash his sins away and come into his heart. Misha believed the gospel that Jesus had died for his sins, and he found peace.

Misha wanted one more thing. He wanted his mom and dad to find Jesus. He asked them to promise they would meet him in heaven. They promised, and soon Misha died. At the grave, his mother and father talked about their promise. Before they went home, they both gave their hearts to Jesus and believed. God responds to people who believe in him. Abraham believed God, and God blessed him. We are blessed, too, when we have faith in God.

*God responds to people who believe in him.*

## ～ Thinking Deeper ～

In 1948, Richard Weaver wrote a book entitled *Ideas Have Consequences*. Weaver's point is that movements and changes in cultures can be traced to the ideas that captivate the culture. It is true in matters of faith. The idea that we are saved by faith and not by works gave rise to the Reformation. That was a reaction to the idea that the Church held salvation in its hands and could dispense it to those who did the proper works. More recently, the ancient pagan idea that the world and its diverse inhabitants have come from original simple forms has been popularized by Darwin and informs the thinking of most public education. The related idea that the world is self-existing and everything can be explained by naturalistic phenomena has captivated a significant portion of human thinking. It was at the heart of Marx's dialectical materialism which led to communism's terror and the human ovens of Hitler's national socialism.

The great Christian idea of righteousness, obtained by faith, opens the door to God's grace and has been a great blessing to the world. We who believe God have the privilege to follow the idea "of the faith of Abraham; who is the father of us all."

# Isaac's Sons

**Bible Reading:** Genesis 25:21-26

## Q37. Who were Isaac's sons?

### A. Isaac's sons were Jacob and Esau.

Gypsies are people who often don't have anywhere to call home, so they move from place to place. In one such family the mother died, leaving the father to raise five boys. They were lonely and sad and lost. But when God looked into that tent, He saw what they would be. There were six preachers in that tent. A time came when the dad heard about Jesus. He put his trust in the truth of the Gospel and became a Christian. In time, all of his boys became preachers. The most famous of them was a great evangelist who was known around the world as Gypsy Smith.

God does great things through families. He was doing something great through Isaac, and it was through Isaac's family that God would bless the world. God can make you a great blessing also. Put your faith in Him.

## Thinking Deeper

God specifically blessed the world through Isaac's son Jacob. Why not Esau? Some see the passage in Romans 9 which says, "Jacob have I loved, but Esau have I hated" as evidence of unconditional election. Adam Clarke makes the significant point that this statement is a quotation from the Old Testament book of Malachi, where the Lord, through the prophet, spoke of the posterity of Jacob and the posterity of Esau. The description of Esau serving Jacob certainly did not fit the individuals, for that didn't happen in their personal lives. It did happen, though, in their national lives in the years when Malachi was prophesying. So if it did not apply to the individuals themselves, then the interpretation that Romans 9 teaches unconditional election must be rejected. God had His sovereign purpose for the nations, but individuals in those nations are free to make own choices.

We can safely conclude that we also as individuals have the responsibility to choose to believe God. It is not predetermined what we will do. God has not made us robots who only act according to a preset program. We are truly free moral agents.

With that said, it was in the sovereign foreknowledge of God to know through which son He would choose to bless the world. That was Jacob. God could see the end from the beginning, and determined that His purposes would be served through Jacob.

*God does great things through families.*

## Q38. What did Esau do with his birth right?

### A. Esau sold his birthright to Jacob for a bowl of pottage.

Jesus told the story of a son who took his things from home and went away to have a good time. He left his home for what he thought was something better. But he ran out of money and ended up starving. He actually ate with the pigs. We know him as the prodigal son. He sold his birthright. He had a good home and a loving father, but he gave it up for something that didn't last. He was like Esau who sold his birthright for a mess of pottage.

What seems like a good idea right now may actually be a very bad thing. It is always wise to consider the outcome before you make a decision. If you are in a Christian family, you have a wonderful birthright. Don't sell it for something that will not last.

### ∼ Thinking Deeper ∼

*It is always wise to consider the outcome before you make a decision.*

In sociology classes in the 1970s, a student would learn some distinctions between upper class society and lower middle class rural society. The upper classes were more into delayed gratification, whereas lower classes were more likely to want instant gratification. This played out morally, where, according to the sociologists, lower classes were less likely to be virgins heading into marriage. If that was true then, it has certainly changed. "Generation Y" youth are characterized by instant gratification and a rejection of the mores of the older generation. The results are not good. A study reported in 2008 that 25% of teenage girls had a sexually transmitted disease. Postmodernism has made lower middle classes of everyone if we use the sociologists definitions of the 1970's.

This is not universally true. Those who honestly follow the Bible understand the value of delayed gratification. The ideals of virtue and purity are not affected by whether we are Baby Boomers, GenXers, or in Generation Y. God's ways are right, and following them brings blessings. Don't sell this wonderful birthright for a mess of postmodernist pottage.

**Bible Reading:** Genesis 26:1-5

# Q39. What did God promise to Isaac?
## A. God promised Isaac what he had promised to Abraham.

Davy wanted to know that he was a Christian. He heard how God was real to his father and mother. He saw the lives of other Christians who were different from worldly people. But was it for him? He tried to be good and read the Bible and pray. But he still wondered. One night he was in a prayer meeting at a camp in the Pennsylvania woods. As he prayed, he asked God to show him that he could know he was saved. A Bible verse came into his mind. "Behold, I stand at the door and knock. If any man hear my voice, and open the door, I will come in..." He opened his heart and sensed something very special. Jesus really did come in! What God had done for his parents and other Godly people was for him, too.

God made promises to Abraham, and he confirmed them to Isaac. God shows that his love continues from generation to generation. What God has done for others, He will do for you. Trust Him.

## Thinking Deeper

What does God want to perpetuate through you? If you are a "first generation" Christian, God wants you to "raise up the foundations of many generations." Abraham was the first of many who believed God and was therefore counted as righteous. The faith was passed on from one to another. But it had to start somewhere. If you are the first, you can be a great blessing to generations to come.

What of you who are in the line of blessings because one of those in your family tree was righteous? You are to find the faith of your fathers, keep it, and transfer it to the generations to come. "Teach it to your children, and your children's children." Jesus said that if you have been given much, much will be required of you. That means you are to keep the legacy going.

Many of us have been given the heritage of holiness. We believe God has an experience with Jesus for us that produces victory over sin in our daily lives. We believe God wants us to be a happy people because of His grace. We believe God wants us to be a reflection of the Lord Jesus Christ. What a great inheritance! Let's find it, keep it, and pass it on.

*God made promises to Abraham, and he confirmed them to Isaac.*

# Q40. How did Jacob get the blessing from Isaac?

## A. Jacob deceived his father and got the blessing.

Nicholas sneaked out of his house to play hockey when he was supposed to be studying. His father found out where he was and drove to the hockey rink. He watched his son play, then drove home. When Nicholas got home, his father asked him where he had been. "Over at my friend's house studying," he lied. "But I was at the hockey game and watched you play," said his father. Nicholas tried to trick his father. "Dad, you're not going to believe this, but there's a boy in school that looks just like me!" His dad was not deceived. He gave Nicholas a well-deserved whipping.

Jacob was a great deceiver. He got the blessing from his father because he acted like he was Esau. But there was One who saw through the deception. God did. Don't ever think you can hide from God. He knows everything.

## ∼ Thinking Deeper ∼

Neither Jacob nor Esau were great examples of virtue when they were young. Esau was willing to sell his birthright for a mess of pottage. Jacob was a deceitful conniver. Why would one of them be used to further God's plan? One thing we know is that God doesn't see what we see.

Raymond was a failure as a husband, as a father, and as a neighbor. He was an alcoholic who couldn't hold a steady job. His health failed, and he had no self esteem. Would God use a man like him? God sees the end from the beginning. He saw what Raymond would be, and God called him. One day Raymond came to himself. He confessed that he was lost and needed a savior. He called on the Lord, and the Lord heard him. Raymond was saved that day. He became a new man, a loving husband, a good father, and a minister of the Gospel. Why did God use Raymond? Because he saw what he would become.

God saw what both Esau and Jacob would become. He saw that Esau would marry pagan wives and become the head of a wild nation. He saw that Jacob would eventually become a humble believer. He chose Jacob in spite of Jacob's failures because He knew what Jacob would become.

God knows you and what you will become. If you humble yourself, He will do great things in you.

*God knows you and what you will become. If you humble yourself, He will do great things in you.*

**Bible Reading:** Hebrews 12:11-17

**Questions in Review**

**Q37. Who were Isaac's sons?**
    **A. Isaac's sons were Jacob and Esau.**
**Q38. What did Esau do with his birthright?**
    **A. Esau sold his birthright to Jacob for a bowl of pottage.**
**Q39. What did God promise to Isaac?**
    **A. God promised Isaac what he had promised to Abraham.**
**Q40. How did Jacob get the blessing from Isaac?**
    **A. Jacob deceived his father and got the blessing.**

The story of Peter Rabbit is about a family of rabbits. Flopsy, Mopsy, and Cottontail obey their mother and are rewarded by a nice meal at the end of the day. But Peter disobeys and has a very scary adventure. He goes to Farmer McGregor's garden where he is chased by the farmer. In his escape he loses his nice new clothes and barely escapes with his life. That night, instead of eating the wonderful supper with his family, he is sick in bed. The story reminds us that there are good rewards for obedience and bad rewards for disobedience. But maybe there is more to the story. If Peter goes on like he started in the story, where will he end up? Maybe, like his father, in Farmer McGregor's wife's stew.

Jacob and Esau came from the same family, but ended up a lot different. What was the difference? Jacob finally loved and obeyed God. Esau seems to have forgotten God's ways. It is important to choose to live for God.

> *Jacob and Esau came from the same family, but ended up a lot different.*

## ⌁ Thinking Deeper ⌁

Was it Isaac's fault that Esau went after pagan wives? Can we blame him for failing in raising his son? Some point to the proverb which says "Train up a child in the way he should go: and when he is old, he will not depart from it" as a proof that Isaac failed Esau. In the same way it may be assumed that it is to Isaac's credit that Jacob turned out as a man of faith. Others say that the free will of each son must be considered. Think about what the proverb says. What can a parent do? "Train up a child." Just as dogs can be trained to do specific things, children can be trained to do certain things. Train a child how to wash hands and when that child is old, he will wash his hands. The parent can train the child but cannot save the child. Only God can.

Training can give the child an advantage even spiritually because training can dispose a child to accept authority. But that is not what saves. Each child must come to the point of personal faith. That is not an issue of training. So we must reserve judgment on Isaac, just as we must reserve judgment on others who may have a wayward child. We had rather see the faith of Isaac who is remembered in Hebrews 11. "By faith Isaac blessed Jacob and Esau concerning things to come."

THE CHILDREN OF ISRAEL

**Bible Reading:** Genesis 28:10-17

## Q41. What did God tell Jacob when he dreamed of a ladder to heaven?
### A. God gave Jacob the blessing of Abraham and Isaac when he dreamed of the ladder going to heaven.

A small boy dreamed that he looked up into the sky and a very large foot appeared coming out of a cloud. The foot looked like it was a human foot and it had the color of skin. But it was so large that the boy thought it might be God's foot! The dream seemed so real that he wondered if it was true. But he never dreamed it again, and he never saw a large foot coming out of a cloud when he was awake. Did the dream have a meaning? Probably not. The boy had heard about Jesus coming in the clouds, and maybe that's what made him dream what he did. But the dream wasn't necessarily a sign from God, because that was over fifty years ago.

Most of your dreams do not have meanings, but Jacob's dream was different. Before there was a Bible, God sometimes spoke to people in dreams. God was showing Jacob about heaven. God was calling Jacob to believe in Him. He is calling us to believe in Him, too. Sometimes He still uses dreams. More often, though, God speaks to us through the Bible.

## ∽ Thinking Deeper ∽

Jacob's encounter with God began as a dream. When he awoke, he realized that God had been there. "Surely the Lord is in this place." Most of us will never have a dream like Jacob did. That doesn't mean we won't encounter God. Each of us, as an individual, must have an encounter with God. Each of our children must also have an individual encounter with God. It is one thing to hear what God has done in the past and to see how God has influenced the lives of family and spiritual mentors, but it is another thing to have a personal encounter with the God of Abraham, Isaac, and Jacob.

Although Jacob had heard of God's covenant with Abraham and Isaac, he needed his own experience with God. Jacob's encounter was unexpected. "Surely the Lord is in this place; and I knew it not." God confronts people in His own time. Jacob was discerning enough to realize that God had met him. He responded to God's initiative. Jacob certainly wasn't perfect when God called him, and the process he went through to make him the man God wanted him to be was a long one. At Bethel, Jacob began moving toward God. And it was because He was going toward God that God blessed him. As one has said, "God is not as concerned about where we are as the direction we are headed." If we head God's direction, God will bless us.

*Before there was a Bible, God sometimes spoke to people in dreams.*

**Bible Reading:** Genesis 32:24-32

# Q42. What new name did God give Jacob at Peniel?

## A. God changed Jacob's name to Israel.

Did you ever hear of Jonny Appleseed?  He was famous for planting apple trees when America had frontier country.  His real name was John Chapman.  Did you know that famous gangster Billy the Kid's name was really Henry  McCarty? Geronimo, the famous American Indian, was really Goyathlay.  Tiger Woods is really Eldrick.  Bill Clinton's name was William Blythe before it was changed.  Some people change their names. Why? Maybe they are ashamed of something in their past.  Maybe they just don't like the sound of their name.  Maybe they become famous, and a new name sticks to them.  Whatever the reason, sometimes people do change their names.  The reason Jacob's name was changed was because God changed it.  God blessed Jacob with a new heart and a new name.

## Thinking Deeper

Jacob had his name changed to Israel.  His name was changed because God changed it.  Jacob meant "heel holder" or "supplanter."  That's what he was before he knew God.  He grasped his brother's heel when he was born.  He grasped his brother's birthright, and he grasped his brother's blessing.  But God changed his heart when he wrestled at Peniel.  God told him his name would not be Jacob anymore, but Israel, which meant "God prevails."  When God prevails in a person's life, his life is changed for the better.  That doesn't mean that his circumstances are always better or his bankbook is always better, but the person becomes better.  Jacob had the mark of God in his life.  In a physical sense, he may not have been better off because he walked with a limp from then on.  But he became a better man.

Jay was a professional man who made a lot of money and had a way about him that turned things in his favor.  He also had vices.  He was a sinner.  However, God arranged circumstances that drew his attention to his deep need.  Jay came to the place where he knew that God was dealing with him.  His encounter with God changed him.  His wild days were over.  He had a new heart.  God does that with people who listen to Him.  He makes them better.
"Therefore if any man be in Christ, he is a new creature: old things are passed away; behold, all things are become new" (2 Cor. 5:17).

*When God prevails in a person's life, his life is changed for the better.*

**Bible Reading: Genesis 35:22c-26**

# Q43. How many sons did Jacob have whose families became known as "the children of Israel?"

## A. Jacob had twelve sons whose families became known as the children of Israel.

A father in Kansas was told that perhaps he had too many children. When he looked around the table during mealtime at each one of his children, he couldn't think of one he wanted to get rid of. He loved them all.

A man named Dr. Annesley had twenty-four children. His twenty-fourth child was a little girl. She was named Susanna. When she grew up, Susanna married a man named Samuel Wesley. After she was married, she had nineteen children. Her fifteenth child became a great man. His name was John Wesley. He was the minister who began the Methodist Church. That was over 200 years ago. Some people still have families with lots of children. In Bible times many people had lots of children. Jacob had twelve sons and at least one daughter. Remember his name was changed to Israel? After his sons grew up and had children, all their families together were known as the Children of Israel. God has used these large families to bless the world.

## ∽ Thinking Deeper ∾

Families can be a blessing. They can also bring heartache. A study was done of the descendents of Jonathan Edwards, the great New England preacher, who had married a godly woman. Some very influential people came from that family. One hundred of them were in some kind of ministry related profession including preachers, missionaries, and teachers. Sixty became doctors, fourteen were college presidents, and sixty-five became college professors. Three became United States senators, thirty became judges, one hundred became lawyers, and seventy-five were officers in the Army or Navy.

Another study was done of a family by the name Jukes. Among their descendents one hundred twenty-eight became prostitutes (who gave venereal disease to four hundred forty others), sixty became thieves, one hundred forty became criminals, at least two were murderers, and sixty-four spent time in what was known as the poorhouse.

A family can have a wonderful influence, but it is important that the foundation is on the Bible. Jesus said when we build our house on the rock of his sayings, our house will stand firm. The great thing about the power of God is that someone with faith can start a new family line which is godly. No matter what your past, you can "raise up the foundations of many generations."

> *A family can have a wonderful influence, but it is important that the foundation is on the Bible.*

**Bible Reading:** Acts 7:9-15

## Q44. Where did the children of Israel go when there was a great famine?

### A. The children of Israel went to Egypt when there was a great famine.

Two boys got on a train in Pennsylvania bound for the state of Washington. All they had with them was a couple of sandwiches. They hadn't thought to take much money with them. The trip lasted over two days. When they got to Chicago they were really hungry. But they still had many, many miles to go. One of them had a few coins and at a station bought some crackers. That helped them, but they were still hungry. After a night and a day, as they were going through the Rocky Mountains, they felt starved. Another night came and they got some sleep, but woke up still hungry. The day dragged on as they went through eastern Washington and on west. By the time they got to the train depot in Seattle, they were famished. A family friend met them with a car. He knew they were hungry because their mother had called. Their first stop was a steak house. How those boys ate! Their famine was over.

Israel's sons went to Egypt to find food because of a great famine. God provided food for them, but they had to go a long way from home to get it. They would stay in Egypt for 400 years.

*God provided food for them, but they had to go a long way from home to get it.*

### ⁓ Thinking Deeper ⁓

Some famines have been used for political advantage. In 1932 and 1933 the Russian communist government orchestrated a famine in Ukraine that killed millions of people. The government noted people who were somewhat successful, or capitalistic. These kulaks were undesirable since they didn't fit in with the plans for equalization. Many were taken prisoner, ushered away and never seen again. Those who were left were put on collective farms. Houses, lands, and grain were taken by the government.

People who were left on their own land were required to produce a certain quota of grain to be given to the government. The collective farms were also given quotas. These quotas in Ukraine were set so high that all the grain was taken by the communists and shipped elsewhere. Not even seed grain was left for the people. Horses, cows, babies, children; all were starving. Horses were allotted only straw to eat, yet put to work as normal. Soon they were dead. People all over Ukraine were starved because the government stole their grain and did nothing to help them. Some Ukrainians were able to escape and survive. Ten million of them did not.

This is one of many dark chapters in the history of communism. Whereas true Christians have historically gone to places stricken by famine with relief, communists actually produced a famine to further their political goals.

**Bible Reading:** Psalms 4:1-8

**Questions in Review**

**Q41. What did God tell Jacob when he dreamed of a ladder to heaven?**
   A. God gave Jacob the blessing of Abraham and Isaac when he dreamed of the ladder going to heaven.

**Q42. What new name did God give Jacob at Peniel?**
   A. God changed Jacob's name to Israel.

**Q43. How many sons did Jacob have whose families became known as "the children of Israel?"**
   A. Jacob had twelve sons whose families became known as the children of Israel.

**Q44. Where did the children of Israel go when there was a great famine?**
   A. The children of Israel went to Egypt when there was a great famine.

Far up north there are large furry animals called musk oxen. One of their enemies is the wolf pack, which will attack a young musk ox. The way the older animals protect their young is to make a circle with young in the center. The big oxen stand with their heads outward, so that the wolves cannot get to their young without facing the heavy horns of the adults. As long as they maintain their circle, the wolves cannot get to the young. But if an ox gets nervous and leaves the circle, the wolves get an opportunity to attack a single animal. It is important for the oxen to stand as a group against their enemies.

Your family can be a place of safety, as long as you stay under God's protection. Don't get nervous and run away from God. Stay in the circle of God's safety.

*Your family can be a place of safety, as long as you stay under God's protection.*

## Thinking Deeper

In 1948, Richard Weaver wrote a book entitled *Ideas Have Consequences*. Weaver's point is that movements and changes in cultures can be traced to the ideas that captivate the culture. The idea that we are saved by faith and not by works gave rise to the Reformation, reforming the church's view of works righteousness. More recently, the ancient pagan idea that the world and its diverse inhabitants have come from original simple forms has been popularized by Darwin and informs the thinking of most public education, as does the idea that the world is self-existing and everything can be explained by naturalistic phenomena. That idea is not without consequences. It was at the heart of Marx's dialectical materialism which led to communism's terror and the human ovens of Hitler's national socialism.

The great Christian idea of righteousness, obtained by faith, opens the door to God's grace and has been a great blessing to the world. We who believe God have the privilege to follow the idea "of the faith of Abraham; who is the father of us all."

*THE CALL OF MOSES*

**Bible Reading:** Exodus 1:7-14

# Q45. Why did the king of Egypt mistreat the Children of Israel?

### A. The king of Egypt was afraid that the Children of Israel would rebel and flee.

"Do you believe in God?" asked Yevgenia's teacher. Each student in the class was asked the same question. Each student said, "No", until the teacher asked Yevgenia. "Yes," she answered. "We believe in God." Yevgenia was a Russian girl attending the public school when Stalin implemented a plan to erase the name of God from the Soviet Union. Her teacher was doing her part to help promote atheism. "Don't you know how stupid it is to believe in God when science has proved that the Bible is nothing but a fairy tale?"

Yevgenia felt sorry for her teacher. "She doesn't believe in God because she doesn't know Him, and these other students don't believe in God because their parents don't know Him." Her mind wandered to her humble home, a two room log cabin where she had often seen her mother on her knees praying for her five girls and three boys. Yevgenia was convinced that her mother knew God and that God answered prayer. She maintained her faith.

Like communists, the Egyptians did not want the Israelites to worship God. They wanted to keep them as slaves, so their lives would be difficult.

## ⮜⮞ Thinking Deeper ⮜⮞

In one village* in Russia, a Christian man allowed his house to be used as a place where Christians would worship God. The communist leaders were angry. The house was next to a public school and the officials said they were afraid school children might somehow be harmed by Christian teaching. So they chased the people out and bulldozed the house. The communists did not want people to believe in God, and they didn't want children to know about God.

*Like communists, the Egyptians did not want the Israelites to worship God.*

Attacks on our faith have been increasing. People who believe the God of the Bible created all things are often considered to be ignorant. Popular atheists, Richard Dawkins, Sam Harris, and Christopher Hitchens have written scornfully about believers. The spirit of Stalin lives on. Harris said if he could get rid of either rape or religion, he'd get rid of religion. Dawkins implied that being raised Catholic is more destructive on a child than being abused by a Catholic priest. Hitchens claims that religion poisons everything. Hitchens tightly clings to Marx's idea that religion is "the opiate of the people." It's really the other way around. After Communism was in power in Russia for seventy years, one could hardly find an unpolluted body of water in the Soviet Union. Not Christianity but Marxism has been very proficient in poisoning things.

*The village was named Barnaul, in Siberia. This account is found in Anita Deyneka's book, *A Song in Siberia*, David C. Cook, 1977.

# Q46. Who was born in Egypt during this hard time?

### A. Moses was born in Egypt during the hard time of the children of Israel.

A new little baby was coming to Jonny's house. He already had two sisters, but now another was on the way. His parents wanted him to be ready, so his mother asked, "Jonny, how would you like to have a new baby?" He thought about it and then said, "No, I want to keep the one we have." Of course they were going to keep the little girl they already had, but they were getting a new baby, too. When Jonny understood, he was excited to have a new baby coming.

Before Moses was born, his parents, Amram and Jochabed, already had two children. Miriam and Aaron were their names. They must have been excited when their new brother was born. God had a plan for Moses. He would lead the people out of Egypt where they were slaves. God has a plan for everyone. He has a plan for you.

*God has a plan for everyone. He has a plan for you.*

## ∽ Thinking Deeper ∽

Some Calvinists believe that God has predetermined everyone's lives and choices, so that only the elect are able to choose to follow God. Others are predetermined to only choose rebellion. On the other end of the spectrum are the Deists, who believe that God made the world, put the natural laws in place, and then left it to run on its own. They see no divine intervention. The truth, as the Bible reveals, lies between these extremes. God made the world and its laws, but gives each individual the freedom to make choices. If the person chooses to follow God, He will intervene in that person's life and in circumstances. If the person chooses to reject God, God will still work circumstances out so that His ultimate will is done, despite the individual's poor choices.

The French Revolution occurred in a climate of unrest by the commoners in France who were disenchanted with the ruling class. This division was fueled by the atheistic underpinnings of the Enlightenment and its intellectual philosophers. The result was The Bastille, the guillotine, and the bloody deaths of multiplied thousands.

During the same time, England had similar societal divisions with the threat of bloodshed. But there was a difference. John Wesley was born when the seeds of divisiveness and hatred were already spread throughout England. God had a plan. When Wesley understood salvation by grace, he began preaching it to the masses. The results were amazing. Instead of a revolution, England had a reformation. The gospel transformed the culture. As He did with Moses in Egypt, God used Wesley in England to promote God's ways and accomplish His intentions. Don't underestimate the plan and power of God, even in dire circumstances. He is working out His purpose.

**Bible Reading:** Exodus 3:1-6

# Q47. At the burning bush, who spoke to Moses?

## A. The God of Abraham, Isaac, and Jacob spoke to Moses at the burning bush.

Two boys decided it was a good day to burn their field. The grass was dry and there was some wind. They took some matches and lit the grass. The fire burned fast – faster than they had expected. Soon it was roaring across the field toward a woods. Pine trees stood in that woods, and they would burn hot and fast. They got shovels and burlap sacks soaked in water and began fighting the fire. Others came to help. They prayed for God to help stop the fire. Just at the right time, the wind died down and the fire slowed. They were able to put it out. The boys were very thankful that God helped them put out the fire.

Moses saw a fire, but it didn't burn the bush, and it didn't spread. He knew he was seeing a wonderful thing. Then God spoke from the burning bush. Moses hid his face. He was afraid. It was God! Moses listened, and God told him that he was the God of his fathers. Moses heard God, and became a special messenger for God. Listen to God's voice. He has something special for those who hear Him. "I will hear what God the LORD will speak: for he will speak peace unto his people, and to his saints" (Psalm 84:8a).

## ⟨∼ Thinking Deeper ∼⟩

Yuri Gagarin was the first man to orbit the earth in space. He was a Russian cosmonaut whose accomplishment on April 12, 1961 was used as a propaganda piece by Russian leader Nikita Krushchev. He is quoted as saying, "Gagarin flew into space, but didn't see any God there." Instead of proving atheism, Krushchev inadvertently echoed the Bible, which says, "No man hath seen God at any time; the only begotten Son, which is in the bosom of the Father, he hath declared him" (John 1:18).

If we want to see what God is like, we must go to Jesus. Jesus, by his own existence, has declared God. The Hebrew writer spoke of the Son as "the express image of his person." That is, Jesus in human form was a "precise reproduction" of the Father. Jesus said that even his spoken words were the Father's words. "...Whatsoever I speak therefore, even as the Father said unto me, so I speak" (John 12:50). If Krushchev had really wanted to know about God, he should have gone to Jesus. Jesus shows us the Father. Jesus speaks the Father's words. He is our way to God.

Moses saw a different manifestation of God in the burning bush. Although he heard God's voice, he still didn't see Him. God told Moses, "Thou canst not see my face: for there shall no man see me, and live" (Exodus 33:20). Others in old times had different kinds of encounters with God. But when Christ came, things changed. "God, who at sundry times and in divers manners spake in time past unto the fathers by the prophets, hath in these last days spoken unto us by his Son" (Hebrews 1:1).

*Listen to God's voice. He has something special for those who hear Him.*

**Bible Reading:** Exodus 3:7-10

# Q48. What did God ask Moses to do?

## A. God asked Moses to bring the people out of the land of Egypt.

"Jenny, take the cows to the fields and watch them today. You must make sure they don't get lost. And bring them home before dark." Jenny's mother gave the small girl her instructions, packed her a lunch, and sent her off. Jenny wasn't happy. It was lonely in the fields, and the dark woods was close by. Besides, the other children were able to go to school, and now she would get behind. Somehow she managed to get through the day. As evening was coming, Jenny noticed that the cows had wandered off toward the dark woods. How could she find them? She began to cry. Just then a neighbor man happened by. "Just go on home," he said. "The cows will come home when it's time for milking." Jenny went home, and sure enough, the cows came just at dark. Jenny had done a hard job for a little girl.

When God told Moses to lead the Children of Israel out of Egypt, it was a big job. Moses didn't think he could do it, but God said He would go with him. With God's help, Moses did what God asked him. You, too, can do great things that God asks you to do because "with God, nothing is impossible."

> *You, too, can do great things that God asks you to do because 'with God, nothing is impossible.'*

## ⌁ Thinking Deeper ⌁

There is a new round of skepticism regarding the historical truth of the Exodus. What Jewish people have held as true through millennia, and the Old Testament recorded and reiterated as fact, is being questioned as to its historicity and considered as mere mythology. In other words, they are saying that the Exodus never really happened. The issues raised are highly important. If Exodus is not true, then all the other Biblical references to it are based on myth. Even the Ten Commandments come into question. For the postmodernist who wants to continue his self-centered existence with no accountability to anyone but himself, what a great relief to find that the there are no true proscriptions to his hedonism. "Eat, drink, and be merry, for tomorrow we die."

This kind of dismissing of the Bible and other historical documents is a familiar tactic of those who want reasons not to believe. The enemies of the Jewish people, for example, find it convenient to deny that the Holocaust ever took place. Such denial provides them relief from dealing with the images of skeletons in mass graves and films of people dying in gas chambers. Denial allows them to discount the testimonies of eyewitnesses as well as first-person accounts of people who survived the butchery of those grim days. They can renew their anti-Semitism with vigor without the inconvenient reminder of the inhumanity of their hatred.

When skeptics deny Exodus, they conveniently relegate the commandments to mythology, and then can excuse their lying, thieving and adultery as normal, acceptable behavior. Skepticism is convenient for those who love the ways of sin. How inconvenient for the skeptics, though, if the Bible is true, for it says "the wages of sin is death."

**Bible Reading:** Hebrews 11:24-26

**Questions in Review**

**Q45. Why did the king of Egypt mistreat the Children of Israel?**
  A. The king of Egypt was afraid that the Children of Israel would rebel and flee.
**Q46. Who was born in Egypt during this hard time?**
  A. Moses was born in Egypt during the hard time of the children of Israel.
**Q47. At the burning bush, who spoke to Moses?**
  A. The God of Abraham, Isaac and Jacob spoke to Moses at the burning bush.
**Q48. What did God ask Moses to do?**
  A. God asked Moses to bring the people out of the land of Egypt.

A talented girl who was a good student walked from home every morning to get to school. But she didn't like her walk to school. Often she was followed by bullies who made fun of her and called her names. It kept happening day after day. She told her mother that she didn't want it to keep happening. The school really couldn't monitor the streets in the morning, so the boys kept teasing her. Finally, she told her mother she was afraid and just didn't want to go. After she thought about it, her mother decided that the little girl didn't have to go to school. She could be taught at home.

The Children of Israel were treated badly by the Egyptians. God heard their cry and raised up Moses to lead them away from their trouble. "The LORD also will be a refuge for the oppressed, a refuge in times of trouble" (Psalm 9:9

*Jacob and Esau came from the same family, but ended up a lot different.*

## Thinking Deeper

Some governments outlaw the expression of Christian beliefs. Others endeavor to silence Christian thinking. For example, hate speech laws in Canada have made it mandatory for Focus on the Family Radio to tape alternate programs if the normal programming deals with homosexuality. Making any kind of judgment on that activity is considered "hate speech." Canadian broadcasters risk their licenses if they air the program.

One place that is unfriendly to ideas of faith is the science class in government schools. The concept that macro-evolution could even be questioned is too outrageous for the Darwinists to contemplate. Some scientists argue that the complexity of the cell with the information mechanism in DNA and RNA looks like it has been designed. The government schools will not let that be considered because if it has been designed, then there must be a Designer. Saying that might "establish religion." What are the alternatives? We still have the option to redress our grievance. In the meantime, Christian parents need to look seriously at Christian schools, or teaching the children at home. Maybe Dad and Mom need to be Moses, and lead the children out of Egypt.

**PLAGUES ON EGYPT**

**Bible Reading:** Exodus 4:29-5:2

## Q49. What did Pharaoh say when Moses gave God's message to let His people go?

### A. Pharaoh said he would not let God's people go.

A teen-aged boy had been going with a bad crowd. He was doing some wrong things like taking drugs. One day he went to the park. Some people were singing about Jesus. He stayed to listen. He heard a message from the Bible that told him he could be saved if he gave his heart to Jesus. He wanted to do that, so he asked for prayer. Later, he went home and told his parents. They were not happy. "We do not want you to be a fanatic." It seemed like they would rather have their son be wild and take drugs than follow Jesus.

Pharaoh didn't want the Israelites to worship God. He liked it just fine to have them as slaves. Some people have hard hearts against God. They don't want others to worship God. They are like Pharaoh, who wouldn't let the people go.

## Thinking Deeper

Some atheists are more strident in their hatred of God than others. Sam Harris, for example, said that if he were given the choice to get rid of either rape or religion, he would get rid of religion. Does that mean he would applaud all churches for changing into training grounds for violent predators of women? It is not clear whether or not he cheered on the Catholic priests who were preying on young boys. After all, they were acting more in keeping with rape than with religion.

Not all atheists go that far. Sir Julian Huxley said that even though he didn't believe in God, he noticed that people acted better who were religious than those who weren't. He was somewhat of a pragmatist in that regard. Even though he believed religion was a lie, he wanted others to follow it because it made them act better.

Much has been made over Barna's research that showed the divorce rate among evangelicals being higher than among the general population and even among atheists. Those statistics failed to consider an important fact. Fifty percent of atheists don't bother to get married. They live as though the institution of marriage doesn't exist, so their break-ups aren't reported. When that is factored in, the divorce rate among atheists is twice as high as that of evangelicals. As much as evangelicals have compromised divorce, they still act a whole lot better than atheists.

Christians should not allow themselves to fall prey to the intimidation of atheists. When atheists cite statistics to prove they do better with marriage, they are flat out wrong.

*Pharaoh didn't want the Israelites to worship God.*

**Bible Reading:** Exodus 12:3, 5, 7, 12-13

## Q52. How did the Israelites escape the plague of death?

### A. The Israelites put lamb's blood on their doorposts. When God saw it, He passed over that house and spared the firstborn.

This is an old story. A mother bird was sitting on a nest of newly hatched chicks when a snake spotted the nest and began climbing the tree. That snake wanted to eat the little birds. The father bird saw the snake coming and flew away. Higher and higher came the snake, while the mother bird just sat very still on the nest, covering her little ones. By now the snake was climbing out on the branch where the nest was. It crept very slowly toward the mother bird and her babies. The snake slithered closer and closer, its tongue flitting in and out of its mouth and its beady eyes fixed on the nest. Suddenly there was a flutter of wings. The father bird flew right to the nest in front of the snake with a red leaf in his beak. He placed the leaf on the nest, covering the mother and the little baby birds. The snake came right to the edge of the nest and stopped. The red leaf was poisonous to the snake. It quickly turned and crawled back down the tree and away in the grass. The father bird had saved his family with a special red leaf.

God told the Israelites that a plague of death was coming to Egypt at midnight. All the firstborn children would die throughout the land. But God gave them instructions to take the blood of a lamb and put it on the doorposts. God said, "When I see the blood, I will pass over you." He gave them a way of safety during the plague. The fathers in Israel saved their children from death by covering their house with the blood of the lamb.

> *Fathers have a very important responsibility regarding the welfare of their families.*

## ⤳ Thinking Deeper ⤲

Fathers have a very important responsibility regarding the welfare of their families. In the case of the Passover, the father was responsible for taking a lamb for the house. He was to paint the door posts and lintels. Dads have a great opportunity to provide protection for their families. But an absent dad will open the door to great trouble.

A study done of teens in new Zealand and the United States concluded that girls whose fathers were absent in the home were far more likely to become promiscuous and end up being pregnant without being married. That one factor, an absent father, was the significant predictor of promiscuity. British Justice Secretary, Jack Straw, linked youth involvement in gangs with absent dads. Other social problems like drug abuse, violence and crime have been shown to have a direct link to fathers absent from the home.

Christian fathers, taking the lead in spiritual matters in the home, have a powerful protective influence for good on their families.

**Bible Reading:** Romans 5:8-11

**Questions in Review**

**Q49. What did Pharaoh say when Moses gave God's message to let His people go?**
A. Pharaoh said he would not let God's people go.
**Q50. What did God do to Egypt when Pharaoh did not let the people go?**
A. God sent plagues on Egypt because Pharaoh would not let the people go.
**Q51. What was the last plague on Egypt?**
A. The last plague on the people of Egypt was the death of the firstborn in every household.
**Q52. How did the Israelites escape the plague of death?**
A. The Israelites put lamb's blood on their doorposts, and when God saw it, He passed over that house and spared the firstborn.

A man and his wife in Australia went to a creek to go swimming. Suddenly a crocodile about eight feet long grabbed the lady. Her husband knew he had to help. He jumped on the crocodile's back. It released the lady, and swam off, leaving eight open wounds from its sharp teeth. The police investigating the attack said that the husband's actions saved his wife. He was a brave man.

Moses gave the Israelite fathers instructions to save their families. Fathers who loved God and loved their families followed the instructions. They protected their families with blood on the doorposts of their houses. Fathers are supposed to protect their wives and children. There are many enemies of God and families. Fathers must be brave to fight against evil enemies.

*Fathers are supposed to protect their wives and children.*

## ∾ **Thinking Deeper** ∾

Suppose two men were on the side of a raging river and both saw a boy struggling to keep above water. One man held a rope with a life preserver tied to it. The other man had nothing in his hands. As the boy swept past them to the falls, neither man did anything. Which one was more to blame for not saving the boy?

A man is to provide for his family. "But if any provide not for his own, and specially for those of his own house, he hath denied the faith, and is worse than an infidel" (1 Timothy 5:8). When an Israelite father was told of the need to paint the blood of a lamb on the doorpost, he had to act before midnight when it would be too late to save his firstborn. That man would be worse than an Egyptian, because the Egyptian had no warning and no escape from the plague. The Egyptian didn't receive the Word from the Lord about protecting his family, whereas, the Israelite father had the warning and the instructions. If he failed to provide for his home, it is logical to conclude that he was worse than the Egyptian father. Fathers must think ahead about protecting their families with the truth of God's Word.

THE RED SEA CROSSING

**Bible Reading:** Exodus 12:29-33

# Q53. What did Pharaoh tell Moses after the plague of the firstborn?

### A. Pharaoh told Moses to take the people away from Egypt and serve the Lord.

Dan and Dave were wrestling on the living room floor. Dan was older and quite a bit bigger than Dave. He didn't have trouble pinning Dave after they wrestled for a while. What he did have trouble doing was to get Dave to give. He had him down, and asked, "Do you give?"

"No," answered Dave in a strained voice.
Dan just clamped down harder. Finally, Dave couldn't move, and he could hardly get his breath. "Do you give now?"

Dave felt like he had claustrophobia. He started feeling panicked. He had to get out. But he couldn't move. "I give!" he panted. That's when Dan let him up.

That's just a little idea of how Pharaoh must have felt. He had lasted through nine plagues, and still wouldn't listen to God. But after the tenth plague, he'd had enough. He let God's people go. Pharaoh would have been much wiser to obey God before God ever sent the plagues. It never pays to disobey God.

*Pharaoh would have been much wiser to obey God before God ever sent the plagues.*

## ∼ Thinking Deeper ∼

God will do great things for His people. He allowed the Israelite women to spoil the Egyptians by borrowing their precious jewels and clothing the night of the Passover. When they left Egypt, they had vast wealth. God did great things against Egypt on behalf of the Children of Israel. He sent the plagues and put a difference between the Egyptian homes and the Israelite homes. On the night of the Passover, God provided a way for the Israelite fathers to protect their homes from death. The father would take the blood of the lamb and put it on his doorposts and lintel. That was the sign God was looking for. He would pass over that house and not bring death.

The great things God does for us also must be under the covering He gives us. We must be under the blood of Christ. It is the blood of Christ that cleanses us from all sin. It is the blood of Christ that speaks to God on our behalf. It is the blood of Christ that protects us from Satan's attacks. "And they overcame him by the blood of the Lamb, and by the word of their testimony" (Rev. 12:11). God will do great things for us as we are under the blood of Christ.

## Q54. How did God lead the Children of Israel after they left Egypt?

### A. He led them with a cloud by day and a pillar of fire by night.

A man was in a great woods one day, trying to go to a certain place by a lake. However, he had no compass, and the day being cloudy, he couldn't see the sun to get directions. He wandered here and there and soon got the impression that he was going around in circles. Eventually, he came across an Indian who offered to help him find his way. The Indian looked around for a while, and then headed off. Every so often he would look up into the clouds. After they had gone for a time, they came to the lake at exactly the place the man wanted to go.

"How did you find this place so surely?" asked the traveler. The Indian pointed to the sky.

"Take notice of the clouds above the lake" explained the Indian. "They are a different color than the clouds above the land. I could see the map of the lake in the clouds."

God had a special way to lead the Children of Israel. He had a cloud that went before them in the day, and a column of fire at night. They could clearly see the way God was leading.

> *They could clearly see the way God was leading.*

### ∼ Thinking Deeper ∼

In 2002, a major fire broke out in the barns at Woodbine Racetrack in Ontario, Canada. Workers went into the barns and led the horses out. Thirty-four horses died in the fire. What was strange was that most of those horses had been led out of their barns. When they were left to themselves, they ran back into the fire, where they perished. Why? Speculation is that under duress they fled to what had been up to then a safe place. They went to what was familiar. But it turned out to be destructive.

God led the Israelites out of Egypt. However, He didn't lead them on the shortest route to the Promised Land. "God led them not through the way of the land of the Philistines, although that was near; for God said, Lest peradventure the people repent when they see war, and they return to Egypt" (Exodus 13:17). Think about it. The plagues were in Egypt. Death was in Egypt. Paganism was in Egypt. But God knew that as soon as the way would get rough, the Israelites would want what had been familiar. Like a horse running back into a burning building, they would likely run back to Egypt.

When we encounter times of stress, it is no time to run back to the fire. It is no time to give up on God and go back to the devil. Even though we face upheaval, committing ourselves to God's protection is the safe place. "The name of the LORD is a strong tower: the righteous runneth into it, and is safe" (Proverbs 18:10).

**Bible Reading:** Exodus 14:5-9

# Q55. Where did Pharaoh's army catch up to the Israelites?

## A. The army came upon Israel at the Red Sea.

The preacher drove up to a house in the country to make a visit. He left his car and walked to the porch. He knocked on the door. No one answered so he turned around and walked back toward his car. Suddenly, a big dog with a bad bite came around the corner and ran straight toward the preacher. With the dog after him, the preacher raced to his car, opened the door and jumped in, just before the dog caught him. The preacher breathed a sigh of relief, thankful to God he hadn't been bitten by the dog.

It wasn't long after the Children of Israel left Egypt that the Egyptian army began chasing them. Pharaoh had changed his mind about letting them go. He wanted them as slaves again. The Israelites fled to the Red Sea. That's where the Egyptian army caught up to them. Israel needed God's help to save them from the Egyptian army. Where can we go when we are chased by our enemy? We can go to God for help. "God is our refuge and strength, a very present help in trouble" (Ps. 46:1).

## Thinking Deeper

Dirk Willems is one of the best known martyrs of the Anabaptist tradition. He had been baptized as a child, but when he was an adult he had come to personal faith in Christ and felt the need to be baptized as a believer. His re-baptism was viewed as an affront to the church, so he was arrested and put unto prison. He languished in the jail for some time and lost quite a bit of weight due to the austere conditions. One day he tied some rags together and made a rope long enough so that he could escape. His route to freedom was across a pond that was frozen over. As he was crossing, he was spotted by a guard, who followed him across the pond. Because he was so light, Willems made it to land. The guard, however, broke through the ice. Hearing his cries, Willems stopped and looked back. His Christian heart of compassion was stirred by the sight of the guard struggling in the icy water. Willems went back and rescued him. The guard, now out of personal danger, captured Willems and returned him to prison. Later, Dirk Willems was burned at the stake. His compassion for his enemy has been a great challenge to Christians through the centuries.

The other part of the story, that the guard would turn on his rescuer, is a reminder of the mind set of people like Egypt's Pharaoh. They "shut up the kingdom of heaven against men: for [they] neither go in [them]selves, neither suffer...them that are entering to go in" (Matthew 23:13).

In all these things, God writes the last chapter. Dirk Willems was awarded the martyr's crown. Israel was saved by the parting of the Red Sea.

*It wasn't long after the Children of Israel left Egypt that the Egyptian army began chasing them.*

**Bible Reading:** Exodus 14:23-31

## Q56. How did God save Israel from Pharaoh's army?

### A. He made a way through the Red Sea for Israel, and then drowned the Egyptian army.

The spider spun its web carefully. Some of the threads it spun were sticky. Others were not. So that the spider would not get caught in its own web, it knew which threads were not sticky, and only walked on them. When the web was ready, the spider went to a special place to hide and watch. After a time, an insect flew into the web and got stuck. The spider ran to the insect, carefully avoiding the sticky threads of the web. It spun threads around the insect. Then the spider waited. It could have a fresh meal anytime it wanted. The spider's web was a place it could be safe, but where other insects would be captured.

The Red Sea was a safe escape for Israel, but a place of destruction for the Egyptians. When the Egyptians had the Israelites trapped beside the Sea, God opened a way for Israel to escape on dry land with the walls of the sea on either side of them. When the Egyptians followed, God caused the walls of water to come together. All the Egyptians in the sea were drowned. The same sea that was used to save God's people was used to destroy their enemies.

*The same sea that was used to save God's people was used to destroy their enemies.*

## ∼ Thinking Deeper ∼

"Let's go to Siberia. Perhaps things will be better there," suggested the Russian husband. He was offering his wife a possible alternative to having their children continue in the public school where their faith was openly attacked. Stalin had launched a five year plan to eliminate the name of God from the Soviet Union.

Instead they decided to go to the capitol and ask permission to leave Russia. The officials looked at their file-- a large family with two students almost ready to become teachers, the father a small business man—and decided that there was no possibility that this fine Soviet family could leave Russia.

Disappointed, the family turned to prayer. Could God intervene on their behalf and free them from oppression? Of course He could.

God used the government to answer their prayers. Government quotas, taxes and fines ruined the businessman, and his children were all thrown out of school. They decided to go again and ask if they could leave Russia. Now the officials saw a family that was a drain on the Soviet system, and issued their passports. The family lost no time leaving Russia. And it's a good thing, because four months later the Red Army troops came into the village, dragged off almost all of the men, and they were never seen again.

But this Christian family was safe in America, a testimony to the fact that God can "part the Red Sea" for anyone who trusts in Him.

**Bible Reading:** Exodus 15:1-13

**Questions in Review**

Q53. **What did Pharaoh tell Moses after the plague of the firstborn?**
A. **Pharaoh told Moses to take the people away from Egypt and serve the Lord.**

Q54. **How did God lead the Children of Israel after they left Egypt?**
A. **He led them with a cloud by day and a pillar of fire by night.**

Q 55. **Where did Pharaoh's army catch up to the Israelites?**
A. **The army came upon Israel at the Red Sea.**

Q 56. **How did God save Israel from Pharaoh's army?**
A. **He made a way through the Red Sea for Israel, and then drowned the Egyptian army.**

What happened when the Children of Israel went through the Red Sea was a miracle. How could walls of water stand up? It was a miracle. That is something that God does. A man had a wicked heart. He was mean to his family. His children were afraid of him. Then he heard about Jesus. He was sorry for his sins and asked Jesus to forgive him and come into his heart. His heart was changed. He became kind and gentle. His family was no longer afraid of him. This mean man had a miracle happen to him, God changed his heart.

God can work in your heart, too. "Therefore if any man be in Christ, he is a new creature: old things are passed away; behold, all things are become new" (2 Corinthians. 5:17).

*Standing amidst these possibilities is that the Bible is true and accurate.*

## Thinking Deeper

Biblical archaeologists argue about the place of the Red Sea crossing and the accurate date. Some look for naturalistic ways to explain the ten plagues that precipitated the Exodus. Some of these archaeologists are not Christians but deal with Biblical issues because archaeology veers into the Biblical story. The problems archaeologists encounter are numerous. It has been thousands of years since the Exodus. There are bits of historical records from the time, but they can be explained from various perspectives. The exact location of crossing the Red Sea has been rigorously debated. Out of all this come various conclusions: the plagues and the Red Sea crossing were rare but natural phenomena; the whole idea is mythical; only part of the Biblical record is valid. Standing amidst these possibilities is that the Bible is true and accurate.

Archaeology is a bit like other scientific efforts that deal with history. Conclusions about the observations are constantly being adjusted and re-evaluated due to new findings. These conclusions should always be viewed with skepticism, especially when they contradict the Biblical record. As has been said, the Bible is "an anvil that's worn out many a hammer." There is a reason for that. "Thy word is truth"(John 17:17).

## THE WILDERNESS

**Bible Reading:** Exodus 16:10-15

# Q57. How did God feed the Children of Israel in the Wilderness?

## A. He sent them manna from heaven.

When a robin wakes up in the morning, it needs to get some food, especially if it has baby robins in the nest. It can't go to a grocery store to buy food. It has to go find it. What if there was no food for the robin to find? It would starve and so would the little robins in the nest. But robins find food. When a robin hops around on the ground, it will stop every once in a while and cock its head to one side. It is listening. Sometimes it hears the sound of an earthworm crawling. The robin will hop toward the earthworm and grab it. Sometimes the worm is partly in a hole in the ground. The worm will try to go underground and the robin will pull on it. Usually the robin wins, and has a food to take to the nest. God has made things in the world so that birds have food to eat without going to the store.

When the Children of Israel were in the wilderness, they didn't have stores where the people could buy food. God provided them food called manna. It came down from heaven every day for forty years. It was a special miracle that God did so that the people wouldn't starve to death. "[God] had commanded the clouds from above, and opened the doors of heaven, And had rained down manna upon them to eat, and had given them of the corn of heaven" (Psalm 78:23,24).

## ∽ Thinking Deeper ∾

How is it that for thousands of years there has been enough food for the robins, and enough food for the worms and other things that robins eat? How is it that there are enough mice to feed the red-tailed hawks, the foxes, and the coyotes? How is it that there are enough shrimp and krill in the oceans to feed the whales? How can the right plants be there to feed the right kind of insects? How come there are milkweeds so that there can be monarch butterflies? These are only a few of the millions of questions that could be asked about the balance of nature. The truth is that this is a complex world we live in with incredible interdependency among a wide array of life forms.

Evolutionists claim that all these forms evolved, many of them separately, against impossible odds, to the point where this complex interdependent eco-system works just nicely, all glory to Darwin. These same people claim that they can have a robust morality springing from the same Darwinian fount.

On the other hand, God created the heavens and the earth, and the seas and everything living. He put everything in its place and set the balance of nature. Though interrupted and corrupted by the fall of man and the flood, God still worked out an incredibly balanced eco-system that has worked quite well for a long time. How he fed the Israelites in the wilderness for forty years is another example of His ability to supply needs. "But my God shall supply all your need according to his riches in glory by Christ Jesus" (Philippians 4:19).

*When the Children of Israel were in the wilderness, they didn't have stores where the people could buy food.*

**Bible Reading:** Exodus 17:1-7

# Q58. In what way did God provide water for the Israelites?

## A. God brought water out of the rock when Moses struck it with the rod.

How long can you live without eating? Some people have gone for forty days without food. How about water? Some people say you will die in three or four days. Others say you could live maybe as long as a week. One thing is sure. Without water you won't live very long.

The Children of Israel lived for forty years in the wilderness. Some of the places they went had no water. When they came to a place called Rephidim, there was no water. The Lord told Moses to lead the people to Horeb, another name for Mt. Sinai. He told Moses to take his rod and strike a rock. Water came out of that rock. It must have been a lot of water. Thousands and thousands of people were able to have water to drink.

God made water come out of a rock. God can do miracles that man can't explain. God brought "forth water for them out of the rock for their thirst" (Nehemiah 9:15). God watches out for His people.

## ❧ Thinking Deeper ❧

*If there is no God, then there are no miracles.*

Adam Clarke has an interesting note regarding this incident, which has been described as possibly the greatest miracle Moses was involved with. Clarke credits a Dr. Priestly with these words. "This supply of water…was a most wonderful display of the Divine power. The water must have been in great abundance to supply two millions of persons…There are sufficient traces of this wonderful miracle remaining at this day. This rock has been visited, drawn, and described by Dr. Shaw and others; and holes and channels appear in the stone, which could only have been formed by the bursting out and running of the water. No art of man could have done it, if any motive could be supposed for the undertaking in such a place as this." (*Clarke's Commentary*, Vol.1)

The controversy between unbelievers and people of faith regarding Biblical claims often rests on the possibility of God doing miracles. If there is no God, then there are no miracles. But if there is a God, the God described in the Old and New Testaments, then miracles are not only possible, but to be expected. God is all powerful and can do what needs to be done. Water out of a rock? No problem. God later turned water into wine. Feeding hungry Israelites with manna? No problem. God later fed 5,000 with a few loaves and fish. If there is a God, there is no problem with the possibilities of miracles. "For with God nothing shall be impossible" (Luke 1:37).

**Bible Reading:** Exodus 19:1-6

## Q59. What did God promise Israel if they would obey his voice?

### A. He promised that they would be a special people if they kept His covenant.

A boy was playing at the edge of the lawn. There were trees and jungle near the house. His father came outside and was watching his son. Suddenly the father's eyes grew large. He spoke in a quiet voice. "Son, do just as I say. Drop to the ground and begin crawling toward me. Do it now." The boy did not question the instructions. He had been trained to obey his father's voice. He dropped to the ground and crawled toward his father. After he had crawled for several yards, he heard his father say, "Now, get up and run to me." The boy ran to his father.

"Daddy, why did you make me crawl?" asked the boy. The father pointed to a tree. Just above where the boy had been playing was a branch. On the branch, looking down, was a very dangerous snake.

"Son, I'm glad you obeyed me when I spoke to you. I didn't want to shout because I didn't want to startle the snake. You did well when you followed my instructions." The boy hugged his dad. He was glad he had obeyed.

God told Israel that they would be specially cared for if they obeyed His voice. As long as they listened, God helped them. God will help us as we obey His voice.

 **Thinking Deeper**

God is a covenant keeping God. That means He keeps His promises. When He promised special blessings to the Children of Israel, He gave them special blessings. However, later in their history Israel came to the place where they were not given such special blessings. Was it because God failed to keep His covenant? No. It was because this covenant was conditional. "If ye will obey my voice indeed, and keep my covenant, then ye shall be a peculiar treasure unto me." God made the promise, but it was based on the people obeying His voice.

It is popular to speak of God's unconditional love. And it is true that God does love the world, even "while we were yet sinners." But God's love for man does not mean that God will bless man in disobedience. Out of His love, God offers salvation to the penitent sinner. But God does not dispense His blessings without the proper heart condition in man. We cannot expect to be protected as God's special treasure if we disobey His voice. Jesus loved the Rich Young Ruler, but allowed him to go away sorrowful. God's love reached out to the young man, but that didn't mean the young man responded. Yes, Christ's unconditional love reached out to that young man, but he did not force his love upon him. If we will receive the special blessings of God, we must be those who obey God's voice.

> *God is a covenant keeping God. That means He keeps His promises.*

**Bible Reading:** Exodus 19:17-20

# Q60. Who did God call up to Mt. Sinai to receive the law?

## A. God called Moses to receive the law.

James Moore was already exhausted. He had ridden 140 miles west to the relay station. Now someone needed to bring another sack of mail back. But the Pony Express rider who was to take the eastbound mail had been killed. It was up to James to bring the mail back. So he took the saddle, and in ten minutes started back east. When he got back to his station, he had ridden on pony express horses for 280 miles. He was one of the Pony Express heroes.

Before airplanes and postal trucks, the Pony Express took mail by horse and rider between Missouri and California. They claimed that the mail could make it in ten days or less. An advertisement looking for riders read like this: "Wanted: Young, skinny, wiry fellows, not over 18. Must be expert riders, willing to risk death daily. Orphans preferred. Wages $25 per week."

These young riders had the important job of carrying mail by horseback. Sometimes they went through dangerous territory. Some riders were attacked by Indians. Yet they managed to get the mail to its destination.

*God gave the law so that His people would know what was right and wrong.*

God called Moses up to Mt. Sinai. Moses was to receive the law from God. The law told people how to live. Moses was a faithful man. He brought God's message to the people. The most famous part of that message is what we call the Ten Commandments. Moses did an important job for God when he brought the commandments to the people.

## ⟿ Thinking Deeper ⟾

God gave the law so that His people would know what was right and wrong. Specifically, God gave the law because people are disposed to do wrong. From birth we go the wrong way. So that we would know where we've done wrong, God gave the law. "The law was added because of transgressions." Man doesn't need the law to do wrong. Man needs the law to show him just how wrong he is. In fact, people generally think they are pretty good. Proverbs says that "every man will declare his own goodness." When the law is added, though, that goodness fades. The Apostle Paul said "when the commandment came, sin revived, and I died."

Moses brought the law from God to the people. It showed them their wickedness. Only when they realized their sin could they appreciate the sacrifices made for sin. The law does the same today. God in mercy sends the law so that we can realize our need for His grace. When we see the depth of our need, we will appreciate the wonderful provision in Christ to meet that need.

**Bible Reading:** Nehemiah 9:19-21

## Questions in Review

**Q57. How did God feed the Children of Israel in the Wilderness?**
   A. He sent them manna from heaven.
**Q58. In what way did God provide water for the Israelites?**
   A. God brought water out of the rock when Moses struck it with the rod.
**Q59. What did God promise Israel if they would obey his voice?**
   A. He promised that they would be a special people if they kept His covenant.
**Q60. Who did God call up to Mt. Sinai to receive the law?**
   A. God called Moses to receive the law.

It was in the days before there were McDonald's that a family of six children were riding in their station wagon with their mom and dad. "I'm hungry," said one of the boys. One of the girls said she was hungry too. In fact, everyone in the car was hungry. They were a long way from home. The mom whispered something to the dad, who stopped at a grocery store. She went inside. In a short time she returned with a paper sack. In it was a loaf of bread, meat, and a sack of potato chips. They thanked the Lord for the food and then had baloney and potato chip sandwiches. They were glad for something to eat.

The Children of Israel had no McDonald's and no grocery stores when they were in the wilderness. God provided what they needed. God will supply our needs, too, if we trust Him.

*The Children of Israel had no McDonald's and no grocery stores when they were in the wilderness.*

## Thinking Deeper

S. D. Herron, founder of Hobe Sound Bible College, preached a message in which he compared the manna God sent from heaven for Israel in the wilderness to the Word of God. Two of his major points were 1) God told the people to gather manna every day, and 2) yesterday's manna is not good for today. Brother Herron encouraged getting the "manna" of the Word of God fresh every day. There is enough for everyone. It is as important to read the Bible as it is to eat food. "I have esteemed the words of his mouth more than my necessary food" (Job 23:12).

Brother Herron's second point was that if we rely on what was in the past, like manna, it could breed worms. Although Moses had told the people not to store the manna for the next day, "some of them left of it until the morning, and it bred worms" (Exodus 16:20). Each generation needs to find the Word fresh for them. Just because our parents found the truth is no indication that we have found it ourselves. This generation must find the manna fresh for itself. Each one of us must personally find and receive the Word of God. "Thy words were found, and I did eat them; and thy word was unto me the joy and rejoicing of mine heart" (Jeremiah 15:16).

**Bible Reading:** Exodus. 20:7-11

## Q62. What are the third and fourth commandments?

A. 3. Thou shalt not take the name of the Lord thy God in vain.
   4. Remember the Sabbath day to keep it holy.

A little boy walked on the street with a college student. The student was saying some words that the little boy didn't understand. He had never heard his parents use those words. When the boy repeated the words, the college student laughed. The boy also thought it was funny. He said the words again, louder. Just then the boy heard his mother call his name. She was not happy. She told him the words were bad words. She wanted him to remember not to say bad words. She put some soap in his mouth. It tasted horrible. "Don't say those words again!" she warned. That was the last time the boy ever said those words. He learned that bad words should not be repeated.

God told His people not to say anything that would be disrespectful to God. Don't misuse the name of God, or Jesus. Never say anything bad about the Holy Spirit. God is too holy to have His name used in a wrong way. And God's day is too holy to be used just for pleasure and work. God's name and God's day are to be kept holy.

*One day in seven is to be reserved for the worship of God and the fellowship of the believers.*

## ～ Thinking Deeper ～

Why do Christians worship on Sunday, and not on Saturday, which was the traditional Jewish Sabbath? There is a scriptural reason, and there is the example set by the early church. The Bible designates Sunday as "The Lord's Day." John wrote that he "was in the Spirit on the Lord's Day" (Rev. 1:10), the day of celebration of the Resurrection of Christ. When Paul the Apostle gave instructions for taking the offering, he said that it should be reserved to be collected on the first day of the week (1 Cor. 16:2). This time of meeting became so regular and so expected of the early Christians that Ignatius noted in 110 A.D. that believers in Jesus were "no longer observing the Sabbath, but fashioning their lives after the Lord's Day." Justin Martyr in the same century said "Sunday is the day on which we all hold our common assembly." Among other early Christians who recognized the change to Sunday worship were Ignatius, Bardaisan, Cyprian, Eusebius, and Clement.

Early church history reveals that the practice of the primitive Christians was the practice of Sunday worship. One day in seven is to be reserved for the worship of God and the fellowship of the believers. That is the New Testament and early church fulfillment of the commandment to keep the Sabbath holy.

**Bible Reading:** Exodus 20:12-14

# Q63. What are commandments five, six and seven?

### A. 5. Honor thy father and thy mother.
### 6. Thou shalt not kill.
### 7. Thou shalt not commit adultery.

Billy and his brother Joey went to Sean's house to play Legos. But when they got there, Sean turned on the TV. "Joey," whispered Billy. "We're not supposed to watch things like that. Those people are doing bad things."

"I don't care," said Joey. "I'm going to watch it." Billy decided to go home. When he got up to leave, Joey grabbed him. "Don't go. You'll ruin everything if you go home. Just stay here." When Billy tried to pull away, Joey pushed him down. Billy started to cry.

"What's wrong with you guys?" asked Sean. Joey had forgotten that Sean was there. Now he felt bad. He had been selfish and disobedient and mean. The brothers left Sean's house.

"Billy, I'm sorry for being mean. Please forgive me," said Joey, as they walked home.

When the boys got home, Joey confessed to his mother what he had done. She told him he needed to ask God to forgive him, too, because he had broken God's commandments.

When we are mean, or selfish, or disobedient, we must confess that to God because we are breaking His commandments. "If we confess our sins, he is faithful and just to forgive us our sins, and to cleanse us from all unrighteousness" (1 John 1:9).

*When children dishonor their parents, they violate the Fifth Commandment.*

## ⟶ Thinking Deeper ⟵

When children dishonor their parents, they violate the Fifth Commandment. A father told his son, "I'm giving you something much more valuable than thousands of dollars. I'm giving you a good name. That name carries a reputation that has been built over many years. Keep it." When someone sins, he dishonors the reputation of his parents. Vidkun Quisling's name had no particular connotation in Norway until he collaborated with the Nazis. Now the name Quisling is on the same level as the name Benedict Arnold. Both Vidkun's and Benedict's parents' names have been dishonored.

God's commandments have been given to show us what the boundaries are to right living. Going outside of the boundaries brings a lot of trouble to a lot of people. God gave his commandments because He has our best interest at heart. "O that there were such an heart in them, that they would fear me, and keep all my commandments always, that it might be well with them, and with their children for ever!" (Deut. 5:29)

> **Bible Reading:** Exodus. 20:15-17

## Q64. What are the last three commandments?

### A. 8. Thou shalt not steal.
### 9. Thou shalt not bear false witness against thy neighbor.
### 10. Thou shalt not covet.

"Don't steal anything, no matter how small," said the father. "Don't even steal a paper clip. You'll just have to take it back." His little girl listened carefully. She knew that it wasn't worth stealing. She was careful not to take things that were not hers. Stealing is taking things that do not belong to you. God told us not to steal. The father helped his little girl understand how important it is to keep God's commandments.

Bearing false witness is saying things about someone else that are not true. God says we should never do that.

God also says that we should not desire to have what someone else has. That is coveting. If another person has something nice, don't wish you had it. Be thankful for what you have and respect what belongs to others.

God's laws help us get along with other people.

*God's laws help us get along with other people.*

### ～ **Thinking Deeper** ～

A certain priest was looking back over the years he had heard people in the confessional. He recollected that the confessors bared their souls over breaking almost all of the commandments. He noted with some wonder that the exception was the tenth commandment. Seldom, if ever, had he heard someone confessing to breaking the commandment on coveting. Why do people find it so difficult to admit to coveting?

You can covet someone's house without stealing it. You can covet someone's wife without committing the act of adultery. You can covet someone's position without actually tearing their character apart by falsehood. But covetousness can lead to all of those sins. That's why it is wrong to covet. It is difficult to know when you are coveting. Covetousness is a sin of the heart. It resides inside of your thought life and can take hold of your motives. The first commandment establishes God's position as authority. The tenth commandment is a check on the inner self to see if we've really given God the authority. Are we bringing our thoughts into the obedience of Christ? Are we letting Him direct our steps by his commandments? "Make me to go in the path of thy commandments; for therein do I delight" (Ps. 119:35).

**Bible Reading:** Matthew 22:35-40

**Questions in Review**

**Q61. What were the first two commandments?**
   A. 1. Thou shalt have no other gods before me.
       2. Thou shalt not make unto thee any graven image.
**Q62. What are the third and fourth commandments?**
   A. 3. Thou shalt not take the name of the Lord thy God in vain.
       4. Remember the Sabbath day to keep it holy.
**Q63. What are commandments five, six and seven?**
   A. 5. Honor thy father and thy mother.
       6. Thou shalt not kill.
       7. Thou shalt not commit adultery.
**Q64. What are the last three commandments?**
   A. 8. Thou shalt not steal.
       9. Thou shalt not bear false witness against thy neighbor.
       10. Thou shalt not covet.

A little boy was banging a spoon against the leg of a table. His mother told him to stop. He kept banging the spoon. His mother made sure he heard what she said. "Young man, if you bang that spoon on the table leg one more time, I'm going to open the window and throw you out!" The little boy's eyes grew big as he deliberately hit the table leg with the spoon. His eyes never left his mother. She didn't hesitate, but picked him up, carried him to the window, opened it and with a little push threw him out. The little boy landed in a rather soft snowdrift that the mother knew was outside of the window. That boy learned a lesson. Mother meant her words.

*God meant what He said. It is important to keep his commandments.*

God meant what He said. It is important to keep his commandments. Jesus said, "If you love me, keep my commandments" (John 14:15). We show our love to God by keeping His commandments.

## ◕ Thinking Deeper ◔

Among present day atheists are those who argue that they can be just as moral as people who believe in God. The morals of any society are based on what are called the mores (pronounced morays) of the people. Mores are those actions that the society as a whole have deemed proper. How do atheists decide what is moral? They say the majority of society decides the standard. The controlling force to cause people to conform to the morality is the policeman. So if you violate the morality, worry about the policeman. In communist Russia, Nazi Germany, and Caligula's Rome that worked for a time with awful results.

The Christian's inner belief in God is a much more powerful incentive to do right than the outward fear of a statist policeman.

# EXPERIENCES IN THE WILDERNESS

**Bible Reading:** Exodus 32:1-6

## Q65. What did the Children of Israel do while Moses delayed coming down from Mt. Sinai?
### A. When Moses delayed coming, the people made a golden calf to worship.

Poking around in the back room of his father's barber shop, Wes spotted something through the slats of a closet door. Could it be a Christmas present? Wes opened the door. Yes! It was a race car set! Before he could look really close, he heard the door open from the shop. "Wesley, what are you doing?" It was his father. Wesley quickly closed the closet door. But his father had seen him. Now the surprise for Christmas morning was ruined. Wesley wished he hadn't opened that closet door.

When Moses was up the mountain talking with God, the people got tired of waiting. They wanted something to happen. So they did something very wrong. Instead of being patient, they made an idol – a golden calf. God was displeased and sent destruction on the people. Many people died. It is a warning to us. "The wages of sin is death." (Romans 6:6a)

## ∼ Thinking Deeper ∼

People need to worship. It is a characteristic of humanity through the ages. Even most atheists worship at some altar. For example, it is almost eerie to see the kind of veneration they give Charles Darwin. Do you know there is a "Darwin Day Celebration"? It is advertised as a "global holiday that transcends separate nationalities and cultures." It is a day of "celebrating … the universal understanding we share." That universal understanding, or course, is evolution. Dr. Raymond Parades, Texas Higher Education Commissioner in rejecting Institute for Creation Research application to give online degrees for science educators, reasoned that creation based teaching doesn't give evolution "the proper attention it deserves." Teachers who don't bow to the altar of evolution are unqualified to form the minds of students. Man will worship something. The question is, what or whom? The golden calf became a substitute for worship of the true God. That misplaced worship deteriorated into a copy of paganism, with the accompanying indulgence of the lusts of the flesh in various manifestations.

Within forty days of seeing Moses going to the holy mount, the Children of Israel were violating the first commandment, "Thou shalt have no other gods before me." They worshipped according to their own minds. It is inadequate to worship according to the dictates of our own conscience. We must worship in truth. "Let the words of my mouth, and the meditation of my heart be acceptable in thy sight, O Lord" (Psalm 19:14).

*People need to worship. It is a characteristic of humanity through the ages.*

**Bible Reading:** Exodus 32:15-20

## Q66. What did Moses do when he saw the people dancing before the golden calf?

### A. Moses threw down the tablets, burned and ground up the golden calf.

Did you know that you can zap virus cells with lasers? Scientists have done it in experiments. Viruses can be bad. They can give you a cold. They can make you very ill. How can viruses be cured? Sometimes you must get a lot of rest so that your body can fight off a virus. When medicine can't help, there may be a way to attack viruses by shooting them with lasers. The laser causes the virus to fall apart, but it doesn't harm healthy cells. They are still working on it, but the viruses better watch out. Someone will figure out how to get them!

When Moses came down from God's presence with the Ten Commandments in his hands, he saw the people dancing in front of an idol. The idol needed to be destroyed. Moses was very upset. He threw the tablets down. They broke. Then Moses destroyed the golden calf. Later God called Moses back up to the mountain again for another copy of the commandments. God does not give up on His Word.

God is not happy when people sin. Sin must be destroyed. "The blood of Jesus Christ, God's Son, cleanseth us from all sin" (1 John 1:7).

*God does not give up on His Word.*

### ∼ **Thinking Deeper** ∼

A young man who was seeking God had been listening to hard rock music and was having trouble giving it up. He understood that what he'd been listening to was directly contrary to Christ and the life of "holiness, without which no man shall see the Lord." The early stars of rock music were open about what they were doing. The Beatles said they were more popular than Jesus Christ. A singer named Blondie said rock was one hundred percent sex. Themes of rebellion fitted well with the hippie movement in the sixties and groups like The Rolling Stones sang rebellion into the culture. Another theme of rock music glorified Satanism and the occult. The young man saw the battle between Christ and the message he'd been listening to. The music had him in bondage. Finally, he decided to yield his music listening to God. When he did, he realized he had to get rid of his music. He burned it in a fire.

Sometimes the only thing to do with evil things is to destroy them. Moses knew that the golden calf was a snare. It had to be destroyed. There was no sanctifying it. It had to be ground to powder. There is no negotiating with sin. It must be destroyed. "Knowing this, that our old man is crucified with him, that the body of sin might be destroyed, that henceforth we should not serve sin" (Romans 6:6).

**Bible Reading:** Exodus 35:1-11

## Q67. Why did God ask for an offering to be taken in the wilderness?

### A. God asked for an offering to make the tabernacle.

A little boy wanted to give something in the church offering, but he didn't have anything in his pocket except for a few marbles, so he put them in the offering plate as it passed by. After the church service one of the ushers who was counting the money asked the boy if he wanted his marbles back. The boy said, "No, I gave them to the Lord Jesus." Later, a man heard about the boy's offering. He gave the church one hundred dollars for the marbles. So the offering the boy gave turned out to be far greater than he could have imagined.*

God asked the Children of Israel to give offerings in the wilderness. Some of them gave gold. Others gave valuable animal skins. Oil, spices, incense, precious stones, and fine wood were among the offerings the people brought. They were bringing supplies to make a tabernacle. The tabernacle was made so the people could come and worship the Lord. The people were very willing to give to God's work. "God loveth a cheerful giver" (II Corinthians 9:7b).

*(From Ruth Dow, in *Encyclopedia of 7700 Illustrations*, P. L. Tan.)

## ∼ Thinking Deeper ∼

It has been stated that the measure of a person's commitment is whether or not it has affected his wallet. Someone said, "The last thing to be converted is the pocketbook." On the bright side, converted people have often found great joy in giving. Another popular saying is "you can't out-give God," with its corollary "God will be no man's debtor." These sayings point to the truth that there is genuine blessing in giving to God.

Giving people are more apt to be interested in the work of God. Jesus said, "where your treasure is, there will your heart be also" (Matthew 6:21). If you don't give to God's work, your heart will be elsewhere. Try it. Give a substantial offering to some aspect of the work of the Lord and see whether or not you have an increased interest in that work. You will likely perk up when that particular endeavor is mentioned. Why? You have some of your heart there. Tony Campolo said that when there was flight from the urban churches, his family didn't leave, because his father had bought the offering plates. There was no way they were going to a suburban church. Those plates were in the urban church!

When the Israelites gave of their possessions to build the tabernacle, they had their hearts turned toward the tabernacle. Give cheerfully to the work of the Lord and you'll be surprised how your heart is turned in His direction.

*It has been stated that the measure of a person's commitment is whether or not it has affected his wallet.*

**THURSDAY**

## Q68. If the people sinned, what were they to do?

### A. If the people sinned, they were to bring a sacrifice to be offered to God.

Jason, can I borrow your rod?" asked Eric. "Mine's out of line and I want to fish." "Sure, just be careful with it." While he was fishing, Eric put the rod on the dock and walked away. Suddenly he heard the rod being dragged off of the dock. A big fish must have taken the bait. Before he could stop it, the rod dropped into the water and sank out of sight. What was Eric to do? He couldn't get the rod because the water was too deep. He went home with a heavy heart.

When Eric told his dad what happened, they talked about what to do. They decided that Eric needed to buy a new rod for Jason. Eric got enough money to buy the rod from his savings. He had wanted to buy a new bike, but that would have to wait.

"I'm sorry, Jason," said Eric the next day. "I lost your rod, but here's a new one to replace it." Jason was happy with the new rod, and Eric went home with a clear conscience. He had done the right thing.

*When we sin, we need to make it right with those we sin against.*

When we sin, we need to make it right with those we sin against. We also need to get right with God. God told Israel to bring Him a sacrifice when they sinned. Later on, Jesus became the sacrifice for our sins on the cross. When we confess our sins, we trust in Jesus to cleanse us and forgive us because he died for us. "Christ died for our sins according to the scriptures" (1 Cor. 15:3b).

## ◦◦◦ Thinking Deeper ◦◦◦

Many people endeavor to bring some kind of sacrifice to appease their god. In ancient times people would bring children to the fire god Molech. Sometimes they would pass their children through the flames arising from a fire in the lap of the idol. Other times they might take a child and place it as a complete sacrifice into the god's glowing arms heated red hot by those flames. Hindus have been known to sacrifice children to the god of the Ganges River, who accepted the little victim with a swirl in the water and snap of a crocodile's jaws. Countless sacrifices have been made to appease the many gods that people have invented.

The God of the Israelites asked for a sacrifice. After the example of Abraham offering Isaac and God providing a ram, the Jewish people understood that God does not require human sacrifice. Rather, the sacrifices made were types of the coming sacrifice of the Promised One, the Messiah. "Christ also hath loved us, and hath given himself for us an offering and a sacrifice to God" (Ephesians 5:2) The sacrifice on Jewish altars was not so much them appeasing God, but looking forward to the perfect sacrifice that God himself would provide.

**Bible Reading:** Psalm 106:19-23

**Questions in Review**

**Q65. What did the Children of Israel do while Moses delayed coming down from Mt. Sinai?**
   **A. When Moses delayed coming, the people made a golden calf to worship.**
**Q66. What did Moses do when he saw the people dancing before the golden calf?**
   **A. Moses threw down the tablets, burned and ground up the golden calf .**
**Q67. Why did God ask for an offering to be taken in the wilderness?**
   **A. God asked for an offering to make the tabernacle.**
**Q68. If the people sinned, what were they to do?**
   **A. If the people sinned, they were to bring a sacrifice to be offered to God.**

Three boys taking a hike had gone farther from home than ever before, and the smallest became frightened. He started to cry out. An older boy asked him what good that would do. "Maybe someone will come and help," suggested the little boy. But no one did. They had to trudge along themselves until they finally found their way home. The little boy was really glad to get home.

When the Israelites were in the wilderness they didn't have a place they could really call home. Everything was new. They had to learn about God's law and how to deal with their sins. But they kept following God. Even in the wilderness, God was there. It is important to keep walking with God, even when things are strange. "The LORD of hosts is with us" (Psa. 46:7).

*It is important to keep walking with God, even when things are strange.*

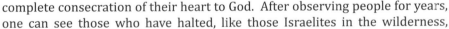

## ⟨⟩ Thinking Deeper ⟨⟩

Some people, in what is called "the wilderness state," have walked with Christ but have little spiritual feeling. They may even question, "where is God?" That can sometimes be a helpful description of one who has not made a complete consecration of their heart to God. After observing people for years, one can see those who have halted, like those Israelites in the wilderness, because of unbelief. Yet others persevere and go on to the Promised Land.

However, it is also an observation that people who have "entered Canaan" sometimes experience such a state. The way through the wilderness is the way of faith. The promises of God, regardless of one's state of grace, are to be taken by faith, not by the senses.

A godly man was overheard praying, "Lord, I take you today as my sanctification." He was affirming faith in God's promises in the present tense. "Let us labour therefore to enter into that rest, lest any man fall after the same example of unbelief" (Hebrews 4:11).

GENERATIONS IN THE WILDERNESS

**Bible Reading:** Leviticus 26:14-16; 32-33

## Q69. What did God promise would happen to the Israelites if they disobeyed Him?

### A. Their enemies would live in their land, they would be scattered, and a sword would follow them.

"Don't build your house on that land. It is not solid. If you build your house there it will be ruined and you won't be able to live in it." This warning was given to people in parts of the city of Fairbanks, Alaska. Some people listened and made sure they had solid land to build on. Some didn't listen to the warnings. If you travel up the mountain on a small road near the city, you come to a house that is broken in the middle. The people built it on a place where the ground was not solid. Now the house is ruined and no one can live in it. They should have listened to the warnings.

The Children of Israel should have listened to God's warnings. He told them what would happen if they didn't follow Him. Sure enough, after many years, they forgot God's ways and followed idols. The time came when they were chased out of their land. God's word came true. It is always the right thing to follow God's word.

## ❧ Thinking Deeper ❧

God's word contains several types of prophecies. Some are very specific, to be fulfilled in specific ways. For example, the prophecy in Psalm 22 that the Messiah's hands and feet would be pierced is very specific in its description of the kind of death Jesus would die. Other prophecies are more general. That is, they have a wider application than just to one individual. Yet these prophecies are precise enough for us to be able to clearly observe their fulfillment. The prophecy that God made concerning Israel's disobedience identified three clear results: 1) their enemies would live in their land. That happened. Israel was inhabited by non-Jews for many years. 2) They would be scattered among the heathen. It is interesting that after the land of Israel was re-established in 1948, people of Jewish descent came "back to Jerusalem" from nations all over the globe. 3) The sword was drawn after them. The history of the violent persecution of Jews is legendary. There was the Roman destruction of Jerusalem in 70A.D. , the 11th Century slaughter in the Rhineland, then later the great persecution against Jews in France and Spain. Later Russia became party to anti-Jewish bigotry and violence, and in the 20th century the Nazis pursued to the death millions of European Jews. *

God's warnings are to be heeded, because His prophecies will be fulfilled. It is a lesson to us to learn His Word with care and hold His declarations of future things in awe. Jesus said, "The scripture cannot be broken" (John 10:35).

> *God's warnings are to be heeded, because His prophecies will be fulfilled.*

*See McDowell, Josh, *Evidence That Demands a Verdict*, Campus Crusade, 1972, pp.329, 330.

**Bible Reading:** Numbers 13:1-2, 30-33; 14:6-8

## Q70. After Moses sent spies into Canaan, what report did they give?

### A. Joshua and Caleb gave a good report, but ten spies gave an evil report.

Larry's mother told him to look at the beans. There were a lot of them. But Larry wanted to play, not pick beans. He came back in the house. "Mom, I don't think they are quite ready yet. Maybe they'll be ready tomorrow." Just then Larry's older brother Ben walked into the room. "Oh, Mother," said Ben. "I looked at the beans last night and I'm sure we need to pick them before they're too old." Mother looked at Larry. "Young man, you march right out there and pick those beans. I would have asked Ben to help you, but since you weren't honest with me, you must pick them all by yourself."

Later, as he was picking beans in the garden, Larry felt awful. He not only had to work harder because he had to do it alone, but he had a heavy heart because he had not been truthful.

The Bible says that "the way of the transgressor is hard." The wilderness was hard for the Israelites because they listened to the evil report of the ten spies instead of trusting God.

*The walk with Jesus is a journey.*

## ∼ Thinking Deeper ∼

The walk with Jesus is a journey. The experience of Israel approaching Canaan is a type from which we are to learn lessons for our journey. When they heard from the spies, they found two contrasting reports. One came from Joshua and Caleb, who focused on the abundant blessings in the Promised Land evidenced by samples of the fruit of the land. They showed off "a branch with one cluster of grapes, and they bare it between two upon a staff." The second report came from the ten who focused on the giants in the land. Compared to them, they said, "we were in our own sight as grasshoppers." The giant of unbelief destroyed them before they ever faced any giant in Canaan. In contrast, Joshua and Caleb were able to receive the blessings of Canaan because they believed God.

As we walk with Jesus, we can either focus on the blessings available, or stop because of giants in front of us. Can you believe God to cleanse your heart from all sin? Can you lay hold on the blessing He offers in going into the "Land of Canaan?" Can you believe for a baptism of perfect love? Or do you so fear your own weakness, or your own coldness of heart, or your own past performance that you can't believe? Look at the blessings God promises, not the giants. "For ye have need of patience, that, after ye have done the will of God, ye might receive the promise" (Heb. 10:36).

**Bible Reading:** Numbers 14:26-33

## Q71. What happened to the generation that refused to enter Canaan?

### A. They died in the wilderness, but their children went in after forty years.

Squanto was an American Indian. He had been kidnapped by some bad men and taken to England. After some time he sailed back to America. When he landed, he looked for his tribe. He couldn't find them anywhere. A sickness had come upon them and they all died. Squanto was very sad. He lived with another tribe. Then he learned that the Pilgrims had come. They were living on the land of his tribe. Squanto went to help them. He showed them how to fish. He helped them plant crops. He was a great blessing. Squanto overcame the great sorrow of the whole generation of his people that had been lost.

The generation of the Children of Israel that refused to enter Canaan when God led them were lost in the wilderness. They never made it to the Promised Land. "So we see that they could not enter in because of unbelief" (Hebrews 3:19). Only Joshua and Caleb made it. The next generation obeyed God and went into Canaan. It is important to obey God when He speaks.

 **Thinking Deeper**

If you had been twenty years old when God told the generation they would be forty years in the wilderness, you would have known that your life span could not exceed sixty. If you married, you would never have a house to live in and land of your own. But if you were nineteen, you had hope that sometime in the future, there was a land waiting. If you obeyed God, you could get to that land and find your own place. God made that clear. One generation would be gone, and the next would have the hope of the promise.

Those four decades in the wilderness were not without God's intervention. The people had a daily reminder of His provision through manna. They were led by the cloud and the fire. As the years went on, they had to have noticed something unusual about their clothing, because at the end of that time, God reminded them with these words: "And I have led you forty years in the wilderness: your clothes are not waxen old upon you, and thy shoe is not waxen old upon thy foot" (Deut. 29:5). God made their clothes and shoes last beyond any reasonable expectation. The miraculous evidence of God's presence was with them.

Miracles were a daily part of that journey through the wilderness. As long as we walk in faith, God is with us in our journey today, even when we encounter dry times. He is there. He is our help and our provider and our defender. "Fear not: for I am with thee" (Isa. 43:5a).

*It is important to obey God when He speaks.*

JOSHUA LEADS THE PEOPLE

**Bible Reading:** Joshua 1:1-6

## Q73.  After Moses died, who led the Children of Israel?

### A. Joshua led the people after Moses died.

A preacher named Adrian Rogers told the story of a man who was bragging that he had cut the tail off of a man-eating lion with his pocket knife. Someone asked him why he didn't cut off its head. "Because someone else had already cut off its head," he answered. That man wanted people to think he was brave, when he really wasn't.

When Moses died, God chose Joshua to lead the Children of Israel. Joshua wasn't a man who bragged about what he did or what he would do. It seems that Joshua may have been somewhat fearful about being chosen to lead the people. God told him to "be of good courage" (Joshua 1:6a). It is important for us to trust God when we are asked to do something new. If we trust in our own strength, we are sure to fail. Joshua trusted God. God made him a good leader.

## ↬ Thinking Deeper ↫

When God chose Joshua to lead the Children of Israel, He gave him a great promise: "s I was with Moses, so I will be with thee" (Joshua 1:5b). Then God told him to "be strong and of a good courage." Again He told Joshua, "Only be thou strong and very courageous" (Joshua 1:7a). And just to make sure he didn't miss the point, God repeated, "Be strong and of a good courage." So Joshua turned to the people and began to instruct them. They responded by accepting his leadership, and then added a word of encouragement. "Be strong and of a good courage" (Joshua 1:9a)

What makes a good leader? If Joshua's installation is a clue, then good leadership requires strength and courage. The strength is derived from the Word of God. "This book of the law shall not depart out of thy mouth; but thou shalt meditate therein day and night, that thou mayest observe to do according to all that is written therein: for then thou shalt make thy way prosperous, and then thou shalt have good success" (Joshua 1:8). God wanted Joshua to be strong in the Word. A good leader will have the Bible as his guide and the controlling force in his life. He will derive his strength from the Word of God. A wrong leader will ignore the Bible and promote his own thinking and agenda.

A good leader will also be courageous. It takes courage to consistently apply the truth of the Bible to the circumstances of life. It takes courage to lead a family in godliness when the world is filled with evil. It takes courage for a church leader to hold to the Bible when others are ignoring parts of it that are not currently popular. Joshua's success as a leader was based on his fidelity to the word of God.

*It takes courage to consistently apply the truth of the Bible to the circumstances of life.*

**Bible Reading:** Joshua 2:1-7

# Q74. Why did Joshua send two spies to Jericho?

### A. Joshua sent spies to view the land.

Spies have been around for a long time. You may have heard of Nathan Hale, a spy who worked for the Patriots during the American Revolution. He was caught by the British. Before he was hung, he is quoted as saying, "I regret that I have but one life to give for my country." Some spies are women. One woman spy was a singer who wrote information on the back of her music. She used invisible ink. Some spies smuggled documents by hiding them in their shoes, or hiding tiny film inside of coins that they had cut into two sides, hollowed out, and then glued them back together.

Joshua sent two spies to see what Jericho was like. They were to find information that would be helpful when the Israelite Army invaded the land around Jericho. Like all spies, they would be in danger if they got caught. God helped the spies through a woman named Rahab. God cares about His people. If we trust Him, He will help us.

## ∽ Thinking Deeper ∽

Some people think that Joshua sent only two spies because of what happened forty years earlier. That's when twelve spies were sent to look at the Promised Land. Ten out of twelve brought back an evil report. Joshua and Caleb brought back a good report. The people were persuaded by the evil report, and forty years were spent in the wilderness while that generation of unbelievers died off.

Joshua did things differently. It is likely that he picked two spies he could trust, rather than picking spies from each tribe. He wanted an accurate report. But he also wanted people who would see things through eyes of faith. Another difference is that these spies were sent secretly. They didn't come back and give a report to all of the people. They were sent out by Joshua to be his eyes and ears. When they returned, they reported directly to him. "And they said unto Joshua, Truly the LORD hath delivered into our hands all the land; for even all the inhabitants of the country do faint because of us" (Joshua 2:24).

It is not necessarily wrong to find things out about the enemy. It would have been helpful in the Scopes Monkey Trials, for example, had William Jennings Bryan found out about the character of pro-Darwinist lawyer Clarence Darrow. Darrow's personal character was very suspect, and had that been known, certain aspects of the trial could have been changed. It may have been helpful, in another example, had Christians known that anthropologist Margaret Mead was having an affair while she was doing research in the South Pacific. Her research was showing that young people in "pristine" tribes had no inhibitions sexually. Why should it come as a surprise, more than fifty years later, to learn that her conclusions were flat out wrong? A little spying by the good guys might have helped.

*Joshua sent two spies to see what Jericho was like.*

**Bible Reading:** Joshua 2:8-18

# Q75. What did Rahab do with the scarlet cord?

## A. Rahab used the scarlet cord to help the spies escape and as a sign for her safety.

In 1949, a cruise ship named the S S Noronic was docked in Lake Ontario. Late one night it caught on fire. Many people were trapped on the top deck of the ship. They tried to escape, but the stairways were too dangerous to use. They found ropes which they threw over the side of the ship. One rope broke because too many people tried to climb down at one time. They fell into the water and were rescued. Other ropes held as person after person climbed down to safety. Some people perished in the fire, but many were saved because they escaped by a rope.

When the two spies Joshua had sent were being chased, they found a place to hide at Rahab's house. She decided that she would help them because she believed that Israel's God was the true God. She helped them get out of the city by putting a scarlet rope out her window and letting them climb down. The spies told her to put the scarlet rope in her window. It would be a sign that the house was to be protected when the Israelite soldiers came. Her faith saved her entire household.

## Thinking Deeper

Rahab's decision to help God's people was based on her faith that the God of Israel was the true God. As she faced the police who had come to search for the spies, she was making a decision. If she helped the police, she risked the destruction sure to come to Jericho. If she helped the spies and was found out, she could be in trouble with Jericho's forces. She had heard about the God of Israel and His power. She decided to help the spies. In haste, she hid them on her roof, covering them with stalks of flax. In haste, she hid her actions, covering them by words that denied she knew where they were. We could condemn her for lying, or commend her for helping God's people. The inspired writer of Hebrews, in the great chapter on heroes of faith, commended her for her act. "By faith the harlot Rahab perished not with them that believed not, when she had received the spies with peace" (Heb. 11:31).

It is helpful to see what kind of faith Rahab possessed. It was more than an awareness that Israel's God was powerful, because the other Jericho inhabitants believed that, and their hearts melted. She believed with the kind of faith that caused her to throw in her lot with God's people. Rahab chose to identify with the people of God and therefore "perished not with them that believed not" (Hebrews 11:31).

> *Rahab's decision to help God's people was based on her faith that the God of Israel was the true God.*

**Bible Reading:** Joshua 3:10-17

## Q76. How did the people cross the Jordan River?

### A. The people crossed on dry ground in the midst of the Jordan River.

Davy was four years old and on his first fishing trip. His mother had brought him to the creek. He tried fishing, but nothing bit. So he put down his rod and looked for something else to do. A tree leaned far out over the water. Davy thought he might try to climb out a ways. It wasn't hard climbing because the tree was leaning so much. Suddenly he lost his grip. Splash! He fell into the water. His mother had to pull him out. Since they were wet, they had to go home. The fishing trip was over.

Normally, if you are in a creek or a river you will get wet. But the Children of Israel went across the Jordan River and stayed dry. God stopped the water and they walked on dry land. As long as the priests stood in the river bed, it stayed dry. Only after all the people crossed over and the priests followed did the water return. God made a way for them to cross the Jordan River.

 **Thinking Deeper**

*As long as the priests stood in the river bed, it stayed dry.*

There is a humorous story that made its rounds about the Israelites crossing the Red Sea. A skeptic explained that what they crossed was really the "Reed Sea," and the wind dried up only about four inches of water, enabling the crossing on relatively dry ground. After this explanation, a man jumped to his feet and exclaimed, "This is even a greater miracle than I thought. God drowned the whole Egyptian Army in four inches of water!"

Trying to explain some of these Biblical accounts by employing unusual natural phenomena encounters a major problem when it comes to explaining the crossing of the Jordan River. The Bible states that the water was piled up in a heap upstream, and dried up downstream. There is no mention of wind. The only explanation is some kind of invisible barrier placed exactly where it was needed so that the Israelites could cross. The hand of God comes to mind. God directly intervened, or the whole account is non-real mythology.

Deists claim that God is not involved in the affairs of men or nature. He made it all and then walked away. Modern "scientism" proponents take the same view of issues of nature. They don't object at all if we believe in a God that has nothing to do with nature or science. But if we propose that God is involved, they become agitated, to put it mildly. So the Jordan Crossing becomes an interesting issue. If the Biblical account is accurate, then Deism is exposed as false.

**Bible Reading:** Psalm 32:6-11

**Questions in Review**

**Q73. After Moses died, who led the Children of Israel?**
　　**A. Joshua led the people after Moses died.**
**Q74. Why did Joshua send two spies to Jericho?**
　　**A. Joshua sent spies to view the land.**
**Q75. What did Rahab do with the scarlet cord?**
　　**A. Rahab used the scarlet cord to help the spies escape**
　　**and as a sign for her safety.**
**Q76. How did the people cross the Jordan River?**
　　**A. The people crossed on dry ground in the midst of**
　　**the Jordan River.**

After the Revolutionary war, George Washington was asked to become the first President of the United States. He seemed rather reluctant to take on this great position. After he agreed, his hesitancy was still rather obvious to his friends. In a letter to Henry Knox, dated in April of 1789, he wrote, "My movements to the chair of Government will be accompanied by feelings not unlike those of a culprit who is going to the place of his execution." Washington has been considered to have been one of our greatest presidents.

Joshua led the people when God gave him the job. He did what God asked him to do. God told Joshua that He would be with Him. Joshua became a great leader in Israel. If God puts you in a place where you are a leader, He will help you do a good job. The word to Joshua is to encourage all of us: "I will be with thee: I will not fail thee, nor forsake thee" (Joshua 1:5b).

> *If God puts you in a place where you are a leader, He will help you do a good job.*

## ～ **Thinking Deeper** ～

Joshua was installed as leader by God. When his leadership became known, it was confirmed by the people. He was soon tested. Israel came to the Jordan River. After the miracle crossing, it was obvious to all the people that the Lord was truly with Joshua. "On that day the LORD magnified Joshua in the sight of all Israel; and they feared him, as they feared Moses, all the days of his life" (Joshua 4:14). There was only one Moses when he led the people. And there was only one Joshua when he was chosen. Moses was "the meekest man that ever lived" and Joshua seems to have learned well the lesson of meekness from Moses. By way of contrast, later kings of Israel were devious men who grasped for power. After David's reign, there were few men who understood the importance of waiting for God's timing and placement of leaders.

Patience, humility, and trust in God's leadership, coupled with strength and courage molded God's leaders. The application of this to our present day is that we are to lead where God places us, and not ever try to force our leadership on anyone. Ultimately, leadership is God's business.

CONQUEST OF CANAAN

**Bible Reading:** Joshua 6:17-21, 25

# Q77. How were the Children of Israel able to take Jericho?

## A. When they shouted, the walls of Jericho fell down.

When a large building needs to be demolished, a special crew is hired. They will put explosives throughout the building and hook wires to the explosives. On the day the building is to be blown up, they will make sure no one is in it. At the right time, the wires will be connected to electricity. There will be a loud "boom!" and the building will fall in on itself. It takes careful planning to destroy a building without harming other buildings around it.

They didn't need dynamite to destroy the walls of Jericho. Instead, they marched around the city. Then they sounded trumpets and shouted. At the shout, the walls came down. God brought the walls down. Remember Rahab? She had a scarlet cord in her window. She was to be saved from destruction. Her house was saved even though the rest of the wall was destroyed. God knew how to protect her because she had faith in Him. He will protect us also as we trust in Him.

## Thinking Deeper

One characteristic of the Exodus and the wilderness wanderings of Israel that cannot be overlooked is the divine intervention on behalf of the Hebrews. The instances are overwhelming: ten plagues, the Red Sea parting, pillars of cloud and fire, manna from heaven, water from the rock, the Jordan River dividing, and Jericho's walls falling. Candidly, these events have no natural explanations. They were obviously supernatural.

You can be an unbeliever and contend that the whole business is made up – the Exodus is nothing but a tale. Or you can believe that God is God and that miracles – either large or small – are part of His intervention in the world. "Through faith we understand that the worlds were framed by the word of God" (Hebrews 11:3). If we have that bottom line, then we should have no trouble believing in other lesser miracles, like the Exodus. Furthermore we should then have no trouble believing that God can deliver a sinner from his sins and make him a saint. Those who have eyes that are opened see it all the time.

*They didn't need dynamite to destroy the walls of Jericho.*

**Bible Reading:** Joshua 7:1-12

# Q78. Why did Israel flee from their enemies at Ai?

## A. Israel fled because there was sin in the camp.

"I can beat you at wrestling anytime," a boy said to his younger brother. He was sure he was stronger than his smaller brother. But one day he came down with the flu. He wanted to spend all day in bed. Could he wrestle his brother now? No. He could hardly walk without feeling dizzy. He sure couldn't wrestle his brother, and if he would have tried he would have certainly lost. His trouble was that his own body was being attacked from inside by the flu virus. It took most of his strength to fight off the flu. He didn't have any strength left to wrestle his brother.

After Israel defeated Jericho, they felt strong. They thought that the little city of Ai would not be hard to beat. What they didn't count on was the weakness that came on them because of sin. God was their strength when they fought Jericho. But this time sin was hidden in their camp. God didn't give them strength. So they ran away from the enemy.

We can't be strong in the fight with the devil if we have sin in our hearts. God will not bless us until we repent.

*We can't be strong in the fight with the devil if we have sin in our hearts.*

## ∼ Thinking Deeper ∼

Scandals seem to be part of the national landscape these days. In recent times scandals have reached the levels of political power from President of the United States to senators, representatives, governors and mayors. Why has there been so little preaching to these issues from the church? Think about it: on the religious front priests, preachers, and parishioners have been involved in scandals. The church at large seems to have little to say to the world on the subject of scandals and moral failure. When the church is so drenched with sin, it has little position to deal with the world.

In those classic tales of the knights and gallantry, Sir Galahad is quoted as saying, "My strength is as the strength of ten, because my heart is pure." It takes a man with a pure heart to stand for truth and virtue. The compromised in heart and actions will be ineffective in dealing with the sins of the age. "Achans" in pulpit and pew rob the church of its strength in the battle for glory and virtue. Several years ago one of the nation's most influential daily newspapers was quoted as lamenting that "when we need the church the most, we find it is just like us."

Unless we as the church want to be "cast out and trampled under foot of men," we must regain the position of being "salt with savor."

**Bible Reading:** Joshua 7:19-25

# Q79. How did Joshua deal with sin?

## A. He found the sinner and punished him for his sin.

Rod was saving money in a small box. When he wanted to spend it, he would take out some coins and use them. But he didn't bother taking out the pennies. After a while, he noticed that his jar was full of pennies. Rod knew he couldn't buy much with pennies. He also knew that his brother Rob was saving dimes in his box. So Rod took both boxes and hid under the steps, where he switched his pennies for Rob's dimes. Then he put Rod's box back where it belonged. For the next several days Rod was able to buy things again. But one day his brother Rob decided he had saved up enough dimes to buy what he had been saving for. When he opened his box he found pennies instead of dimes. For some reason he immediately knew what had happened. He went right to Rod. Needless to say, Rod paid dearly for his actions.

When Joshua realized that there was sin in the camp, he didn't wait to deal with it. He found out who had sinned. Achan had stolen things that were supposed to be given to God and buried them in his tent. Joshua found out and punished Achan for his sin. We can't get away with sin. Sin will be punished.

## ❦ Thinking Deeper ❧

Sin is not always punished as swiftly as it was in Achan's case. Many people who are very blatant sinners live long lives and seemingly don't pay for their sins. The psalmist considered this and it almost made him lose his faith. "But as for me, my feet were almost gone; my steps had well nigh slipped. For I was envious at the foolish, when I saw the prosperity of the wicked" (Ps. 73:3,4). What are we to think when evil people triumph and seem to enjoy the evils of sin and don't reap its fearful consequences?

For one thing, we don't really know what goes on in their lives behind closed doors. The college community surrounding Penn State University is affluent. It is also marked by great tolerance for "alternative lifestyles" (translate that to mean sin). There is a sense of aloofness to spiritual things in that community. Yet, these intellectual elites have issues beneath the surface. One Christian man found that family troubles in that community were rife. Homes of these university types were marked by dysfunction. Their children were rebels, addicts or drop-outs. Pride and affluence masked the reality of heartache and spiritual poverty.

Another truth must also be factored in. These so-called elites will one day stand before God and give an account of their lives to Him. What will be their defense when they stand before Him who has said He "resists the proud but gives grace to the humble" (I Peter 5:5b)? The psalmist was finally brought to his senses when he thought this over. "Until I went into the sanctuary of God; then understood I their end. Surely thou didst set them in slippery places: thou castedst them down into destruction" (Psalm 73:17, 18).

*We can't get away with sin. Sin will be punished.*

> **Bible Reading:** Joshua 11:15-23

## Q80. How much of the land did Joshua take?

### A. Joshua took all the land that the Lord told him to take.

On September 16, 1893, an amazing thing happened on the border of Oklahoma. Thousands of people were stationed along that border, waiting for a signal. Right at noon, the sound of a gun started a race. It was a race for land. People raced into Oklahoma and staked a claim to land that they got to first. The race for land became known as the Oklahoma Land Rush.* When people came to land they liked, they could claim it and then begin to settle the land.

Actually, that was only one of several times the government allowed people to race for land in Oklahoma. Some of the people went in before the race and staked a claim. People from Oklahoma are sometimes called "Sooners," nicknamed after those people who got there too soon.

The land God promised to Israel was divided among the twelve tribes. But first they had to conquer the land. Years before, God had promised Abraham this land. The Lord was with Joshua as he took all the land God told him to take.

*"The Oklahoma Land Rush of 1893," Eyewitness to History, www.eyewitnesstohistory.com (2006).

### ∾ Thinking Deeper ∾

Christians often speak about going deeper with God. After coming into God's family there is a lot for a new Christian to learn. The follower of Jesus is to learn all the things Jesus taught His disciples. The experience of the new birth is the beginning. Letting God have control of a person's heart, soul, mind and strength is the foundation for building a life that is pleasing to God. The conquest of the whole person for God is the goal of Christian discipleship.

Israel's conquest of Canaan is a picture of the Christian's conquest of his life. There are places to be conquered, areas to be cleared out, thinking to be changed, actions to be altered, and motives to be purified. It is the transformation of the whole person that is the challenge. These things take time. Sanctification is both crisis and process. The yielding of a Christian's will completely to God is foundational to the ongoing process of conforming him to the image of Christ. When the Holy Spirit fills the heart of the believer, that believer is at the beginning of seeing ongoing changes, "from glory to glory," in his whole life.

Israel was in the Promised Land when they had all the conquests before them. We gain much by being filled with the Spirit, but the conquest continues. Don't be discouraged when you see new ground to gain. It is God's purpose to continue His work in us, to make us more and more like the Lord Jesus Christ.

*Israel's conquest of Canaan is a picture of the Christian's conquest of his life.*

**Bible Reading:** Psalm 25:1-5

## Questions in Review

**Q77. How were the Children of Israel able to take Jericho?**
    **A. When they shouted, the walls of Jericho fell down.**
**Q78. Why did Israel flee from their enemies at Ai?**
    **A. Israel fled because there was sin in the camp.**
**Q79. How did Joshua deal with sin?**
    **A. He found the sinner and punished him for his sin.**
**Q80.  How much of the land did Joshua take?**
    **A. Joshua took all the land that the Lord told him to take.**

A young boy got in trouble for being disobedient.  His dad gave him a whipping for what he had done.   "You don't love me," whined the boy.  The dad was quiet for a moment.  Then he said, "That's not true.  I gave you a spanking because I love you too much to allow you to be disobedient." The father had read the proverb that says "He that spareth his rod hateth his son: but he that loveth him chasteneth him betimes [from time to time]" (Pro. 13:24).

God brought punishment to Israel when there was sin in the camp.  He wanted them to come back to Him.  If nothing happened to them, they would not know how wrong they were to disobey.  Israel did what they needed to do.  They got rid of the sin.  God will bless us as we turn our hearts to Him.

## ❧ Thinking Deeper ❧

God helped Israel cross the Jordan and take Jericho.  But when there was sin in the camp, God withdrew His help and the people fled before their enemies.  However, God did not abandon them.  When they dealt with sin, the Lord blessed their efforts again.  They were able to continue their conquest of the Promised Land.

We cannot afford to countenance hidden sin.  It is sure to bring defeat, destruction and desolation.  Whole churches have felt the chastening rod of God as a result of covering over secret sin.  There is reason to believe that some Christian businessmen have lost God's favor in their business because they countenance secret sins that they have "buried under their tent."  Every Christian must honestly live his life, in the open and in secret, with the constant awareness that "thou, Lord, seest me."  But we must not despair when sin is revealed.  Deal with it.  One has said that God does not bless a man based on where he is, but on the direction in which he is headed.  "Draw nigh to God and He will draw nigh to you."  Then continue to take the land that God has laid before you.

*We cannot afford to countenance hidden sin.*

## ISRAEL AS A YOUNG NATION

**Bible Reading:** Judges 2:11-19

# Q81. What did the children of Israel do after Joshua died?

## A. They forsook the Lord and served false gods.

An old man lived by himself on a piece of land. The government decided to build a road through the land and offered him a price for it. He would not take the money. The government offered him even more money. He told them he would not sell his land at any price and they could not make him leave. They finally sent a man called a "troubleshooter." He sat down with the man and talked with him. He asked him why he was so attached to the land. The old man told him that in his fireplace was a fire that had never gone out for generations. He had promised not to let it go out. Now the government was trying to make him break his promise. When the "troubleshooter" found that out, he told the old man that they could keep the fire going until he was moved into a different house. Then they would take the fire from the old house and carry it to the new one. This satisfied the old man. He was able to keep his promise.

When Joshua died, the people forgot about God. They didn't keep their promise to serve only the Lord. They turned to false gods. They got into trouble because of their sin. They should have kept their promise. We should learn from that example and keep our promises to God. "For I give you good doctrine, forsake ye not my law" (Pr. 4:2).

## ～ Thinking Deeper ～

The book of Judges records the "cycles of sin" of the Children of Israel. When they forgot God, they would turn to idols. The Lord would then allow an enemy to conquer them. They would live in bondage until they called on the Lord. The Lord would answer their prayer and send them a deliverer, or judge. The Lord would give them freedom from bondage, and a period of rest. Again they would turn from God and the cycle would restart. This distinct cycle happened at least five times. Adam Clarke observed that we should learn from these events 1) not to presume for God is just, and 2) not to despair, for God is merciful. It is from these events that we get the histories of Othniel, Ehud, Deborah with Barak, Gideon, and Samson. These judges arose to help Israel in times of oppression.

The debate between Calvinists and Wesleyans about the possibility of backsliding was answered by one cynic who said that Calvinists don't believe in backsliding, while Wesleyans do and practice it freely. The truth is that there are far too many who do backslide. And the results are not good. God actively "resists the proud." It is the proud who thinks he "has need of nothing" while in reality he is spiritually impoverished. The oppression of sin can only be lifted when men call upon the Lord for deliverance. But the oppression can be lifted, for God "gives grace to the humble." The answer to backsliding is to daily "walk humbly with our God."

*For I give you good doctrine, forsake ye not my law' (Pr. 4:2).*

**Bible Reading:** 1 Samuel 3:7-21

## Q84. Why did God call Samuel?

### A. God called Samuel to be a prophet of the Lord in Israel.

A fourth grade class was asked by the teacher to write an answer to this question: "What do you want to be when you grow up?" Many of the students wrote about what kind of job they wanted to have, like being a nurse, or a firefighter, or a cowboy. One boy thought about the question. He didn't know what he wanted to be. But he was a Christian and knew that the Lord had a plan for his life. He wrote his answer. "When I grow up, I want to be what Jesus wants me to be."

When Samuel was a little boy, his mother brought him to the temple. He was to serve the Lord under a priest named Eli. One night Samuel heard God calling him. He answered, "Speak, for thy servant heareth." Samuel was willing to be whatever God wanted him to be. God had a plan for Samuel. He wanted him to be a prophet in Israel. Samuel was faithful to God when he was a young boy, and he remained faithful all his life. God also wants us to be faithful.

### ∽ Thinking Deeper ∾

God gave Samuel a special calling. He was chosen to bring people the word from the Lord. He was in a culture that had been heavily influenced by paganism. Time and again the Children of Israel had abandoned God and embraced idols. They lost the blessing of the Lord and were sold into slavery to other nations. When they called on the Lord, He heard them and raised up judges to deliver them. This cycle lasted until Samuel was called. Samuel had the Word of the Lord to give to the people. Under the anointing of the Holy Spirit, Samuel was able to apply God's truth to the people. He prophetically spoke to his people in his time. He spoke God's word with boldness.

People of God face a variety of temptations. One of them is to take on the belief systems of the culture in which they live. Often the culture has practices and expectations that are contrary to the Bible. God's call for His people is to come out of their culture into the Christian community. The preacher is to be like Samuel in calling the people away from the pagan ways of the present culture. He is to speak God's Word with boldness. He must point out where the culture is in violation of God's law. And he must call the people to decide to follow God's Word instead of following cultural norms. "Choose you this day whom ye will serve" (Joshua 24:15).

*People of God face a variety of temptations. One of them is to take on the belief systems of the culture in which they live.*

**Bible Reading:** I Thessalonians 1:5-10

**Questions in Review**

**Q81. What did the children of Israel do after Joshua died?**
   **A. They forsook the Lord and served false gods.**
**Q82. What caused Israel to serve false gods?**
   **A. They married women who were unbelievers.**
**Q83. How did people decide what to do in the days of the Judges?**
   **A. They did what was right in their own eyes.**
**Q84. Why did God call Samuel?**
   **A. God called Samuel to be a prophet of the Lord in Israel.**

At recess the students were playing scooter dodge ball. A boy was hit by a ball that was thrown by a girl. As he sat at the sidelines watching, he said "Get her!" The teacher said one word: "Revenge." He knew she was right. He wanted revenge on the girl and he knew that was wrong. It was a game to be played by certain rules and she had played by the rules. He should not have those bad feelings toward her just because he lost the game. It hadn't occurred to him that his feelings were wrong until the teacher said that one word.

Without the Word of God being spoken to them, Israel did what was right in their own eyes. God sent Samuel to give them His Word so they would know that their ways were wrong. God sends us His Word so that we can know the difference between right and wrong. "Order my steps in thy word: and let not any iniquity have dominion over me" (Ps. 119:133).

## Thinking Deeper

A young man building a wall mixed the mortar and began putting the rocks in place. After some time, he checked the strength of the wall. To his dismay, he found that the wall crumbled with a slight amount of pressure. On checking, he found that instead of mortar he had been using a bag of gray lime. It looked like mortar, but had no strength at all. He had to start over with real mortar. Then the wall was strong, and stayed in place for years.

When Israel was doing what was right in their own eyes, they did what was wrong. They had no strength under pressure. Without being built on the solid foundation of the Word of God, they crumbled in the face of opposition. God called Samuel to proclaim His word to Israel. Invariably, spiritual movements have a man of God calling people back to the Word. Luther led Europe's Protestant Reformation with the phrase "sola scriptura." Wesley became known as a man of "One Book." If a man will lead his family in godly ways, that man will be a man who brings them to the Word of God. "Thy word is a lamp unto my feet, and a light unto my path."

*Without the Word of God being spoken to them, Israel did what was right in their own eyes.*

# ISRAEL'S KINGS

**Bible Reading:** 1 Samuel 15:16-23

# Q85. Why did Saul lose his kingdom?

### A. Saul lost his kingdom because he rejected God's Word.

Some basketball players are over seven feet tall. They have to duck to walk through a door without hitting their heads. Saul was a big man. He was "head and shoulders" above everybody else. But Saul didn't think he was special. When he was chosen to be king, he was little in his own eyes. But Saul began to think that maybe he was pretty special, since he was the king. After a while, he began doing things that were wrong. He did not listen to Samuel, who told him what God wanted him to do. Instead, Saul did things his own way. Saul didn't obey God. His story has a sad ending. Samuel told him he would lose the kingdom. He got so far away from God that he went to a witch for advice. Finally, his life ended when he fell on his own sword.

We can learn a lesson from Saul's life. If we want God's blessing, we must obey His word. If we reject God's Word, we can expect a sad ending to our lives. "He, that being often reproved hardeneth his neck, shall suddenly be destroyed, and that without remedy" (Proverbs 29:1).

 ## Thinking Deeper

A major church denomination continued to send liberal preachers to a rural church where the people still believed in the Bible. When they sent a feminist woman to pastor the church, not enough people came to the services. The denomination decided to close the church and put the building up for sale. That was not an isolated incident. Many churches in that denomination closed. What was the trouble? It is clear that they harmed themselves by their liberalism.

Theological liberalism denies the major truths of the Bible: the Bible is man's book, not God's; the stories in the Bible are not true; the commandments should be seen as help in making decisions, but should be adjusted to the situation; Jesus was a great teacher and moral example, but wasn't born of a virgin; He was the son of God only in the same way that we all are sons of God; there is no such thing as salvation from sin; and being born again is a concept followed by the misguided and ignorant.

On consideration, why would anyone go to a church filled with such unbelief? And why would God bless such a church? This denomination which had once been a powerful force in America for godliness has followed in the footsteps of King Saul, who once had walked with God, but later rejected His Word. Like Saul, they have ended up with no heart for God. Rejecting God's Word is exactly the way to lose a kingdom, and a church.

> *If we reject God's Word, we can expect a sad ending to our lives.*

> **Bible Reading:** Psalm 9:1-10

## Q86. What was it about David that made him special to God?

### A. David was "the apple of God's eye" because he served God with his whole heart.

A father called his children around him and asked, "Who will help me clean out the car?" Only Joey volunteered. "I'll help," he said. The other children wanted to play. The next day the dad was trimming the hedges around the house. "Who wants to help me?" he asked. "I will," said Joey. He was the only one. The others went off to play. When morning came, the father said, "Tomorrow I'm going early to our cabin to get ready for our vacation. I can only take one of you children with me. Who wants to go?" All the children volunteered. They wanted to go on the adventure. Dad thought a minute and then said, "I have decided to take Joey."

Why did the dad pick Joey? He could depend on Joey. Joey was a real help.

David was special in God's eyes because he loved God with his whole heart. God will treat anyone special who serves Him with his whole heart. You too can be one of His special people.

*God will treat anyone special who serves Him with their whole heart.*

## ⟲ **Thinking Deeper** ⟲

What is it to have a perfect heart? It is not to have a perfect record, for David's acts in the matter of Uriah were certainly less than perfect. It is not to have perfect judgment, for David greatly miscalculated in the matter of his son Absolom. It is not to have perfect wisdom, for David foolishly discarded wise advice and numbered his people. Yet David is considered as one who had a perfect heart.

To get at what that means we must look at those who were later contrasted with David, who did not have perfect hearts. David is used as the standard of comparison. Of Abijam it is written that "his heart was not perfect with the LORD his God, as the heart of David his father" (1 Kings 15:3). What did he do? He disregarded God's word. Other kings did great evil in departing from God's ways. Most never repented. In contrast, David had great respect for God's word. "David did that which was right in the eyes of the LORD, and turned not aside from any thing that he commanded him all the days of his life, save only in the matter of Uriah the Hittite"(1 Kings 15:5). And in that matter, when David was confronted, he deeply repented, as is evidenced in Psalm 51.

A perfect heart is one which follows God wherever God leads, and desires whatever God desires. A perfect heart will always lead one away from evil and to holiness.

**Bible Reading:** 1 Kings 11:1-13

# Q87. Why was Solomon's reign partly good and partly bad?

### A. Solomon served the Lord with a divided heart.

The farm boy was proud to be driving a tractor. He was even more proud to be pulling a wagon with his sisters riding. He looked back at them so they would know what a good job he was doing. Suddenly he felt the wheels hit something. Quickly he turned and saw that he had veered off the lane and was riding on a hedge. He stepped on the brake but it was too late. The hedge was flattened. He had not been concentrating on driving, and now he had ruined a hedge. He learned an important lesson. When driving, it is important to keep your attention undivided.

Solomon had his heart divided between pleasing the God of his father David, and pleasing all the wives he had married. Those wives worshiped strange gods. Solomon began building temples to those gods for his wives. Solomon allowed the evil of false religion to enter Israel. His heart was divided. He opened the door to trouble for Israel.

 **Thinking Deeper**

Dr. Gailyn Van Rheenen wrote an article in which he observed that in Africa some Christians profess faith in Jesus, yet as many as 69% still have a deep belief that their safety and provisions depend on the spirits of their departed ancestors. That blending of two different religious belief systems is called syncretism. Lest we think that the Africans are somehow more prone to syncretism than Westerners, consider how prevalent is the blending of belief in some form of creationism with some form of Darwinism. It is safe to say that most Christian colleges in America hold to theistic evolution, and are committed to the basic principles of Darwinism. A mid-western theological seminary prominently displays large dictionaries of evolution, with no offsetting volumes from a creationist perspective. What is that if it is not syncretism?

Another description for syncretism is accommodation of truth and error. That is what afflicted Solomon. He wanted to please God on the one hand and please his foreign wives on the other. It led to a strange amalgam of beliefs, which was the undoing of Israel. Solomon sowed the seeds of instability with his syncretism. His son reaped the harvest of grievous division.

We would do well to reject the water from the poisoned wells of secularism in favor of the pure Word of God. Mixing truth and error always leads to compromise of truth.

> *Solomon had his heart divided between pleasing the God of his father David, and pleasing all the wives he had married.*

**Bible Reading:** 1 Kings 12:12-20

## Q88. What happened to the kingdom after Solomon's reign?

### A. After Solomon's reign, the kingdom was divided between Israel and Judah.

It wasn't Darin's fault that his mom and dad got a divorce. But he felt like maybe if he had been a better boy they would have stayed together. He loved them both. Sometimes he stayed with his mom and sometimes he stayed with his dad. Darin wished they could be together all the time. But that didn't happen. Even though he didn't show it, Darin was sad a lot. His parents were divided, and Darin was in the middle. It was much better for Darin when his mom and dad were together. Divorce is a sad thing.

After Solomon died, his son took his place. But he was not a wise king. Because he did wrong, the kingdom was divided. It was sad that the kingdom was divided. It is sad when families are divided. God wants families to stay together. "What therefore God hath joined together, let not man put asunder" (Matthew 19:6b).

*Solomon's son Rehoboam did a foolish thing when he listened to the advice of his peers instead of the advice of the elders.*

### ❧ Thinking Deeper ❧

Abraham Lincoln, the American President during the Civil War, had one great vision for America. He was committed to keeping the United States united. Yet, Lincoln had a cousin who fought for the Confederates. His own family had divided loyalties. There are numerous examples where relatives fought on opposite sides of that war. Some have called it the "Brother's War." It was a bleak time in the nation's history when the people were so divided. Israel had such a time.

Solomon's son Rehoboam did a foolish thing when he listened to the advice of his peers instead of the advice of the elders. Had he put the people's needs first and eased their burdens, he would have been a beloved king. Instead, he put his own desires first and made life hard for the people. That led to a division between the northern and southern kingdoms. Ten northern tribes separated themselves from Judah and retained the name Israel. They installed their own king, Jeroboam.

Where was God in these divisions? One of the conundrums of the American Civil War was that sincere Christians fought valiantly on both sides. Some people ascribe the whole war to the judgment of God on the nation because of its sins. It is quite clear that the division of Israel into two kingdoms was God's judgment on Solomon's compromise with false gods. "... thus saith the LORD, the God of Israel, Behold, I will rend the kingdom out of the hand of Solomon...Because that they have forsaken me" (1 Kings 11:31, 33a).

God's expressed desire for His people is that they be united. Jesus prayed for unity. "I in them, and thou in me, that they may be made perfect in one" (John 17:23a). God's will for His people is unity, not division.

**Bible Reading:** Proverbs 3:1-8

**Questions in Review**

**Q85. Why did Saul lose his kingdom?**
    **A. Saul lost his kingdom because he rejected God's Word.**
**Q86. What was it about David that made him special to God?**
    **A. David was "the apple of God's eye" because he served God with his whole heart.**
**Q87. Why was Solomon's reign partly good and partly bad?**
    **A. Solomon served the Lord with a divided heart.**
**Q88. What happened to the kingdom after Solomon's reign?**
    **A. After Solomon's reign, the kingdom was divided between Israel and Judah.**

King Midas who made a wish that whatever he touched would turn to gold. A fairy gave him that ability. He began touching things and they turned to gold. But when he touched something that his little girl loved and it turned to gold, she was sad. Trying to give her comfort, he gave her a hug. He watched in horror as his daughter turned to gold with a golden tear on her golden cheek. Then the king decided he had made a big mistake. In the story, the fairy gave him another wish. Whatever he touched would become normal again. He changed everything back, starting with his daughter. They were happy to have things back to normal.

*Have you asked the Lord what He thinks?*

Many of the kings of Israel did not realize how they were harming the people and their land. Most of them never did turn to God. They brought destruction to their land. They should have changed. God would have been pleased, and the people would have been blessed.

## ⤙ Thinking Deeper ⤚

After the kingdom of Israel was divided into the northern kingdom of Israel and the southern kingdom of Judah, each nation had its own kings. Israel had nineteen kings. Judah had twenty kings. It was not said of even one of Israel's kings that "he did that which was right in the sight of the Lord." That statement was only said of eight of the kings of Judah. The other twelve did evil. The results were trouble, war, poverty and captivity. God did not bless the evil ways of people he had called his own. It is not a light thing for any people who name the name of Christ to compromise with the false philosophies of the world. One writer observed that some preachers fear being unpopular more than they fear God. It is not only preachers. Who do we really want to please?

A woman asked Dr. Yocum a question about a certain standard of appearance. He turned the question to her: "Have you asked the Lord what He thinks?" Asking for direction from God presupposes searching the scriptures and applying them. Interestingly, the woman had not taken the time to see what God has to say on the subject. If we would have the blessing of God, we must seek to do what is right in His sight.

GOD'S PROPHETS

**Bible Reading:** 1 Kings 16:29,30; 17:1; 18:1,2,17,18

## Q89. Why did God send Elijah to the King?

### A. God sent Elijah with a word from the Lord.

Many years ago businesses would hire boys to take messages from one place to another. They would run with the message, or sometimes they would ride a bike. One messenger boy was riding his bike when a car swerved on the road and hit him. The boy was killed. That was in the year of 1906. Messenger boys had important work to do, even though it was sometimes dangerous.

God called Elijah to be His messenger to Ahab, the king of Israel. He told Ahab that the trouble Israel was having was because of their sinful ways. Ahab didn't want to hear the message. He wanted to kill Elijah. God protected His messenger.

Sometimes God's messengers were killed. Yet faithful messengers continued to give God's word. It is important to be faithful to God. Death is not the end of everything. God's messengers will be rewarded. God said, "Be thou faithful unto death, and I will give thee a crown of life" (Revelation 2:10b).

# **Thinking Deeper** #

Preachers are to fulfill the role of ambassador. An ambassador's job is not to make the message more acceptable. It is not to change the message. Rather it is to relay God's message to the recipients as accurately as possible. The worst possible motive for being a preacher is to make the gospel relevant only to the "felt needs" of people. The preacher who does that will omit the parts of God's message that are unpopular or that are considered to be offensive. There was a popular gospel song that disparaged so-called "irrelevant preaching" with a phrase that went something like this: "Don't want to spend my life a preachin' sermons/ that give answers to the questions no one's asking anywhere." The problem is precisely that people don't ask the right questions. It doesn't matter if people are not asking how to be reconciled to God. The job of Christ's ambassadors is to give precisely that message: "be ye reconciled to God."

*A true ambassador carrying God's message will give warnings that are apply to the circumstances of people.*

A true ambassador carrying God's message will give warnings that are apply to the circumstances of people. Failure to give the message accurately will bring trouble to the messenger. "So thou, O son of man, I have set thee a watchman unto the house of Israel; therefore thou shalt hear the word at my mouth, and warn them from me. When I say unto the wicked, O wicked man, thou shalt surely die; if thou dost not speak to warn the wicked from his way, that wicked man shall die in his iniquity; but his blood will I require at thine hand" (Ezekiel 33:7,8).

**Bible Reading:** 1 Kings 18:19-29

## Q90. What was the contest on Mt. Carmel?

### A. The contest on Mt. Carmel was to see which was the true God.

Years ago people would test a coin to see if it was the real thing by biting it. Some people thought that if the coin was real, their teeth could leave a mark on it. That may have worked with gold, since gold is naturally softer than most metals. People also used to say, "Don't take any wooden nickels." It was a phrase warning people about taking worthless money. This became popular during the Great Depression.

The people of Israel had to decide who deserved their worship – Baal or God. Elijah told them that they should make a test. The God that answered by fire was the true God. Elijah's God answered by fire. The people knew that He was the true God. It is important that we follow the true God. Jesus said, "I am the way, the truth, and the life" (John 14:6a).

*It is important that we follow the true God. Jesus said, 'I am the way, the truth, and the life' (John 14:6a).*

### ❦ Thinking Deeper ❧

J.P. Thomas, a Christian evangelist from India, gave a message regarding miracles. He recounted several miracles he had witnessed in India. Several Hindu students listened to his message. When it was over, they argued that they had seen miracles in other religious traditions that were not Christian. Thomas responded that it is possible for certain phenomena to happen in other religions. But he went on to say that a miracle where a person is changed from a sinner to a righteous person, where selfishness turns to giving, where there is a new spirit of righteousness marked by a new attitude where love fills the heart, "this kind of miracle I've never seen except in the Christian religion."

There are going to be false prophets who claim miraculous confirmation to their claims. But the Bible warns of "the working of Satan with all power and signs and lying wonders"(II Thessalonians 2:9b). The true test of the Christian gospel is the test of divine love. I Corinthians chapter 13 records all that is possible without this love: speaking in tongues, understanding mysteries, faith to remove mountains, ultimate self-sacrifice. All these are possible without divine love, and without divine love we are nothing and all these things gain us nothing. The true God is love, and reproduces that love in His followers.

**Bible Reading:** 1 Kings 18:30-41

# Q91. What convinced the people that the Lord was God?

### A. Fire from heaven revealed the true God.

"What if a man walked through my door and told me he was Jesus, and then said that I should jump out of the window? How would I know what to do?" A student asked that question because he wanted to obey God, but didn't want to do something foolish. What is the answer to his question?

The answer is that the Bible has told us how Jesus would come back. He is coming in the clouds, and there will be a trumpet sound and a loud voice. "Every eye shall see him," the Bible says. In fact, Jesus said that "if any man shall say to you, Lo, here is Christ; or, lo, he is there; believe him not" (Mark 13:21). Jesus is coming just like He said He would. Don't believe anyone else who claims to be Jesus, or who tells something about Jesus that is different than what the Bible states. There is only one true Jesus, just like the Bible says.

Elijah was God's prophet. God helped him devise the contest with the prophets of Baal. God worked through Elijah to show who God really was. The false prophets could not get their god to answer, because Baal did not exist. The true God answered by fire. Elijah served the only true God.

 ## Thinking Deeper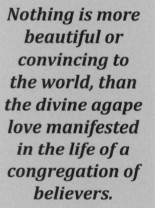

Mormons testify to having a "burning in the bosom" in confirmation to their question about whether their doctrine about their church is true. "I know that it's true," said one of their missionaries. Several decades ago Indian mystic Guru Majaraji had a following of people who were convinced because they would experience a "shot of nectar" as they became one with the vibrations of the universe. They spoke of being "blissed out." The prophets of Baal were convinced enough that they were right that they cried aloud all day, cutting themselves with sharp lancets to enhance the quality of their prayers.

*Nothing is more beautiful or convincing to the world, than the divine agape love manifested in the life of a congregation of believers.*

Human experience is a poor way to decide on what is true. The confirmation that Elijah received was more than inner experiential confirmation. It was demonstrated so that all could see. God answered by fire and there was no trickery, psychology, or demonic interference.

God spoke to the fathers in time past in various ways ( Heb. 1:1). Now He speaks through His Son. We do not look for outward fire, though Pentecost had that manifestation. We look for the evidence that God has marked a person through the Word of the Son. That mark is divine love, lived out in the daily walk by people who have humbled themselves before Him and have found His grace. Grandmother Zernov, on having found the theology of the Free Methodists, said, "It is the most beautiful doctrine." Nothing is more beautiful or convincing to the world, than the divine agape love manifested in the life of a congregation of believers. "The greatest of these is love" (I Corinthians 13:13b).

**THURSDAY**

**Bible Reading:** 2 Kings 17:1, 2, 7, 8, 12-14, 18

## Q92. What happened when Israel refused to listen to God's prophets?

### A. Israel was taken into captivity by the Assyrians.

"Boys, don't play around with those hornets." The dad knew what hornets could do. After he went into the house, the boys decided to throw some apples at the hornet's nest. One boy threw a small green apple. It barely missed the nest. Before he could pick up another apple, "wham!" A hornet stung him on the jaw. How that hurt! That hornet must have seen him throw the apple. The boy wished he had listened to the warning.

God warned Israel about their sin. He had told them if they forgot Him and served idols they would lose their land. They didn't listen to God. After many warnings, God withdrew His protection from them. The Assyrians invaded the land and the people of Israel were taken as slaves. They should have listened to God's warnings.

 **Thinking Deeper**

There is a tendency for Christians to become overwhelmed by the culture they live in. It is natural to want to fit in and be liked. It is also important to be friendly and approachable. The danger comes when being friendly and likeable causes Christians to compromise biblical ways in favor of the ways of the culture. Standing for godliness will contrast with the culture at some point. At that point the Christian must make a choice; will I be true to biblical principles or will I opt to fit in with the culture?

In 2008, a preacher in Canada made the decision to be true to the Bible and proclaimed its teachings on homosexuality and lesbianism. For his efforts he was taken to court for "hate speech" and told not to speak out on those issues again. The culture had taken a position in opposition to the biblical position.

There are consequences to a decision to compromise with the culture. Christians who do so will become indistinguishable from the culture. The salt will have lost its savor. It is then good for nothing, said Jesus, but to be "cast out and to be trodden under foot of men."

It is far better to suffer for righteousness' sake and retain the kingdom of heaven (Matthew 5:10).

> *There is a tendency for Christians to become overwhelmed by the culture they live in.*

**Bible Reading:** 2 Timothy 4:1-5

**Questions in Review**

**Q89. Why did God send Elijah to the King?**
   **A. God sent Elijah with a word from the Lord**
**Q90. What was the contest on Mt. Carmel?**
   **A. The contest on Mt. Carmel was to see which was the true God.**
**Q91. What convinced the people that the Lord was God?**
   **A. Fire from heaven revealed the true God.**
**Q92. What happened when Israel refused to listen to God's prophets?**
   **A. Israel was taken into captivity by the Assyrians.**

Two brothers decided to take a shortcut through the countryside. "I think we should go that way," pointed one brother. "No," said the other, pointing in a different direction, "we should go that way." They chose to go somewhere between the two directions. After walking for a long time, they finally came out to a road. They were quite a way off. Their directions were not good. They would have been wise to have used a map and a compass. Or, they could have asked someone who knew the right direction.

The people kept going the wrong way and God's prophets kept pointing them back to God's way. Finally, the people were so far from God that when the prophets gave them God's word, they became angry. They put some of God's prophets in prison and killed others. God saw their wickedness and allowed them to be taken captive. Israel was like a man who "heard the sound of the trumpet, and took not warning; his blood shall be upon him" (Ezekiel 33:5).

It is important that we listen to God's warnings and follow His directions.

*It is important that we listen to God's warnings and follow His directions.*

## Thinking Deeper

Each generation must fight its own battle for truth. Moses stood against Pharaoh. Joshua fought the aliens in Canaan. David fought with the Philistines. The prophets stood against the compromisers in Israel. In our generation we are in a battle with the forces of secularism. The theory of Darwinian Evolution is the basis for the secular worldview. If we are merely products of chance meetings of the right proteins in the right configuration in the primordial soup, then there is no basis for belief in truth. The post-modern mind has essentially given up on the concept of, as Francis Scheaffer put it, "true truth." The battle is between this ever changing secular humanist view of reality, and the unchanging Biblical revelation of truth given by the God who made the world and everything in it in six days. Make no mistake, this is a major battle. It is a battle for the souls of men. The churches must be involved or the battle will be lost.

The Bible encourages us in this battle: "Earnestly contend for the faith which was once delivered to the saints" (Jude 1:3).

TUESDAY

| Bible Reading: Ezra 1:1-6 |
| --- |

## Q94. Who gave authority for the Jewish people to return to Jerusalem?

### A. Cyrus the King of Persia sent the Jewish people back to Jerusalem.

Two boys were swimming in a farm pond. A man who sometimes worked on that farm drove by and saw them. He stopped his car and yelled at the boys. "Who said you could swim in there?" One of the boys yelled back an answer. "Cal did!" The man didn't say anything more. He got in the car and drove away. The boys kept swimming. They were not afraid of someone who was trying to bully them. Cal was the owner of the farm and the pond. They were confident to stay because they had permission from the right person.

When the Jewish people returned to their land, they were confident because they had permission from the King of Persia, the most powerful king in that part of the world. God had put it in the king's heart to send the people to their homeland. "The king's heart is in the Lord's hand."

### ∼ Thinking Deeper ∼

*How real is the Bible?*

How real is the Bible? How much can we use it in actual daily life? Can we make major changes in our lives because of what the Bible says? Daniel believed that the Bible was true in real time history. He believed it was accurate. If it spoke, he was careful to listen. He didn't relegate it to mythology to pick and choose from. He relied on it as historically accurate and presently relevant.

Here is how Daniel looked at the prophecy of Jeremiah concerning the return of the exiles to the land of Israel: "In the first year of his reign I Daniel understood by books the number of the years, whereof the word of the LORD came to Jeremiah the prophet, that he would accomplish seventy years in the desolations of Jerusalem" (Daniel 9:2). Daniel had been reading Jeremiah the prophet who wrote, "For thus saith the LORD, That after seventy years be accomplished at Babylon I will visit you, and perform my good word toward you, in causing you to return to this place" (Jeremiah 29:10). Like Daniel, Ezra had read Jeremiah and understood that events in real history were part of God's plan for Israel.

Don't be mistaken. God is working His will in the world and in your personal life. Don't miss out on His plan. Apply the truths of the Bible as though your personal eternal future is at stake. It is.

**Bible Reading:** Ezra 3:8-13

## Q95. What was the first rebuilding project in Jerusalem?

### A. The first project was rebuilding the house of the Lord.

A widow lady in Mississippi had a very large tree fall on her house because of Hurricane Katrina. Thankfully, it didn't crash all the way through the roof. Other trees were fallen around her property. Some Christian volunteers came to help the lady. They decided that one of the first things to do was to get the tree off of her house so the house could be fixed. The rest of the land could be cleared later. After several hours of work, the tree was off of her house, some plastic was put in place so her roof wouldn't leak, and many of the trees had been cleared off her land. She stood outside her house, weeping tears of gratitude. She was so thankful that things were being repaired. "I didn't know what I was going to do," she said. God saw her need and sent her help.

When the Jews returned to Jerusalem, they saw the whole city in ruins. The first thing that needed to be done was to rebuild the house of the Lord. They began to do the work, and God blessed them. But some people began to oppose them, and the work stopped. Then the prophet Haggai told the people that they should build God's house. They listened to the prophet and completed the work. The people were happy that they had rebuilt the house of the Lord.

## ∽ Thinking Deeper ∽

Is there hope for rebuilding what has been destroyed? Can a backslider come back to faith? Can a family that is divided be rebuilt? Can ruined relationships be repaired? Can a church that has departed from truth return? The story of Ezra indicates that all these are possible.

The people of Judah were so far from God that they were allowed to go into exile. Jerusalem had been destroyed. The temple had been raided and destroyed. Ezra gave the account of them coming back. God blessed their efforts. Even from the far country before they ever returned, God was with them, blessing their desire to come home.

God blesses a man who turns his steps toward the right. It doesn't matter where those steps have been, if he turns them in the right direction, God will bless him. A man was heading toward the bar one snowy day. He chanced to look behind him and saw his young son following him. Deliberately, the boy was planting his little feet into the footprints left by his father. The dad paused, then turned his steps from the bar and went, instead to the church. His family became blessed. What caused God's blessing on that family? It was the direction that the man took.

God will bless you based on the direction you are heading. Past failures can be overcome by present grace. God blesses the rebuilder.

*God blesses a man who turns his steps toward the right.*

**Bible Reading:** Nehemiah 2:12-20

# Q96. What was the second rebuilding project in Jerusalem?

### A. The second project was to rebuild the walls.

The city of New Orleans was flooded by water during Hurricane Katrina. A major reason was that levees broke. A levee is a barrier between the water and the land that is built to keep the land from being flooded. When the levees broke the water that was held back poured into the city. There was so much water that some people had to climb to their roof tops to keep from drowning. Many people were rescued. After the flood, the people had to rebuild their homes. After that they had to work on the levees. If the levees don't get fixed, the houses will be flooded again in the next big storm. It is important to repair the levees.

When the Jews returned to Jerusalem, they began their work by repairing the temple. But the walls of the city were broken down. To keep the enemies out, they had to repair the walls. Nehemiah was the leader. He made sure that the great work of repairing the walls was completed. Nehemiah trusted in God to protect them from their enemies while they rebuilt the walls. God was faithful to help them.

*When the Jews returned to Jerusalem, they began their work by repairing the temple.*

## ⌁ Thinking Deeper ⌁

When a backslider returns to God, he must repair the "house of the Lord." His heart needs to be brought back into a right attitude to God. Whatever a person's past, he must have a humble heart to come into fellowship with God. "God resists the proud but gives grace to the humble" (I Peter 5:5). The humble in heart will be accepted by God. But there is more that needs to be done after the "house of the Lord" is repaired. Just as Jerusalem's walls were needed to keep the enemies from invading the homes of the Hebrews and defiling the temple, so too the barriers against the onslaught of the world must be erected around a person's life.

Take the example of a person who fell into a sin of the flesh. For a time he was held in the grip of a habit that he could not break. Every day he lost the battle to its allurement. But the man humbled himself and sought the Lord, who graciously took him back. Now it is up to that man to build some walls. He must build walls around his entertainment, so he is not unduly tempted. He must build walls around his reading material and his Internet usage. He must be careful where he goes and who he is with. Anywhere there is a possible weakness, he must build walls. Just as God helped Nehemiah do the great work of building the walls around Jerusalem so too God will help the humble man build walls around his life to keep his enemies from destroying him.

**Bible Reading:** Psalm 137:1-4

## Questions in Review

**Q93. Why did Judah go into captivity?**
   A. Judah was captive to the Babylonians because they did evil in the sight of the Lord.
**Q94. Who gave authority for the Jewish people to return to Jerusalem?**
   A. Cyrus the King of Persia sent the Jewish people back to Jerusalem.
**Q95. What was the first rebuilding project in Jerusalem?**
   A. The first project was rebuilding the house of the Lord.
**Q96. What was the second rebuilding project in Jerusalem?**
   A. The second project was to rebuild the walls.

It was a cold and icy morning in Kansas, and the country road was slippery. The driver of a car was pretty careful until he took his eyes off the road for just a second. In that moment, the car started to slip. By the time the driver tried to stop, it was too late. The car went out of control and slammed into a bank. The front of the car was damaged. The driver got help and took his car home, but it looked bad. It took time, energy and money to fix the car. It would have been a lot better had the driver been more careful and never have been in a wreck.

Many years after their city had been captured, the Hebrews were able to return to Jerusalem. It took a lot of time, a lot of effort, and a lot of people to rebuild Jerusalem. They would have been far better off to have obeyed God in the first place. But God was good to them and helped them return.

## Thinking Deeper

When Daniel studied the book of Jeremiah, he understood that the time of the exile of the Hebrews was coming to an end. Soon there would be a return to Jerusalem. We can read what Daniel read (Jeremiah 29:10) and see how he came to his conclusions. The time of the exile was to be seventy years. Think of the people who were born, lived and died without ever seeing Jerusalem. They had never seen the holy places or been where the glory had been revealed. Children were raised in a heathen land without a sense of God's blessing. What kind of fallout did that have? How many people were lost? God's grace brought them back, but that was seventy years and two generations later.

What happens when a home turns from God? How long will it be before someone in that home returns? And what will the cost be of living away from God? It invariably is paid by the children, some of whom are lost, and some of whom are scarred from the years away. It is good to return, no matter how far one has strayed. It is better to remain faithful and fight the good fight from the beginning to the end.

*It is better to remain faithful and fight the good fight from the beginning to the end.*

PROPHECIES OF THE MESSIAH

**Bible Reading:** Isaiah 7:14

## Q97. What was to be special about the birth of the Messiah?

### A. The Messiah would be born of a virgin.

Every baby is special. Every baby has a purpose in life. The Bible says that God knew each baby before it was born while it was being formed inside its mother. (Psalm 139:15) God knew you before you were born. He knew what you would look like. He knew what color your eyes would be. God made you special. God is so great and so wise that He knows what will happen in the future. That is how He knew about you before you were born.

Long before the Messiah was born, God knew what He would be like. There was something very special God knew about the Messiah. He knew that the Messiah would be born of a virgin. Her name would be Mary. The Messiah would be a miracle baby. God would be His father. God wanted people to know ahead of time what to expect the Messiah to be like. About 700 years before the Messiah was born, God inspired the prophet Isaiah to write that the Messiah would be born of a virgin. Do you know who the Messiah is? It is Jesus.

## Thinking Deeper

Without the virgin birth of Christ, the whole Christmas story would fade into nothing. It is precisely because Jesus would be born of a virgin that Christmas is the season it is. The angels announced the birth because it was special. They came for the express purpose of announcing this one-of-a-kind birth. Mary was visited by the angel because this was a birth like no other. Joseph was visited by the angel for the same reason. The angels came to the shepherds to herald this special birth. It is because Jesus was the virgin-born-son of Mary and the only begotten Son of God that this was the most special of all births that ever happened or ever will happen on earth. These things were prophesied by Isaiah long before the actual events.

Skeptics, agnostics, and atheists attack the virgin birth because it is so crucial to the Christian faith. If it can be shown to be false, the rest of the faith will fall. However, the weight of history, the fulfilled prophecies, the uniqueness of the events surrounding the birth, the singularity of the life of Christ, all undergird the claims to the virgin birth. In the virgin birth, we have a great witness to the supernatural intervention of the Transcendent One in the affairs of men. Earth has had a Divine invasion. As C.S. Lewis said, "God has landed on our shores."

> *Skeptics, agnostics and atheists attack the virgin birth because it is so crucial to the Christian faith.*

**Bible Reading:** Micah 5:2

# Q98. Where was the Messiah to be born?

### A. The Messiah was to be born in Bethlehem of Judea.

Zhang Xiaoyan hoped that her baby would be able to be born. She was a Chinese woman who had been buried for fifty hours by the large earthquake of May 2008. It caused so much damage that almost 70,000 people were killed. She said that while she was trapped, she kept hoping that somehow she would be rescued. Her greatest wish was that even if she died her baby would live and be born. Her wish came true. Rescue workers finally got through to her. She was taken to a hospital where she gave birth to a healthy little girl. She named the girl Ai, which means love.

Not everyone is born in a hospital. Some people were born at home. Some babies have been born in the car on the way to the hospital. The Bible gave a prophecy about the Messiah's birth. He was to be born in a certain city. When the Hebrews wanted to see where their Messiah would be born, they went to the Bible. The prophet Micah said the Messiah would be born in the little city of Bethlehem of Judea.

 **Thinking Deeper**

This prophecy of Micah is very specific. There were two cities named Bethlehem identified in the Old Testament. There was a Bethlehem in the territory assigned to the tribe of Zebulon (Joshua 19:15). That was not the Bethlehem where the Messiah would be born. Micah pointed to another city, Bethlehem Ephratah, as the place. Unger refers to Bethlehem Ephratah as "the ancient name of Bethlehem in Judah. Genesis 48:7 documents Unger's case: "And as for me, when I came from Padan, Rachel died by me in the land of Canaan in the way, when yet there was but a little way to come unto Ephrath: and I buried her there in the way of Ephrath; the same is Bethlehem." So Micah clearly settled on the Bethlehem in Judah's territory as the birthplace of the Messiah, distinguishing it from the Bethlehem in Zebulon's territory.

Why is this important? Because God wanted to make clear to us that He knew exactly where and when He would fulfill His promises. He was not making guesses. He was showing exactly how things would happen. How did He know, hundreds of years before, where the Messiah would be born? He knew because He is God. He knows the end from the beginning. He made specific prophecies so that their fulfillment would be confirmation that all of His plan is unfolding according to His will. "In the fullness of time, God sent forth His Son..."

*Why is this important? Because God wanted to make clear to us that He knew exactly where and when He would fulfill His promises.*

**Bible Reading:** Deuteronomy 18:15; Isaiah 61:1-2a

# Q99. What kind of ministry was the Messiah to have?

### A. The Messiah would be a prophet and a preacher.

Sometimes parents want to decide what their children will do when they grow up. One father wanted his son to do well in school. But his son was the poorest student in the class. His father was very unhappy with him. It looked like his son would be worthless. But his father was wrong. Winston Churchill was not the best of students in his school, but he became one of the best leaders in the world during World War II.

Long before the Messiah ever came to earth, Moses wrote about what He would do when He grew up. Moses wrote the book of Deuteronomy around 1460 B.C. In it, he predicted that when the Messiah came He would be a prophet. Seven hundred years later, Isaiah also wrote about the Messiah that was to come. He said He would be a preacher of good news. The Holy Spirit inspired both Moses and Isaiah to describe what kind of ministry the Messiah would have when He came to earth. His words would be awesome and gracious. He would tell things to come, and He would give good news to people who truly wanted to know God.

## Thinking Deeper

When King David sinned, who was to make him accountable? Of course, the Holy Spirit is faithful. However, David somehow either missed the promptings of the Holy Spirit, or ignored them. In his case, it took the prophet Nathan to bring him to account for what he had done. Of course, the Holy Spirit moved Nathan to speak to David, so ultimately it was the promptings of the Spirit that got David's attention. In David's case, the Holy Spirit's work was effective through the prophet Nathan.

The ministry of a prophet was two-fold. The prophet would foretell events that would follow. Also, the prophet would apply truth directly to the circumstances of life. Jesus did both in His ministry. He prophesied the destruction of Jerusalem, which came to pass in 70 A.D. when Rome invaded. He also spoke directly to the circumstances of people. He applied Scripture to the Pharisees, spoke pointedly to His disciples, and preached good news to the poor. Jesus perfectly fulfilled the prophecies of God's anointed prophets.

In the present, the church with its spiritual gifts has the responsibility of fulfilling the ministry of prophet and preacher. There are individuals in the church, often "prophets, evangelists, pastors and teachers", who are specifically called to bring the Word of God to bear on circumstances. As the prophets of old, and Jesus in His earthly ministry, the church must faithfully apply God's truths. The present age needs the prophetic ministry of the church.

*The Holy Spirit inspired both Moses and Isaiah to describe what kind of ministry the Messiah would have when He came to earth.*

**Bible Reading:** Psalm 41:9; Isaiah 50:6; Zech. 11:12

## Q100. What would happen at the end of the Messiah's life?

### A. He would be betrayed, sold, and shamed.

"You'll never amount to anything!" Jimmy's dad yelled. Tears stung Jimmy's eyes at his father's words. He wanted to please his dad. Instead, everything he did made his dad angry. However, Jimmy grew up and did amount to something. He became a good husband and a loving father. His dad was wrong about him. It's good that Jimmy didn't give up when he was young. Sometimes dads don't know what is going to happen. But God always knows.

God the Father knew what would happen to the Messiah. The Holy Spirit moved on the prophets to write about what would happen when the Messiah came. The Messiah would be kind and loving, but evil people would treat him badly. The Messiah would know what would happen to Him. But God also promised to help Him when the bad people hurt Him. God was right. Things turned out just like He said they would. If you trust God, He will also watch over you.

*If you trust God, He will also watch over you.*

### ❧ Thinking Deeper ❧

About 1000 years before the Messiah was born, David wrote a psalm predicting that the Messiah would be betrayed by a very close friend. Three hundred years later Isaiah prophesied that the Messiah would be openly shamed and spit upon. In another two hundred years, Zechariah wrote that the Messiah would be betrayed for thirty pieces of silver.

These prophecies are notable on several levels. How could people from three different centuries write accurately about the same person who would not be born for hundreds of years to come? How could one prophecy be so specific that it detailed the exact amount for which the Messiah would be betrayed? How could they all know that the Messiah would suffer at the end of his life? The only explanation that makes sense is that God knows the future and has revealed bits of it. Despite the claims of contemporary psychics, God is the only One who knows the future. Trust God. "But he knoweth the way that I take: when he hath tried me, I shall come forth as gold" (Job 23:10).

**Bible Reading:** Isaiah 9:6-7

## Questions in Review

**Q97. What was to be special about the birth of the Messiah?**
   **A. The Messiah would be born of a virgin.**
**Q98. Where was the Messiah to be born?**
   **A. The Messiah was to be born in Bethlehem of Judea.**
**Q99. What kind of ministry was the Messiah to have?**
   **A. The Messiah would be a prophet and a preacher.**
**Q100. What would happen at the end of the Messiah's life?**
   **A. He would be betrayed, sold, and shamed.**

A family kept getting more children so they had to sell their car and buy a bigger one. One day while they were shopping the children saw their old car. They ran to it car like it was a long lost friend. How did they know it was the same car? They noticed it was the same make, model and color. Something else made them positive it was the same car. There was a long dent below the doors from an accident. They recognized their old car!

How would people know who the Messiah would be? God made a lot of prophecies in the Bible about him. The Bible told where he would be born, that kings would come to visit him, that he would be a preacher and a prophet. It also said that later in his life he would be betrayed for thirty pieces of silver. When the Messiah came, people who were looking for him would recognize who he was. If they read the Bible, they would know what to look for.

## ∽ Thinking Deeper ∽

It appears that God wanted to make the coming of the Messiah so clear that anyone with an opened mind would recognize who he was. God did not hide what He was going to do. He spelled it out clearly. Reading through the Old Testament is rewarded by finding clues about things yet to come.

What are the probabilities that the prophecies about the Messiah could be fulfilled by chance? Peter Stoner calculated that just eight of the prophecies being fulfilled in one person has the probability of 1 X 10 to the 17th power. Stoner said that happening by chance would be like covering the state of Texas with silver dollars two feet deep. Mark one of them with an X and then stir them up. The chance of a blindfolded man picking up that one silver dollar are the same as eight prophecies being fulfilled by chance in one person.* But there are many more than eight prophecies. The probabilities of them being fulfilled by chance are so remote that it is impossible. The fulfillment of the Old Testament prophecies is a great evidence that God is behind those sacred writings. "Every word of God is pure" (Pr. 30:5).

*Referenced by Josh McDowell in *Evidence that Demands a Verdict,* Here's Life Publishers, 1979, p.167.

*Jacob and Esau came from the same family, but ended up a lot different.*

*PROPHECIES OF THE MESSIAH II*

**Bible Reading: Psalm 22:16b**

# Q101. How would the Messiah die?
### A. The Messiah would be crucified.

Very few people know how they will die. It is not the kind of information we usually want to know. One little boy was about four years old when he heard that a neighbor man died. It made him feel badly. He looked up into the night sky at the stars and thought, "I wish I would never have to die." As he grew up, though, he kept hearing about others who died. Dying was something that happened – all the time. When that boy became a man, he heard about having eternal life. He opened his heart to Jesus, and was born again. After that, he wasn't afraid of death. He had hope of living forever. That hope was because Jesus, the Messiah, died for his sins.

The Messiah knew how He would die. The prophets wrote about it many years before He was born. He would die for the sins of all people. And He would die by being crucified. The death of the Messiah was part of God's plan to bring salvation to man. God planned it before the world was ever created. He was the "Lamb slain from the foundation of the world" (Revelation 13:8b).

 **Thinking Deeper**

One of the earliest accounts of crucifixion comes from as far back as the 7th century B.C. where the Persians apparently practiced it. (There are some who suggest that crucifixion may have happened much earlier, citing Pharaoh hanging his former baker on a tree. Whether or not that was crucifixion or historical conjecture is probably debatable.) Later, the Romans used it much more extensively. It is quite interesting that David, who wrote Psalm 22, described the crucifixion of the Messiah with the words, "they pierced my hands and my feet." This was about 300 years before the Persians practiced it. The Jewish people certainly did not practice crucifixion. So David's prophecy about the Messiah being crucified is significant.

This prophecy is so significant that it is no wonder skeptics attack it. According to some skeptics, the word "pierced" should instead be translated "like a lion." Those who deny that Psalm 22 is a Messianic Psalm promote this view. But one fact stubbornly resists their explanation. The Septuagint, the Greek translation of the Old Testament written two hundred years before Christ, uses the word "pierced." So there was no "Christian bias" in the translation. Conservative scholars have concluded that there is no reason to question the accepted translation of David's prophecy "they pierced my hands and my feet" (Psalm 22:16b).

*The death of the Messiah was part of God's plan to bring salvation to man.*

| Bible Reading: Isaiah 53:9 |
| --- |

## Q102. Where would the Messiah be buried?

### A. The Messiah would be buried in a rich man's tomb.

Dodge City, Kansas, has a cemetery which is called Boot Hill. In it were buried people who "died with their boots on." That is a way of saying they died while in a gunfight, and they lost. It is claimed that thirty people were buried in Boot Hill, "with their boots on." Another part of the story is that few of these were buried in coffins. The wood to make coffins was too expensive, so when they died, they were buried without a coffin in Boot Hill.

Seven hundred years before the Messiah came, Isaiah wrote that He would be buried in a rich man's tomb. The Messiah would not be a rich person. He would be forsaken by His own people. Yet after He died, He would not be buried where poor people were usually buried. They were taken to a place called the Potter's Field, or the field of blood. Isaiah clearly said that He would be buried in the place where rich people were buried. He would be buried "with the rich." God inspired the prophet to write about how the Messiah would be buried so we would know who the Messiah is.

*Seven hundred years before the Messiah came, Isaiah wrote that He would be buried in a rich man's tomb.*

### ∼ Thinking Deeper ∼

Could a person who wanted to have fame for himself have orchestrated events to make it look like he was the Messiah? That's what some people propose. They don't want to believe that the true Messiah has come and fulfilled all of the prophecies, so they suggest that Jesus fulfilled them on purpose and perpetuated a fraud. But consider some of the prophecies. Could He have fulfilled where He was born by manipulating things? No human could do that. Imagine the difficulty: before He is born, He convinces his mother Mary and Joseph to go to Bethlehem. How could He have done that? He couldn't speak to them, and Morse code was not yet invented, so tapping the message would not have been possible. Actually, the suggestion that He could have fulfilled that prophecy is absurd. Another prophecy states "out of Egypt I have called my son." It is slightly more believable that as a child less than two years old He could have convinced his parents that they needed to flee to Egypt. Again, it is slightly more believable, but that "slightly" is really inconceivable. How many parents move out of the country at the direction of their two-year-old? Could He have manipulated where He was buried? That is conceivable, but highly unlikely. There is no evidence that He had the money to buy a tomb, let alone the tomb of a rich man like Joseph of Arimathea. An itinerant preacher with no money and dwindling popularity could hardly have been buried anywhere but in the place for the lowest class. That would have been the Potter's Field. Actually, to suggest that Jesus fraudulently fulfilled the prophecies to deceive people into believing in Him is absurd. The facts shout that Jesus is the promised one, the Son of God, the Messiah of Israel.

**Bible Reading:** Psalm 16:8-11

# Q103. What would happen to the Messiah after he died?

### A. He would not be dead long enough for His body to decay.

One day some people in a country church noticed a strange smell. It reminded them of the odor of a dead skunk on the highway. They looked around but didn't see anything. Several days passed, and the smell only got worse. Finally, it was so strong that people could smell it throughout the whole church. Something had to be done. After looking everywhere they could think of, they took a flashlight and shined it down a drainpipe that was not yet connected to a rainspout. There was the problem. A skunk had climbed into the pipe, fallen to the bottom, got stuck, and died. It was the worst odor some of the people had ever smelled. That skunk did what all dead things do; it decayed.

One of the prophecies about the Messiah was that after He died, His body would not decay. He would not "see corruption." That means that before a very long time passed after He died, He would be raised out of the grave. The Messiah was going to be different than any other religious leader that had ever lived and died. He was going to rise in a short time and be alive again. He would rise from the dead.

 **Thinking Deeper**

The Bible records more than one resurrection from the dead. The prophet Elijah was instrumental in raising the son of the widow's daughter from the dead. Elisha, who received a double portion of Elijah's spirit, was involved in two resurrections. One was the son of the Shunamite woman, and the other is recorded in 2 Kings 13:21. "And it came to pass, as they were burying a man, that, behold, they spied a band of men; and they cast the man into the sepulcher of Elisha: and when the man was let down, and touched the bones of Elisha, he revived, and stood up on his feet." These accounts indicate that God has the power to raise a person from the dead.

*These accounts indicate that God has the power to raise a person from the dead.*

The prophecy regarding the Messiah indicates a difference. The boys that the prophets raised from the dead eventually died. The man whose body touched Elisha's bones and revived, died at a later date. They were buried. Like all flesh, they decayed. The Messiah would be different. He would die. He would rise from the dead. But He would never die again. 'I am he that liveth, and was dead; and, behold, I am alive for evermore, Amen; and have the keys of hell and of death" (Revelation 1:18).

*THE BIRTH OF CHRIST*

**Bible Reading:** Luke 1:26-35

## Q105. What was special about the birth of Jesus?

### A. Jesus was born of a virgin.

Moms and dads often tell their children if a new brother or sister is coming into their family. One mother asked her little boy if he would like to have a new baby in the house. The boy thought for a little while and then answered, "I want to keep the one we have." He thought he might have to give up his little sister if a new baby came. His mommy explained to him that they would keep his baby sister, but get a new baby brother, too. The boy thought that would be fine.

God wanted Mary to know that she was going to have a baby. He wanted her to know that her baby would be special. He wanted her to know that this baby would have a special Father. God sent an angel with the message that this baby was going to be the Son of God. Mary was happy she was going to be the mother of a special boy. But she was not proud. She humbly gave thanks to God that He had chosen her.

We should be thankful for the special things God gives to us. It is always good to be thankful.

## ❧ Thinking Deeper ❧

Jesus was unique in history. He was the Son of God, and he was the Son of man. He was born of a woman but did not have a physical, earthly father. The Bible always ascribes sin that is passed down through the generations to Adam. Adam is the one through whom the sinful nature descends. Jesus came as the second Adam. He had no inherited sinful nature. As God, Jesus was holy. As man, Jesus was sinless. Being a sinless man, the second Adam, Jesus was perfectly qualified to die for the sins of the descendents of the first Adam. Jesus was the only human being in the history of the world who was qualified to die for the sins of others. Everyone else had his own sins, thus would not qualify to die as a substitute sacrifice for others. Jesus is the only possible sacrifice for the sin of mankind. This is why the virgin birth was so critical to God's plan of salvation. Without the virgin birth, there would be no one qualified to die for the sins of man. Without the virgin birth, there would have been no incarnation. "God with us" would not have happened. But it did happen. "But when the fullness of the time was come, God sent forth his Son, made of a woman" (Galatians 4:4a). Jesus was born of a virgin. Thank the Lord for his wonderful gift.

> *We should be thankful for the special things God gives to us. It is always good to be thankful.*

**Bible Reading:** Matthew 1:18-25

# Q106. How did Joseph know what name to give Mary's baby?

## A. The angel of the Lord told Joseph to name the baby Jesus.

If Chinese parents name their child Lifen, it is likely that they are happy to have the baby. Lifen means "beautiful fragrance." But what would you think if the name was Yun, which means "cloud"? The Algonquin name Kimi means "secret." Who knows what the parents thought when they gave that name? The Zapotek tribe family who named their child Nayeli didn't want any question about how they felt: it means "I love you." Some Russian parents named their fourth child Yevgeniya, indicating she was quite a proper child. Her name means "well born."

Another family had expectations for their little girl when they named her Nadya, which means "hope." Your name most likely has a meaning, also. You could ask your parents why they gave you your name.

Mary and Joseph were each told by an angel to name the Christ-child Jesus. The name Jesus means "God is Salvation."

## ∽ Thinking Deeper ∽

When Jesus was given His name, Mary and Joseph were fulfilling the prophecy of Isaiah, which said, "Behold, a virgin shall conceive, and bear a son, and shall call his name Immanuel."

According to Matthew's Gospel, Immanuel denotes that God is with us. God is the only Savior, thus when the name Jesus was given, the whole meaning denoted that God, who is salvation, is with us. God had spoken in the past that He was the only salvation. "...there is no God else beside me; a just God and a Saviour; there is none beside me" (Isaiah 45:21b). Now God has come down, as a baby, to be the Savior of the world. The mystery of the Trinity is revealed in the very name of Jesus. He came, as the Son of God, to be the Son of man, to save man from his sin. If there is only one God, and He is the Savior, and there is only one Savior, and He is Jesus, then Jesus is that God who is the one God. Yet God was in heaven when Jesus was on earth. So the explanation that Jesus, as the Son, came from heaven to be the expresse image of the Father, is explained by the Trinity – three Persons, one God.

*God is the only Savior, thus when the name Jesus was given, the whole meaning denoted that God, who is salvation, is with us.*

**Bible Reading:** Luke 2:1-7

# Q107. Where was Jesus born?

## A. Jesus was born in Bethlehem of Judea.

Do you think it matters where you were born? If you were born in the United States of America, you have privileges that only US citizens have. For example, you can be President of the United States. According to the Constitution, people who were not born in the United States' territory are not allowed to be President. In other things it doesn't matter where you were born. Regardless of where you were born, you are still part of your family, and you are still important to God. It did matter, though, where Jesus was born.

Jesus was born in Bethlehem. The reason that is important is because it fulfilled a prophecy made hundreds of years before His birth. Micah prophesied that the Messiah would be born in Bethlehem. The wise men had two clues that led them to Jesus. Their first clue was the star. They knew it was special and that it would lead them to the new-born king. The second clue was that He would be born in Bethlehem. They got that clue when they went to King Herod in Jerusalem. They found Jesus just where the Bible said He would be born.

 **Thinking Deeper**

Some cities are not very famous. Nothing about them makes them stand out from others. Others are famous for various reasons: Paris for its fashions, London for its bridge and its history, St. Petersburg for its beauty, Pisa for its tower, Venice for its canals, New York for Wall Street, and Washington for politics. Some cities have become famous because of a significant incident that happened there. When we think of Gettysburg, we think of the Civil War battle. Yalta was the site of conferences of the "Big Three" Allied leaders (Churchill, Stalin and Roosevelt). Nuremberg brings the World War II trials to mind. Hanoi is a reminder of Viet Nam prisoners of war. Wittenberg reminds us of Martin Luther and the Protestant Reformation. And Bethlehem reminds us of the birth of Jesus Christ.

*They found Jesus just where the Bible said He would be born.*

Bethlehem was not really very important or famous until Jesus was born there. It was small and historically rather insignificant. But it was also a place mentioned in prophecy. When Jesus was born, Bethlehem suddenly showed up as an important place. King Herod took notice of it, for good when he sent the wise men there, and for evil when he sent his soldiers to kill the little children two years old and younger. Since then it has been famous. Every year at Christmas and Easter it gets national and international notice. Oh, little town of Bethlehem: how significant it has become since the birth of Jesus!

**Bible Reading:** Luke 2:8-18

## Q108. How did the shepherds know that Jesus was born?

### A. The angel of the Lord told the shepherds that Jesus was born.

Early one morning a man answered his phone. "Hello," he said. On the other end of the line no one spoke. Instead he heard someone pushing the numbers on the phone. The tones of the numbers were making a melody – "Mary had a little lamb, little lamb, little lamb..." "What is that all about?" wondered the man. Suddenly he knew. His daughter's name was Mary, and she had been expecting a baby. That was it! His daughter's baby had been born. He started to laugh, and then his son-in-law told him about the new-born child. He knew he had a grandchild because he got a phone call.

The shepherds did not have telephones to hear the news of the birth of Jesus. No one came to them with a telegram. They didn't hear it on the news. They didn't see the morning newspaper. They were shepherds, out in the fields watching their sheep. They got the news in a very special way. They learned that Jesus was born from the angel of the Lord and a multitude from heaven. "And suddenly there was with the angel a multitude of the heavenly host praising God..." (Luke 2:13a).

*The shepherds did not have telephones to hear the news of the birth of Jesus.*

## ❦ Thinking Deeper ❧

For a naturalist, who only considers phenomena that he can explain by natural laws, parts of the Christmas story are clearly unbelievable. The naturalist would not believe in the virgin birth. He would also not believe that angels actually came to the shepherds. Yet he would have a hard time explaining how the shepherds got to the manger the night of the birth of Jesus. There would be no natural reason for them to leave their job of tending sheep. Why would they at random suddenly get up in the night, abandon the sheep, go to Bethlehem, and start poking around in stables looking for a little baby? That's incredible. But if you are a skeptic, you would believe something like that happened. If there are no angelic beings, then something else must have prompted the shepherds. Maybe they got frightened by a lion, fled to the city, and hid in a stable only to stumble onto this unlikely couple with a newborn baby.

Such explanations are highly imaginative, but imagination is the only resort of a skeptic when it comes to the Christmas story. For those who don't keep their minds closed in by the narrow box of naturalism, the story is believable. Something prompted the shepherds to go to the stable in Bethlehem. They said it was a visit from angels. People have wondered at their saying, that night and ever since. Why did the angels choose shepherds, anyway? They had no agenda other than keeping sheep – until they saw the Christ-child. Then that's what they wanted to talk about. Maybe God knew no one else would be so honest in telling what happened. Makes you wonder, doesn't it?

**Bible Reading:** John 1:1-3, 14

**Questions in Review**

Q105. What was special about the birth of Jesus?
   A. Jesus was born of a virgin.
Q106. How did Joseph know what name to give Mary's baby?
   A. The angel of the Lord told Joseph to name the baby Jesus.
Q107. Where was Jesus born?
   A. Jesus was born in Bethlehem of Judea.
Q108. How did the shepherds know that Jesus was born?
   A. The angels told the shepherds that Jesus was born.

Have you ever been on a treasure hunt? Somebody hides clues that lead from one place to another until the last clue finally shows the way to a treasure. One family did treasure hunts on Halloween instead of going door to door and saying "trick or treat." Their mother hid clues in the house upstairs and downstairs, then outdoors to the chicken house, and down the lane to the mailbox. The last clue finally led them to a bag full of all kinds of candy. They were so excited about the treasure hunt that the next year they asked to have it again.

The wise men and the shepherds had clues to lead them to the Christ-child. The shepherds got their clues from the angels. The Wise Men saw a star and followed it. Then they got another clue when they went to Jerusalem and learned that He would be born in Bethlehem. As they followed the clues they finally found Him. He was a great treasure! The Bible says that he was God's gift to man. "For God so loved the world, that he gave his only begotten Son, that whosoever believeth in him should not perish, but have everlasting life" (John 3:16).

> *The virgin birth, the appearances of angels, and the fulfillment of prophecy, all are easily explainable as the works of the God who created the heavens and the earth and the seas and all that is in them.*

## ❧ Thinking Deeper ❧

The belief that we got where we are through the long process of evolution is based on the philosophic position of naturalism. Everything that exists must have a natural explanation. Naturalists struggle with how things began in the first place, but they are valiantly working on things like "string theory" and some kind of oscillation of an energy field as the precursor to matter. They still must come up with where the energy field came from, but certainly someone will invent some idea that also gives a natural explanation for that. With naturalism as a basis for thinking, it is impossible to believe in the supernatural.

In contrast, those who believe that the eternal God spoke the worlds into existence, have no trouble believing that He has supernaturally worked in the world. The virgin birth, the appearances of angels, and the fulfillment of prophecy, all are easily explainable as the works of the God who created the heavens and the earth and the seas and all that is in them. If God exists he can do anything! "Behold, I am the LORD, the God of all flesh: is there any thing too hard for me?" (Jeremiah 32:27).

**EARLY LIFE OF JESUS**

**Bible Reading:** Luke 2:21-33

# Q109. How did Simeon know that Jesus was the Messiah?

## A. The Holy Spirit revealed to Simeon that Jesus was the Messiah.

A Christian lady heard that a young man had cancer. She was concerned and so she prayed about it. Sometime later, while he was still having treatments, she came to the young man and said, "I've prayed for you and I believe the Lord has answered me. You are going to get well." She was right. He did get well. And he had no cancer for many years after that. How did she know? She was in touch with God. God answers prayer. Sometimes God lets His people know what He is going to do. "Call unto me, and I will answer thee, and shew thee great and mighty things, which thou knowest not" (Jeremiah 33:3).

Simeon was an old man who was waiting for the Messiah. He was a man of prayer. God's Holy Spirit showed him that he would see the Messiah before he died. When Mary and Joseph brought Jesus to the temple as a little baby, Simeon recognized that this was the One he was waiting for. Simeon rejoiced to see this special baby. He was at peace to go to heaven. He had seen God's promised One.

## ❧ Thinking Deeper ❧

Mary and Joseph did not come to the temple with Jesus and make an announcement that they were there. They came in accordance with Jewish custom to make sacrifice for the first-born child. What made them different than any other couple who brought a child to present to the Lord? How did Simeon know this couple's child was the Messiah? Just at that time an old woman came. When she saw the baby, she also recognized who He was and broke into spontaneous praise. Did this little family have halos on their heads, as medieval art depicts? No. There is no evidence that anything was different about the couple and their baby. The difference was that both Simeon and Anna were close to the Lord. They had a prayer life. They knew the scriptures. They were led by the Holy Spirit.

Both Simeon and Anna feared the Lord. They had a daily relationship with Him. They had communion with God. As a result, they were in tune with God's Spirit. They heard His "still small voice."

We read that God "is no respecter of persons." Can we know His secrets? Can we be in tune with the Holy Spirit? Yes. The Psalmist wrote, "The secret of the LORD is with them that fear him; and he will shew them his covenant" (Psalm 25:14).

*When Mary and Joseph brought Jesus to the temple as a little baby, Simeon recognized that this was the One he was waiting for.*

**Bible Reading:** Matthew 2:1-10

# Q110. How did the wise men know Jesus was in Bethlehem?

## A. King Herod told them to go to Bethlehem to find the Christ-child.

Three brothers and their sister from America were in a small city in Russia. They were looking for some relatives. They followed directions to a given address, but when they got there, they could not find a house with that number. Somebody told them that the house had been torn down. When they kept asking about their relatives, they found out that the family had moved into a nearby apartment building. So they went to the building and knocked on the door. Sure enough, they found their relatives. They were thankful someone told them the right place to go.

When the wise men came to Jerusalem, they were looking for the Messiah. The star had led them that far, but they didn't know where to go next. So they went to see King Herod. He asked some Bible teachers if they knew where to find the Messiah. They did. He would be in Bethlehem. So the Wise Men went to Bethlehem where they found Jesus.

Do you know that Jesus is at the door of your heart today? "Behold, I stand at the door, and knock: if any man hear my voice, and open the door, I will come in to him, and will sup with him, and he with me" (Revelation 3:20).

*Do you know that Jesus is at the door of your heart today?*

## ❧ Thinking Deeper ❧

Was the star that the wise men followed a natural phenomenon? Speculations include it being a supernova, a conjunction of planets, Venus, and even an alien invasion. There are problems with these explanations. If the star was some exceptional happening thousands of miles away, how could it have led them? Any star, planet, or conjunction of planets anywhere in the sky will give the impression of movement throughout the night as the world turns. But a bright spot slowly moving in the sky is hardly able to lead someone to a specific nation, let alone to the tiny area we call Israel. Even if astronomers confirmed that two planets did appear to come together, that does not explain how that would have led anyone anywhere.

When the wise men were told to go to Bethlehem, we read that "the star, which they saw in the east, went before them, till it came and stood over where the young child was" (Matthew 2:9b). The distance between Jerusalem and Bethlehem is about six miles. Venus is at least forty-eight million miles away from the earth. How could that possibly "go before" the wise men and then "stand over" the place where Jesus was? It's not that God couldn't make it happen – He caused the sun to stand still for Joshua – but it doesn't make sense that a tiny star in space would fulfill the description of the Bible passage. It makes more sense that God did something special for the wise men, something on the order of what He did for the shepherds. The aura surrounding the Christmas story includes the mysterious and miraculous events that brought it all together. The description of the star fits in with that aura.

**Bible Reading:** Matthew 2:13-18

# Q111. Why was Jesus taken to Egypt?

## A. Jesus was taken to Egypt to escape Herod, who wanted to kill him.

"We are moving to America," are the words Jenny heard from her mother. How exciting it was to be going to a new country! In her home country of Russia, Jenny had been attending a school that was run by the Soviet government. Her teacher had been teaching that there was no God, and one day she had made fun of Jenny for believing the Bible. Jenny's mother had prayed that they could find a place to live where they could worship God without fear. Now they were going to America where they could freely worship God. Jenny was grateful that God had answered her mother's prayers. God cares about all of His children.

When Jesus was very young, his parents moved away from their home in Israel. Herod the King had heard from the wise men that a new king was born. Herod was jealous. He sent soldiers to kill the little babies in and around Bethlehem. His plan was to kill baby Jesus. But God spoke to Joseph in a dream and told him what was happening. Joseph took Mary and Jesus and they escaped to Egypt. God was watching out for Jesus, His only begotten Son.

## ∽ Thinking Deeper ∽

Why does God allow evil people to be in power? Why doesn't He just do away with them? Why did He allow Hitler to live to kill millions of people? Why did He allow Stalin and Mao to live to kill multiplied millions of people? Why does He allow wicked people to live to abuse people, to enslave women, to harm children, and to spread diseases that are incurable by their selfish and wild sexual behavior? Why did He allow Herod to live and seek the life of His Son? Why did He allow Herod to kill all of those little children?

These kinds of questions make some people think that God doesn't exist, or worse, if He does that He doesn't care. We can't answer all the questions that surround this, but we do know several things. God exists or we wouldn't even know it was wrong to murder. God cares, or He wouldn't have made a way for Jesus to be taken to Egypt to escape the murderous intent of Herod. There are other things we know from this. The free will of man can be exercised to do great evil, and the results of man's choices will happen. We do reap what we sow. Life is not a game, but very real, and there are very real consequences to the actions of people, whether good or bad.

Even though we can't answer all the questions, we can be part of the solution instead of being part of the problem. The gospel is the good news that evil people can be saved and changed. Despite Herod's attempts to destroy Jesus, God made sure salvation would be provided.

*God was watching out for Jesus, His only begotten Son.*

**Bible Reading:** Matthew 2:19-23

# Q112. In what town was Jesus raised?

## A. Jesus was raised in Nazareth.

David was born in Bellefonte but was raised in State College. Jon was born in El Dorado and Julie was born in Topeka, but they were both raised in Lyndon. Jeana was born in Atchison and Jeffrey was born in Topeka, but they were both raised in Vassar. In this family, only one was born and raised in the same place – Janice, in Melvern. Some children have been born during war and had to move. Others had to move away from their place of birth because their parents changed jobs. There are a lot of reasons why people are not raised where they were born.

Jesus was born in Bethlehem, but was raised in Nazareth. After they left Egypt, Mary and Joseph were afraid to go back to their home area because Herod's son had become king. Maybe they were afraid someone might remember how they had fled and tell the king that they were back. Maybe the new king would remember why his father had killed the babies and get jealous and look for Jesus again. They didn't want to take that chance. They wanted to protect Jesus so they went to Nazareth.

> *Jesus was born in Bethlehem, but was raised in Nazareth.*

## ～ Thinking Deeper ～

During the Presidential election of 1964, Barry Goldwater, the Republican nominee was questioned regarding his birth. The reason for the question had to do with Constitutional requirements for being a U. S. President. One requirement is that the person must have been born in the United States. Immigrants cannot be President. At issue was the fact that Goldwater had been born in Arizona while it was a territory and not a state. The issue was resolved when the courts ruled that being born in a United States' territory, whether or not it was an actual state, met the requirement the Constitution had set. Before people understood that, they questioned Goldwater's qualifications. They needed more information.

There was a question about Jesus being the Messiah from people who apparently knew the Micah passage that stated He would be born in Bethlehem. When Jesus was introduced at the beginning of His ministry, He was known as Jesus of Nazareth. "Can anything good come out of Nazareth?" was the question. How could Jesus be the Messiah if He came from Nazareth? The question was valid. But it was based on incomplete information. Yes, Jesus was from Nazareth, but He had been born in Bethlehem. If they assumed that since He was from Nazareth He was born there, it would have been a false assumption. Knowing more about Jesus resolved the question.

Many issues like this are complicated because we don't have enough information. The Christian faith has withstood many assaults from people who have operated with incomplete information. Don't get nervous about the questions. The Bible has stood the test of time.

**Bible Reading:** I Timothy 4:12-15

**Questions in Review**

**Q109. How did Simeon know that Jesus was the Messiah?**
    **A. The Holy Spirit revealed to Simeon that Jesus was the Messiah.**
**Q110. How did the Wise Men know Jesus was in Bethlehem?**
    **A. King Herod told them to go to Bethlehem to find the Christ child.**
**Q111. Why was Jesus taken to Egypt?**
    **A. Jesus was taken to Egypt to escape Herod, who wanted to kill him.**
**Q112. In what town was Jesus raised?**
    **A. Jesus was raised in Nazareth.**

Anita was playing in the front yard with her little sister Nancy. It was fall, and leaves were all over the ground. Anita buried Nancy with leaves. Just then, their brother walked into the yard. Anita whispered to him, "Go jump on that pile of leaves." She thought he knew Nancy was in the leaves. He thought Nancy was somewhere else. He ran quickly toward the leaves. He was going to jump right on them. Just a second before he jumped, something inside him warned him not to land on the leaves. He jumped over the pile. Suddenly, his little sister crawled out of the leaf pile. He shuddered to think how close he had come to harming her. Then he thought how good the Holy Spirit was to warn him not to jump on the leaves. He had heard that "still small voice."

The people who recognized that Jesus was God's Son were people who listened to God. Simeon listened to God, and welcomed Jesus at the temple. The Wise Men listened, and were led to the place where they found Jesus. Joseph and Mary listened and saved Jesus from Herod. God's Holy Spirit is faithful to speak to His people and help them. He will lead you if you seek Him.

## ～ Thinking Deeper ～

Jesus' birth was unusual in the most literal sense. It was unusual for a baby to be born of a virgin, that just doesn't naturally happen. It was unusual for His name to be Jesus, or "Jehovah is Salvation," who can save others from sin? It is unusual for His place of birth to be predicted from hundreds of years before, who can tell that a significant person will be born in a small town four hundred years from now? It was unusual that shepherds found Him the night of His birth, how many people get a direct message from angels? It was unusual that Simeon and Anna, without any human coaching, recognized that the baby was the Messiah, how many others at the temple recognized Him? It was unusual because Jesus is one-of-a-kind, God's "only begotten Son," the Messiah of Israel, and the Savior of the world, sent "in the fullness of time."

*Jesus' birth was unusual in the most literal sense.*

JESUS AS A YOUTH

**Bible Reading:** Luke 2:40

## Q113. What kind of little child was Jesus?

### A. As a child Jesus was wise and spiritually strong.

Jonathan Edwards was a great preacher in early American history. He preached a famous sermon called "Sinners in the Hands of an Angry God." While he preached, there were men so moved upon that they held on to the pillars of the building to keep from falling. That sermon began what is called The Great Awakening. Thousands of people became Christians during that time. An interesting fact about Jonathan Edwards is that he was saved at young age. He was seven years old when he came to faith and gave his life to God. Another great Christian leader who was saved at a young age was a man named Count Zinzendorf. He was four when he gave his heart to Jesus. Children can come to Jesus. He said, "Suffer the little children to come unto me, and forbid them not: for of such is the kingdom of God" (Mark 10:14b).

When Jesus was a little child, He was spiritually strong and wise. The Bible says that the grace of God was upon Jesus. He showed how a child can live in such a way that the Father in heaven is glorified. You don't have to be old to have God's wisdom. Jesus wants the little children to come to Him.

## ❧ Thinking Deeper ❧

The Bible reveals the dual nature of Jesus – He was "wholly God and wholly man." While Jesus was a small boy, He was developing as small boys do, yet He had the grace of God upon Him. Adam Clarke notes that in this instance, "grace" means that the favor of God was upon Jesus. Even though Jesus was young, He was living a life which God approved. The incarnation meant that the Son of God came to earth and became a human being. As a human, Jesus went through the stages of growth. He had to learn to walk. He had to learn to talk. In all of these stages, Jesus showed a spiritual dimension. He used wisdom.

At the same time Jesus was growing and developing as a human, He was wholly God. The prophecy of Micah 5:2 that tells us Jesus' "goings forth have been from of old, from everlasting." So Jesus existed from eternity. He was God come to earth in the flesh. He was God's revelation on earth. In all stages of the life of Jesus, we see God revealing Himself to man. Jesus as a child revealed God.

> *The Bible reveals the dual nature of Jesus – He was wholly God and wholly man.*

**Bible Reading:** Luke 2:41-50

## Q114. When Jesus was 12, what was he doing in the temple in Jerusalem?

### A. Jesus was doing His Father's business in the temple.

A preacher was traveling with his wife in their car. They were going a long distance and the car was loaded with luggage. They even had boxes piled between them on the front seat. After driving for a while, they stopped for a break. When the preacher was ready to go, he got into the car and drove off. He drove several miles and then noticed that a policeman was behind him with his lights flashing. The minister pulled off of the highway and waited as the officer came to his window. "Sir, where is your wife?" asked the policeman. "Why, right over there in her seat," answered the preacher. "You might have a look over there," responded the lawman. When the preacher looked, he saw her seat was empty. He was relieved when he heard the patrolman say, "She's in my car, right behind you." The rather embarrassed minister was reunited with his wife and they continued their journey.

When Jesus was twelve years old, Mary and Joseph left Him in Jerusalem. They had been to a feast and assumed that Jesus was with other relatives as they journeyed home. After they traveled for a day, they realized that Jesus was not with them. When they returned, they found Him talking to some teachers in the temple. He was talking with them about God's ways. Jesus was doing what the Father in heaven wanted Him to do.

> *This incident in the early life of Jesus lays to rest the idea that Jesus didn't know His purpose in life or His own identity.*

### ❧ Thinking Deeper ❧

Why is this incident in Jesus' life recorded? Although it is somewhat notable that a family member is for a time unaccounted for, that in itself does not necessarily rise to the level of being worthy of inclusion in the inspired record of Jesus' life. Also, it is not unusual for a young person to be asking questions. In this case, though, Jesus was asking questions that were very significant, and His conversation was such that it amazed the hearers. More significant, perhaps, is the answer Jesus gave Mary when she asked why He didn't join the travelers days before when they had left Jerusalem. "I must be about my Father's business." Jesus' answer indicates that He knew who He was. He knew He was the Son of God. His Father was in heaven, and He was on earth doing what His Father had sent Him to do.

This incident in the early life of Jesus lays to rest the idea that Jesus didn't know His purpose in life or His own identity. Jesus knew who He was. He knew what He was doing. He knew it at the age of twelve.

**Bible Reading:** Luke 2:50,51

## Q115. When Jesus spoke about doing His Father's business, how did Mary respond?

### A. Mary treasured these things in her heart.

Two-year-old Julie was standing on a chair and diligently washing dishes in the sink. Her mother saw her and said, "Julie, you're working too hard!" "No," the little girl answered, "I'm working soft." Years later Julie's mother still treasured those cute words. Mothers often remember things their children say. Some mothers keep baby books and write down special sayings of their children. Perhaps your mother has written down things that you have said.

Mary treasured the words of Jesus. She knew that Jesus was special. His words were special. They were words to be remembered. Mary may not have had a baby book where she could write the things that Jesus said, but she did have a place to keep them. She kept them as treasures in her heart.

### Thinking Deeper

Mary had a wealth of things to treasure in her heart. She could remember when the angel spoke to her. That was a treasure. She could remember when she met with her cousin Elizabeth. She could remember when Jesus was born. She could remember the shepherds and their report of the angels. She could remember how Joseph was warned by the angel, how they fled to Egypt, and then later returned to their own land. She could remember the visit by the magi, and the gifts they brought. Now she had a new treasure to add to her heart's collection. She kept His words, astonishing words, as a treasure in her heart.

Mary's example is one worth emulating. We all have things to treasure in our hearts. When you hear the Word of God, that is a great treasure. When the Holy Spirit spoke to you through God's Word, and you came to Jesus, that is a wonderful treasure. When the Word of God continues to speak to you, that is a daily treasure. "More to be desired are they than gold, yea, than much fine gold: sweeter also than honey and the honeycomb" (Psalm 19:10). Keep these things in your heart.

*Mary may not have had a baby book where she could write the things that Jesus said. But she did have a place to keep them.*

**Bible Reading:** Luke 2:52

## Q116. How did Jesus relate to Mary and Joseph when He was entering His teen years?

### A. Jesus was obedient to Mary and Joseph.

Two boys were working with their mother in their garden. They were talking about how it might be easier to run away from home than to keep working.

"Where would you go?" asked the mother.

"We could go somewhere and camp out."

"How would you eat?" she asked.

"We would buy things at the store."

"How would you get your money?" she asked.

"We could plant a garden and sell vegetables."

She looked at her boys and smiled. "Don't you think it would be easier to stay here and work in the garden?" They admitted that she was right.

Jesus was obedient to His parents even though He knew He was the Son of the Father in heaven. He showed how that for young people it is important to be obedient.

Are you obedient to your parents? Do you honor them? If so, then you can expect special help in your life from God.

> *Jesus was obedient to His parents even though He knew He was the Son of the Father in heaven.*

## ⚮ Thinking Deeper ⚮

A college student was ready to graduate and receive his degree. He had a job lined up in his area of study. However, he asked his father what to do. Should he take the job and begin making money? His father gave him some different counsel. "I think you should go back to college and get a Master's degree," he advised. "But I don't want to go back to school again," said the son. However, after thinking it over, he obeyed his father's direction. He enrolled in college for the next semester. Interestingly, it was during that year of graduate education that the student became involved in a youth ministry. Because he listened to the advice of his father, he found direction for his life.

Jesus was obedient to His earthly parents. Even though He was the Son of God, He submitted Himself to His earthly authorities. If that was right for Jesus, how much more important it is for Christian young people to be submissive to the authorities God places in their lives. Being submissive to parents is one way God teaches lessons to His youthful children. God gives direction through authorities. He also gives protection through their wise counsel. Also, being subject to authority is one way to find favor with both God and men.

By being submissive to God-ordained authority on earth, a teen can be in a place to expect blessings from heaven.

**Bible Reading:** Proverbs 2:1-6

**Questions in Review**

**Q113. What kind of little child was Jesus?**
    **A. As a child Jesus was wise and spiritually strong.**
**Q114. When Jesus was 12, what was He doing in the temple in Jerusalem?**
    **A. Jesus was doing His Father's business in the temple.**
**Q115. When Jesus spoke about doing His father's business, how did Mary respond?**
    **A. Mary pondered these things in her heart.**
**Q116. How did Jesus relate to Mary and Joseph when He was entering His teen years?**
    **A. Jesus was obedient to Mary and Joseph.**

Two little boys were playing together. One of them had an idea that he thought might be fun. They would do something that they had never done before. But before they did it, the other boy asked, "Would this really be a good idea?" Then he said, "I don't think this would be wise." His friend listened to him. They likely saved themselves from some kind of trouble. Where did this boy learn wisdom? He learned it from his father, who taught him from the Bible.

The Bible says that when Jesus was just a little boy, He was wise. He didn't do foolish things. He acted in such a way that others could see He made good decisions. His wisdom came from His Father in heaven. If you want to be wise, listen to the Word of God. "For the LORD giveth wisdom: out of his mouth cometh knowledge and understanding" (Proverbs 2:6).

*The Bible says that when Jesus was just a little boy, He was wise.*

## ∼ **Thinking Deeper** ∼

There are some fables handed down from ancient literature about some childhood miracles that Jesus supposedly performed. One told about Jesus making clay birds, and when He finished, He gave them life and sent them off flying. Another had Him striking His neighbors with blindness when they showed themselves to be complainers. One actually had Him cursing a boy for some infraction, and the boy died.

These fables have really nothing to do with the Jesus of the Bible. The descriptions we have of Jesus as a child and entering His teen years reveal that Jesus was wise, obedient, and one who was respected and liked. There is no evidence that Jesus ever did anything that was the least bit questionable. He grew up as a model young man in a home where His earthly parents valued Him and valued His words.

There is another reason that such fables can be rejected. The Bible states that Jesus' first miracle was at the wedding in Cana of Galilee. The claims that there were childhood miracles that Jesus performed are clear contradictions to the Scriptures. When it comes to the truth about Jesus, stay with the facts. The facts are in the Bible.

**JOHN INTRODUCES JESUS' MINISTRY**

**Bible Reading:** John 1:6-8

## Q117. Who did God send to bear witness of the Light?

### A. God sent John to bear witness of the Light.

When you turn on a light switch, you expect your room to light up. That is because the switch is connected to the electricity that comes from the power company. When the power company needs to change something about how electricity is used in your house, they will often call ahead. They will tell you why someone needs to come, what they will do, who is coming, and when they will be there. That way your family will know to expect a worker from the company, and you will recognize who that stranger is.

Before Jesus started His ministry, God sent someone to announce that Jesus was coming. The man God sent was named John the Baptist. He probably seemed a little strange by the way he dressed. He preached to the people. As he was preaching, he introduced Jesus to the crowd of people who came to hear him.

### ∼ Thinking Deeper ∼

When a new political candidate wants to be introduced he will often find someone who is well known and well respected to do the introduction. He may choose a successful businessman, a public official, a war hero, or a famous sports figure. He wants someone to introduce him who will give him credibility. When Jesus began His ministry, God sent a rather unusual person to introduce Him. He didn't send a politician or a sports figure or a businessman. He sent a strange figure, dressed in camel's hair, whose diet was locusts and wild honey.

Jesus was introduced by John the Baptist. John was actually related to Jesus. John's mother was Elizabeth, who was Mary's cousin. John had been preaching to large crowds. He had a group of disciples who followed him. He had a very compelling message that connected with the people in an unusual way. John had been baptizing people who were convinced by his message. Now he turned their attention to Jesus. God sent John for the specific purpose of introducing Jesus when it was time for Jesus to begin His ministry.

*Before Jesus started His ministry, God sent someone to announce that Jesus was coming.*

**Bible Reading:** John 1:19-28

# Q118. Who did John the Baptist say he was?

### A. John said he was a voice crying in the wilderness.

A man climing to be a French government official met with several businessmen to talk about the expense of maintaining the Eiffel Tower. He sold the great French monument to one of the businessmen who was a scrap metal dealer. The trouble was, he was not a French official, but a man named Victor Lustig. He was what is called a con-artist, or an impersonator. He pretended to be somebody who he wasn't so he could get a suitcase full of cash.

People didn't understand who John the Baptist was. They asked him if he was the Messiah. He said no. They asked if he was Elijah. He said no. When they kept asking who he was, he said he was one sent to prepare the way for the Lord. John was not the one people were to follow. He said, "There cometh one mightier than I after me, the latchet of whose shoes I am not worthy to stoop down and unloose" (Mark 1:7). John the Baptist came to help people see that Jesus was the savior.

*Isaiah's prophecy indicated that a voice would cry in the wilderness when such blessings were imminent.*

## ∽ Thinking Deeper ∽

An aria in Handel's Messiah highlights the words "Prepare ye the way of the LORD, make straight in the desert a highway for our God. Every valley shall be exalted, and every mountain and hill shall be made low: and the crooked shall be made straight, and the rough places plain." Handel's exaltation of Jesus recognized the message of Isaiah that was echoed by John the Baptist as he proclaimed the Christ. Isaiah's prophecy indicated that a voice would cry in the wilderness when such blessings were imminent. John the Baptist was that voice.

It is one thing to see the fulfillment of prophecy. It is another thing to be the fulfillment of prophecy. John the Baptist saw the fulfillment of prophecy in Jesus. Jesus was the promised Messiah. John's purpose in ministry was to point out Jesus as the one who fulfilled prophecy. But John was also personally a fulfillment of prophecy. He was the voice in the wilderness. He was the one who was making straight paths in preparation for the Messiah. He was proclaiming the message that all men should repent. The first step to entering that "straight gate" that leads to life is to repent. John the Baptist proclaimed it, just as the prophet said he would.

**Bible Reading:** John 1:29-34

## Q119. How did John introduce Jesus?

### A. John called Jesus the Lamb of God, which taketh away the sin of the world.

Many years ago, when doctors made house calls, a little boy was sick. The boy's mother was concerned so she called the family doctor. The doctor came to visit the boy. When the doctor came to the house, the mother said, "This is Dr. Ishler. He's here to see what's wrong and try to help you get better." The doctor checked the boy and told the mother what to do. Soon, the boy was better. When Dr. Ishler came to his home, the most important thing the boy needed to know about him was that he was there to help him get well. Other things about Dr. Ishler may have been interesting, but he was told the most important thing.

When Jesus came to begin His ministry, John the Baptist told people to look at Him. He was going to tell the most important thing about Jesus. John said He came to take away the sin of the world. That is why He came. That is the most important thing people need to know about Jesus. Jesus came to take away our sins.

## ⌇ Thinking Deeper ⌇

When John said, "Behold the Lamb of God," he was not directly quoting a specific Old Testament prophecy. Neither was John introducing something novel to the Jewish mind with his reference to a lamb taking away sin. They knew about lambs and sin. It was part of their life to take a lamb and have it offered as a sacrifice on an altar as an offering for sin. What John did was to tie together the familiar image of a lamb offering to this specific person as the One who could really take away sin. He was pointing to Jesus as the archetype of sacrificial lambs. All the other lambs that had ever been sacrificed for sin had only been representative of this Lamb, who John identified as the Lamb of God. Jesus was the sacrifice that would satisfy the requirement of God's justice. Sin must be paid for by death, and Jesus would die for all men. Jesus, John said, would "take away the sin of the world." If we are to take this imagery seriously, we can think of a man taking a lamb for his household and bringing it to be slain so that the blood of that lamb can be used as atonement. But instead of a man, now God brings His Lamb to be sacrificed, not for just one household, but for the whole world.

John made a glorious introduction with those words, "Behold the Lamb of God which taketh away the sin of the world" (John 1:29b).

> *He was pointing to Jesus as the archetype of sacrificial lambs.*

**Bible Reading:** John 1:35-42

## Q120. How did John turn his own disciples to Jesus?

### A. John continued to point them to Jesus as the Lamb of God.

S. D. Herron was the founder of Hobe Sound Bible College. He spent time and energy getting young people to go to the Bible College in Florida. Students came and greatly admired Mr. Herron. Then the day came when the students graduated. They left the college to go to the places they felt called to serve Jesus Christ. Brother Herron didn't want them to go to Bible College so they would stay there. He was preparing them to go into ministry, and he was happy when they went to serve the Lord.

As John the Baptist was preaching, he had his own group of followers. When Jesus came, John pointed his followers to Jesus. Jesus was the Messiah. John was happy when his disciples followed Jesus.

## ∼ Thinking Deeper ∼

A mission organization sent a missionary to a foreign field to start a work. He went to a remote city and began working on getting people to come to church. The missions group helped him with finances and encouraged his efforts. Now the rest of the story: this new work was started in a small city within a few blocks of where another group of the same doctrinal persuasion already had a church. With a whole world to win, they chose to go where they might possibly get the benefit of the labors of others. What kingdom were they really building?

Instead of trying to steal someone else's disciples, John the Baptist encouraged his disciples to follow another. He didn't do that because he was tired of the ministry. He didn't do it because he was angry at his disciples. He had found the Messiah! He wanted his disciples to follow Him. John understood his place in the kingdom of God and did his part to see it advanced. We would do well to follow his example.

*Instead of trying to steal someone else's disciples, John the Baptist encouraged his disciples to follow another.*

**Bible Reading:** I Corinthians 3:7-11

**Questions in Review**

**Q117. Who did God send to bear witness of the Light?**
   **A. God sent John to bear witness of the Light.**
**Q118. Who did John say he was?**
   **A. John said he was a voice crying in the wilderness.**
**Q119. How did John introduce Jesus?**
   **A. John called Jesus the Lamb of God, which taketh away the sin of the world.**
**Q120.How did John turn his own disciples to Jesus?**
   **A. John continued to point them to Jesus.**

Three brothers went to a tent meeting with their family. It was the first night of the effort, and they didn't know what to expect of the preacher. They were in for a surprise. This preacher played the accordion like a showman, moving back and forth with the music, playing loud and soft, grand and quiet. Then he preached. He was in the pulpit, then among the pews. He preached in an excited voice. He told interesting and funny stories. By the second night, those three brothers were sitting on the front row. This preacher had their attention.

When John the Baptist came preaching, he was not a normal rabbi. He looked different, preached in a different way, and even ate different food. He got the people's attention. When he introduced Jesus as the Messiah, many people heard his message. God chose an interesting man to introduce His Son.

*Jacob and Esau came from the same family, but ended up a lot different.*

## ～ **Thinking Deeper** ～

A group of young people went to a Pennsylvania drive-in eatery and set up a platform with lights. They sang lively songs, gave testimonies, and then a young man preached a fiery message. Dozens of young people listened to the message. At the end, a young man approached the group. "Why are you so excited?" he asked. "If we weren't excited, how many of you would have listened?" answered one of the evangelists. "You're right," said the youth. "I guess your method worked."

John the Baptist was likely considered unorthodox in his method. "Repent!" he preached to the sinners of his day, and they came to be baptized. "You generation of vipers," he scolded the religious hypocrites, and told them to bring fruits of repentance. He was stern, he was strong, he was different, and he had crowds listening. He got his message across. That is likely why God chose him for his specific task. As Christians we would do well to have enough passion to cause the lost to at least listen to what we say. We don't need wildfire, but we do need fire. We could learn from John the Baptist, the one who prepared the way for Jesus, the Messiah.

# THE BEGINNING OF JESUS' MINISTRY

**Bible Reading:** Mark 1:6-11

## Q121. How was the Trinity involved in the introduction of Jesus' ministry?

### A. The Holy Spirit descended on Jesus the Son, and the Father spoke from heaven.

A hunter was in the woods watching for deer. He was standing very still. A small bird flew to a branch that was right beside him. The hunter could clearly see the feathers, the beak and the eyes of the bird. The hunter didn't move. The bird flew all around him. It is not often that birds come close to people. The hunter felt special that a wild creature would come so close to him.

When John baptized Jesus something special happened. The Holy Spirit came down from heaven. The Bible says that the Spirit came on Jesus like a dove. Just then there was a voice from heaven that said, "This is my beloved Son." The voice came from the Father in heaven. Three persons of the one God were revealed – God the Father spoke, Jesus the Son was baptized, and the Holy Spirit came like a dove. Three persons in one God is called the Trinity.

## ⤳ Thinking Deeper ⤶

Various cults deny the Trinity. Most often their denial focuses on Jesus. They don't believe that Jesus who came in the flesh is the pre-existent and only Son of God who, after He died and rose again, ascended back to heaven from where He had come. In almost every case where the Trinity is denied, Jesus is diminished. When Jesus is diminished, man is increased. Cults will either deify man or assert that man can somehow do something to save himself. If they deify man, then Jesus is diminished and man will eventually be on the same level as Jesus. If they say that man can save himself by some kind of effort, then the need for the cross disappears.

The cults which deny the Trinity end up exalting man and diminishing Jesus. But the Bible says that Jesus "must increase" and that in all things he "must have the pre-eminence" (Colossians 1:18) Historic Christianity has maintained the doctrine of the Trinity because it keeps Jesus in the exalted place that the Father has given Him. In that great truth tradition, we affirm with Reginald Heber that God is "Holy, holy, holy...God in three persons, blessed Trinity."

> *Three persons of the One God were revealed; God the Father spoke, Jesus the Son was baptized, and the Holy Spirit came like a dove.*

**Bible Reading:** Matthew 4:1-11

# Q122. What happened to Jesus just before he began his ministry?

## A. Jesus was in the wilderness forty days and was tempted by the devil.

A man did not eat any food for ten days. He was fasting. To fast means to not eat anything. This man was so hungry that when he saw some cows in a field eating grass he thought, "That grass looks good!" He said to himself, "Why am I thinking about grass? I can eat some real food." He decided to stop fasting and began to eat again. Food sure tasted good to him.

Jesus had been fasting in the wilderness for forty days and was hungry. The devil tried to get Jesus to turn stones into bread. He tempted Jesus. That means he tried to get Jesus to do something wrong. It was not wrong for Jesus to eat bread, but it was wrong for Jesus to listen to the devil. Jesus said, "It is written: Man shall not live by bread alone, but by every word that proceedeth out of the mouth of God." Jesus would not do anything unless God told Him to do it. God didn't tell Jesus to turn stones into bread. After the devil left Jesus, God sent angels with food for Jesus. Jesus didn't yield to temptation. He used words from the Bible to answer the devil. Jesus gave us an example to follow when we are tempted. We can use God's Word to overcome temptation.

*Jesus gave us an example to follow when we are tempted.*

## ～ **Thinking Deeper** ～

Why was it wrong for Jesus to turn stones into bread? Years before this, when he was twelve, Jesus had said to Mary and Joseph, "I must be about my Father's business" (Luke 2:49). It was of the Father that Jesus was directed to the wilderness by the Holy Spirit. It was according to the will of the Father that Jesus was tempted by the devil. When Jesus answered Satan's temptation to turn stones to bread, He knew exactly what He was doing. He was reconfirming that He was on earth for one purpose—to do what His Father said. He was to act only by the words that came "out of the mouth of God". Jesus only did miracles at the will of the Father in heaven. Had He acted on the suggestion from Satan to turn stones into bread, He would have violated His purpose on earth. At the end of His ministry Jesus had a similar temptation when King Herod asked Him to do a miracle. Jesus did nothing. He was committed to His Father's will and His Father's will only.

Here is a great lesson for the Christian. We are to do only what the Father tells us. Listening to the suggestions of other voices opens us up to great trouble. Adam and Eve, for example, listened to the wrong voice. The world is still groaning.

**Bible Reading:** Mark 1:14,15

# Q123. How did Jesus begin His ministry?

## A. Jesus proclaimed that the time had come for the Gospel.

Six-year-old Victor was excited to go to school. It was the first day of first grade. He made sure he was ready. When the bus came, he was on time. That evening when he came home his mother noticed that he was upset. "What's the matter, Victor?" she asked.

"I think they put me in kindergarten," he answered through his tears. "I didn't learn anything all day!"

His mother told him that there was no mistake and that he would soon be learning. Victor was ready to begin. He knew that first grade was the time for learning.

When Jesus was thirty years old, he knew it was time for telling people about the Gospel. The word "gospel" means good news. The good news Jesus talked about is that people can be forgiven for their sins and have eternal life in heaven. In only three years Jesus would go to the cross and die for the sins of the world. Jesus began telling people the good news.

Here is the Gospel in one Bible verse: "For God so loved the world, that he gave his only begotten Son, that whosoever believeth in him should not perish, but have everlasting life" (John 3:16).

## ❧ Thinking Deeper ❧

Jesus came with good news. He also proclaimed that people should repent. In proclaiming the Gospel, He was inaugurating the dispensation of grace. "The grace of God that bringeth salvation" was appearing to all men. At the same time Jesus was continuing the message of truth that had been proclaimed in the Old Testament by the prophets and then by John the Baptist. All men have sinned and must repent. Jesus continued in that prophetic tradition while He began His ministry which would fulfill the good news. He would die as God's sin offering for all mankind. All of the types in the scriptures would soon be fulfilled in Jesus Christ.

> *The Gospel is similar, in that although it is exceptional, it is a continuation of the message that had already been given by the ancient prophets.*

The concept of individual rights guaranteed by the U. S. Constitution has been called "the great American experiment." Ronald Reagan called America "a shining city on a hill." Although American freedom is exceptional in our world, it came into being on the foundation of other earlier documents. Notable among them was the Magna Carta, an English document signed in 1215 A.D. which guaranteed the rights of free men in England. So American Constitutional government is in a real sense a continuation of guaranteed freedoms from years past. The Gospel is similar, in that although it is exceptional, it is a continuation of the message that had already been given by the ancient prophets. In every sense, Jesus fulfilled their message.

**Bible Reading:** John 1:43-52

## Q124. How did Jesus assemble his disciples?

### A. Jesus called people to follow him.

A hunter scared a flock of turkeys. The turkeys flew in all directions. Instead of leaving the woods, the hunter sat down quietly and waited. After several minutes he could hear some turkeys calling to one another. They wanted to get back together. The hunter knew that they would likely come back. In God's animal kingdom, the creatures have ways to call one another together. Mother hens have a special cluck that causes her little chicks to run to her. When a covey of quail is scattered, they will whistle to each other and soon be back together.

Jesus called certain men to follow him. He wanted to teach people how to live to please God. He also wanted to show them how to have faith in God and not in themselves. He chose twelve disciples who would learn God's ways and then be able to teach God's ways to other people. Jesus gave a special call to the men He chose. "Follow me," He said. His disciples came together and followed Him.

###  Thinking Deeper

Jesus had an ongoing ministry with multitudes of people. He healed them and taught them. But when Jesus invested time and energy in building His ways into people, He spent time with just a few. He had his twelve disciples, a few women who followed Him, and about one hundred others who were serious followers. (This number is derived from the number in the upper room at Pentecost.) The ones Jesus spent most of His time with were Peter, James, and John. If you consider who made the most lasting influence of all these, it was these three. They are the ones who had the most to do with the early church in Jerusalem and the beginning of Christian evangelism formation. (Paul came a bit later.)

The point here is that when Jesus wanted to make a lasting impact, He worked with a few. The pattern may be worth considering. Should we try to engage a lot of people? Yes. Jesus did. But that's not how He built His church. To do that, He focused on twelve (and particularly three) men who really learned and were committed to "the Jesus way." If we would make a lasting impact, it is probably better to thoroughly train a few than to exhaust ourselves with a host of people but have no real disciples. Look for people who are committed to "the Jesus way" of living, and make them disciples.

*Jesus gave a special call to the men He chose. 'Follow me,' He said.*

**Bible Reading:** Isaiah 40:1-5

**Questions in Review**

**Q121. How was the Trinity involved in the introduction of Jesus' ministry?**
A. The Holy Spirit descended on Jesus the Son, and the Father spoke from heaven.

**Q122. What happened to Jesus just before He began his ministry?**
A. Jesus was in the wilderness forty days and tempted by the devil.

**Q123. How did Jesus begin His ministry?**
A. Jesus proclaimed that the time had come for the Gospel.

**Q124. How did Jesus assemble his disciples?**
A. Jesus called people to follow Him.

Before an airplane flies, the pilot is to make sure everything works. He walks around the plane to make sure nothing is wrong with it. He checks the wings. He checks the tail section. He checks the fuel. Then he gets into the airplane. He makes sure the engine works. He checks to make sure the controls work. After he has done all of that, he can begin his taxi to the end of the runway where he can take off. Each time before he flies the plane the pilot must check his aircraft to make sure it is safe and ready to fly.

Before Jesus began His ministry, certain things needed to be in place. He had to be introduced as the Messiah. That happened when He was baptized. He had to be prepared by His time in the wilderness and His temptation. Then it was time for Jesus to begin. He told people that the time of good news had come. Jesus was ready to begin His ministry.

*Jesus came to minister to people and to go to the cross to redeem all of mankind.*

## ∽ Thinking Deeper ∽

Christian apologist, John Warwick Montgomery, wrote a book with the title *Faith Founded On Fact*. He argues that the Christian faith is not merely a "pie in the sky" kind of belief, but is a belief rooted in historic happenings, many of which are fulfillments of former prophecies. Jesus came to minister to people and to go to the cross to redeem all of mankind. His mission was well established before He ever came.

Throughout the Old Testament the prophets proclaimed that the Messiah would come to minister grace to the hurting masses while He lived, and to sinful man in His death. If Hebrew seekers had open hearts, they understood who Jesus was when he appeared. Jesus walked in steps that had already been prophesied. From His birth to His baptism, the way had been laid out. God was not doing things to surprise men. He was working to bring his salvation to all men. The person and work of the Messiah had been clearly announced, and everything was in place that the prophets had spoken of. Jesus began His ministry "in the fullness of time."

**TEACHING OF JESUS**

**Bible Reading:** Matthew 5:1-12

# Q125. What did Jesus teach His disciples?

## A. He taught them how to live as part of the kingdom of heaven.

A man stood at the side of the road with traffic whizzing by him. After a little while, he put up his hand. Cars and trucks suddenly slowed down and stopped. Why did they stop? The man was wearing a uniform. He was a policeman. Policemen wear uniforms so that people know who they are. A man wearing that uniform represents the law. When you see a policeman, you know what he represents by his uniform.

Those who are part of the kingdom of God are not required to wear a uniform. In His teaching, Jesus did not tell people to wear certain clothes that said they were Christians. Instead, He taught that if you are part of the kingdom of heaven, you would have a godly spirit. The Beatitudes that Jesus taught us in the Sermon on the Mount show us how to live for God. You can't tell a person is a Christian just by looking at him. But if you are around him for a while and watch how he lives, you should be able to tell if he is a Christian. A Christian represents Jesus by a righteous life.

## Thinking Deeper

Professional baseball players must wear a uniform to play on the team. Each team uniform has a different color or design, but no uniform can be too baggy, or have pants hooked onto the player's shoes. (These are in the contract negotiations of the 2008 baseball season.) There are reasons for uniforms. A baggy uniform could get in the way of the player as he tries to run. Or a baggy uniform gives the batter an advantage. It can be puffed out while the player is batting, making it easier to be touched by a pitch thus sending him to first base. If a player does not wear a uniform which conforms to Major League rules, he cannot play the game.

Are you living according to kingdom guidelines? Jesus taught that the Kingdom of God includes those who live according to God's precepts. In what has been called "the greatest sermon ever preached," Jesus set out the parameters of kingdom living. It is significant that Jesus didn't approach kingdom living as something that we "ought" to do, but rather as a description of how people live who are part of the kingdom. S.D. Herron used to say that any man from the south sitting on his porch and chewing Brown Mule tobacco could tell you how you ought to live. That doesn't make that man a Christian. Basically, Jesus' sermon stated that if you are in the kingdom, this is how you live. If you are not living this way, you are not in the kingdom. It's as straightforward as that.

> *A Christian represents Jesus by a righteous life.*

## Q126. How does a follower of Jesus change the world?

### A. They are like salt and light.

Baby food in jars comes in a lot of flavors. One flavor is squash. The squash is cooked and blended so that it is very smooth. Salt is added, along with sugar, and maybe a little butter. It tastes pretty good. One family decided to make their own squash for the baby. They cooked the squash and blended it so it was very smooth. Then they gave the baby a bite. She made a very bad face and spit out the squash. What was the matter? They didn't add any flavoring; no sugar, no salt, and no butter. Actually, very few adults would have wanted to eat that squash without any flavor. Food without flavoring is often not very good.

Jesus said that Christians are the salt of the earth. We are in the world to make things better. We are here to help when people are hurting. We are here to give to people who are in need. When there is a chance, Christians are to be a blessing. If Christians are not a blessing, what good is it to have Christians? Without salt, food doesn't taste good. Without Christians being a blessing, the world is a pretty sad place. Jesus said, "Ye are the salt of the earth."

*Without Christians being a blessing, the world is a pretty sad place.*

### ∽ **Thinking Deeper** ∾

John R. W. Stott has argued that just as salt has a preservative influence when it is applied to what normally degenerates, so Christianity in the world helps to preserve it from rotting. Similarly, kingdom living in the world shows up its dark places, just as a candle illuminates what hides under the cover of darkness. Jesus' teaching on salt and light presupposes a righteous life as the norm for Christian influence. The normal Christian life is a holy life. The normal Christian ethic is righteousness. The normal Christian morality is truthfulness, virtue, and purity. The normal Christian financial dealing is honesty. The normal Christian relationship is marked by kindness and forgiveness.

What happens when those who claim the name of Christ are unholy, impure, dishonest, unforgiving, and unkind? What happens when lasciviousness, fornication, unpaid bills, judging of others, and a harsh spirit are a significant part of those who are supposed to be examples of kingdom living? They will be rightly condemned as hypocrites. Men will cast them out and trample them underfoot. The world will be without a preservative influence. The darkness will deepen. It is not what we ought to be, but what we are, that counts. Am I the salt of the earth and the light of the world?

**Bible Reading:** Matthew 5:17-20

# Q127. How is living for the kingdom of God different from living by the law?

## A. Kingdom living is more righteous than living by the law.

There is an old story about a little girl who did something wrong. Her mother punished her by making her sit in a corner. The girl sat for a while and then said, "I'm sitting down on the outside, but I'm standing up on the inside." She was outwardly doing what she was told, but in her heart she was not obedient.

Jesus taught us that it is more important to do things from the heart than to just have everything right on the outside. The scribes and Pharisees didn't want anyone to see them do anything wrong. But Jesus knew that they did not have a heart of love for God. In fact, their hearts were hard. They had an outside righteousness, but inside they were sinners. Jesus said that people who were in his kingdom would have hearts that were right on the inside, and would also do the right things on the outside.

## Thinking Deeper

How do we measure righteousness? Is it by keeping outward standards of modesty? That is important, but Muslim women dress more modestly than most Christian women, at least in America. Is righteousness measured by abstaining from alcohol and tobacco? That is certainly healthy, and Mormons have adopted those prohibitions in a large measure. Is righteousness measured by staying by your beliefs and being willing to be persecuted by them? Jehovah's Witnesses are very vocal about their beliefs and are quite willing to endure scorn and ridicule. This is not to take away from these kinds of issues or their place in lifestyle, but notice that it is possible to have these outward lifestyles and not be at all an example of a Christian.

Jesus was clear that those in His kingdom would have a righteousness that exceeded the righteousness of the scribes and Pharisees, who kept the law out of duty and cultural mandate. Jesus did not come to destroy the law. He came to fulfill the law. People in His kingdom keep the law because they love their King. Unless we love the King, keeping the rules of the kingdom falls short of kingdom righteousness.

> *Jesus taught us that it is more important to do things from the heart than to just have everything right on the outside.*

Bible Reading: Matthew 5:21-26

## Q128. What is more important than giving offerings to God?

### A. Living with a Christian attitude toward others is more important than offerings.

You can offer more than money to God. You can offer your singing to God or offer your prayer to God or offer helping others to God. But while you are offering things to God, make sure you have a good attitude toward others. A family was asked to sing in a church. They had several children who sang, but one little boy did not sing with the rest of his family. "Why isn't this boy singing?" they were asked. "We have a rule that if you don't live for Jesus during the week, you don't sing on Sunday," answered the mother. She understood something about what is important to God.

Remember the story of Cain and Abel? Abel offered something to God, and it was accepted. Cain's offering was not accepted, and Cain was so angry that he killed his brother. Cain gave an offering, but it would have pleased God far more if Cain had loved his brother instead of killing him. If you have something to offer to God, it is a good thing. God loves a cheerful giver. If, however, you are offering something to God but have a bad attitude toward another person, God will not be pleased. Make sure you keep in mind what is most important to God.

### ✦ Thinking Deeper ✦

If a person doesn't have a giving attitude, he probably doesn't have the spirit of Christ. The newest believers are told to stop stealing, but rather work so they can give to others in need (Ephesians 4:28). Giving to God is a significant part of the Christian life. Paying tithes and offerings is the one area where God challenges people to test Him. He said to see if He will pour out a blessing on the one who gives. Giving can come in different forms. Whatever you do in your service to God is looked upon as a gift brought to the altar. Yet Jesus said it would be better to stop bringing your gift if you have a bad relationship with someone else. "Leave there thy gift."

A youth leader publicly rebuked one of his students for something that was really insignificant. As the leader prepared to give a Bible lesson, he realized that he should leave his gift and be reconciled to the student. He made a public apology. Only after he received the forgiveness of the student did he feel clear to offer his gift. Don't try to use your gift while you are violating a greater mandate. The greater mandate is to love one another. If you are trying to offer service to God but have a sour relationship, put your service on hold and work on reconciliation.

*If you have something to offer to God, it is a good thing. God loves a cheerful giver.*

**Bible Reading:** John 12:46-50

Questions in Review

Q125. What did Jesus teach his disciples?
A. He taught them how to live as part of the kingdom of heaven.
Q126. How does a follower of Jesus change the world?
A. They are like salt and light.
Q127. How is living for the kingdom of God different from living by the law?
A. Kingdom living is more righteous than living by the law.
Q128. What is more important than giving offerings to God?
A. Living with a Christian attitude toward others is more important than offerings.

A little boy thought that when he asked Jesus in his heart, he would die and go to heaven. One day he was thinking about it. He wanted to be ready for heaven, but wasn't sure he wanted to go so soon. He asked his mother, "Mommy, do you have Jesus in your heart?" "Why, yes," she answered. "Well, you are still alive, and not in heaven," he said. His mother told him that when you ask Jesus into your heart, you are ready for heaven if you die, but that doesn't mean you will die right away. The boy was happy to ask Jesus into his heart.

Being a Christian is more than just getting ready to go to heaven. Jesus taught us how to live while we are on earth. The people who are going to heaven become part of the kingdom of heaven when they trust in Jesus. They don't go right to heaven, but start living like people who are going there. That means they listen to what Jesus says. Jesus said a lot about living in the Sermon on the Mount. He taught us how to live as part of the kingdom of heaven.

*Being a Christian is more than just getting ready to go to heaven.*

## ⟿ Thinking Deeper ⟿

H. E. Schmul once said that it is as important to keep a saint as it is to make one. Included in his meaning is that people need to learn how to live the Christian life. If we don't live like Christians, there is a pretty good chance that we aren't Christian. A big part of the truth that Jesus taught in the Sermon on the Mount is that being consistent as a Christian is an important part of the kingdom of heaven. Someone has said that each of us is either a "part of the problem or part of the solution." Another saying is that "each person is either a missionary or a mission field."

Kingdom living is for all Christians. It is the life of the believer that will tell a story of righteousness. In this evil world, the great contribution of Christians is that they are a force for love, for truth, and for right living. That is the message Jesus proclaimed. Think about the implications: people who claim to be Christians but who do not live the life Jesus described are hardly believable. Kingdom living marks the Christian.

*TEACHING OF JESUS II*

**Bible Reading:** Matthew 5:27-30

# Q129. How did Jesus explain the Seventh Commandment?

## A. Jesus said that a look to lust is breaking the Seventh Commandment

"Does your pastor allow you to have a television?" a lady was asked.

"Oh, yes," she answered, "but he doesn't let us watch it."

The minister wanted people to be careful about what they looked at because Jesus said that looking in a certain way is sin. To lust is to have a strong desire. If a man looks at a woman who is not his wife for the purpose of stirring up a strong desire for her, he has committed adultery in his heart. That's what Jesus said, and committing adultery is sin. A lot of programs on television can easily make someone think things they should not be thinking. Other things can also cause wrong thoughts. We must be careful what we allow ourselves to look at and think about.

Jesus taught us that what is in the heart is most important. It is from the heart that we decide what to do, what to say, and what to look at. The Bible says, "Keep thy heart with all diligence; for out of it are the issues of life" (Pr. 4:23).

## ∽ Thinking Deeper ∾

The scandal of one of the recent U.S. Presidents involving an intern had an insidious twist. The President held that because he didn't technically commit the act of adultery he was not really in violation of the Ten Commandments. He even said that he had studied the Bible on the subject. The trouble with his excuse is revealed in this teaching of Jesus. When he felt an attraction for the intern, he was duty bound by God's laws to say no to the attraction before it got to any physical involvement. He was married and his attraction was to be to his wife. The scandal was first a scandal of the heart before it ever manifested itself. That's why Jesus warned against the look with the intent of lusting. That's where the sin started.

All people, whether young or old, will be held to account not only for their actions, but also for the thoughts of their hearts. The Word of God "is a discerner of the thoughts and intents of the heart" (Hebrews 4:12). It is deceptive to think that keeping certain legalistic, outward limits on action fulfills the requirements of righteousness. Righteousness begins and ends in the heart. Outward actions are merely an indication of what is in the heart. Jesus taught that the seventh commandment is violated by thoughts in the heart. People who have trouble with actions need to look deeper. The problem is in the heart.

*Jesus taught us that what is in the heart is most important.*

**Bible Reading:** Matthew 5:31-32

# Q130. Why is divorce wrong?

## A. Jesus said that divorce was a cause of adultery.

"Why are you having trouble paying attention today?" the teacher asked her student. The student told the teacher that he had been sleeping all night in their pickup truck. "Why did you do that?" she asked. "Mom and Dad were fighting and I didn't want to stay in the house." No wonder that boy had trouble in school! Many times when parents get a divorce they say it will be better for the children not to live with them. But the children don't agree. Over and over children think it's somehow their fault that their mom and dad got divorced, so they are sad, and they blame themselves. When the parents do divorce, they often get remarried. But that is usually bad for the kids. There is a lot of violence and abuse in homes where the children live with someone who is not their parent. Jesus made a very strong statement about divorce. He said when it happens, it causes someone to commit adultery. Divorce is wrong because it causes more sin and more heartache. Jesus loves families and taught that the mother and father should stay together for life. That's how God created things to be in the beginning.

## ⟶ Thinking Deeper ⟵

Why does God hate divorce? (Malachi 2:16) Jesus said that it causes adultery. Sometimes adultery causes divorce. So adultery can be at the heart of divorce as either a cause or an effect. In either case it is a violation of God's seventh commandment.

God has given his laws for the benefit of people. "O that there were such an heart in them, that they would fear me, and keep all my commandments always, that it might be well with them, and with their children for ever!" (Deut. 5:29) The commandments have a twofold benefit: for the parents and for the children. When the commandments are violated, the violation has a generational effect. Both generations, parents and children, suffer. Wives divorced from their husbands have a statistical likelihood to be worse off financially after the divorce. Children of divorce suffer in their childhood from the separations, and then as they grow, as evidenced in higher incidences of social pathologies: drug abuse, alcoholism, physical abuse, divorce. It is no wonder that God hates divorce. It is a violation of His laws that were given for the benefit of mankind.

Not everyone involved in divorce wanted it to happen or agreed to its happening. Some state laws make it hard for one spouse to keep a troubled marriage together, and there is an exception to culpability in divorce (Matt. 5:32; 1 Cor. 7:15). God cares for the abused, and abandoned and does not blame the innocent. But He hates divorce because of the harm and heartache it produces, and because it violates His original purpose for marriage. Defend marriage. Do it God's way.

*When the commandments are violated, the violation has a generational effecttistical likelihood.*

**Bible Reading: Matthew 5:33-42**

# Q131. What did Jesus teach about standing up for yourself or for your rights?

### A. Jesus gave examples of being meek in various ways.

A Christian man was digging a hole in his backyard for a clothesline pole. His neighbor came to him and rather crossly asked him what he was doing. The neighbor complained that he was putting the pole on the wrong side of their property line. The Christian man stopped his work and kindly asked the neighbor, "Why don't you show me where you think I should put it?" The neighbor looked around and then said, "I guess it will be fine to put it where you are digging." By having a meek spirit, this Christian man was able to keep from having trouble with his neighbor.

People often fuss because they want to protect what belongs to them. Jesus taught us to consider the other person above ourselves. Our lives are much happier that way. Remember the song that says "Jesus and Others and You, what a wonderful way to spell JOY."

## Thinking Deeper

It is a good thing to look out for the things that are your responsibility. "Be thou diligent to know the state of thy flocks, and look well to thy herds," said the wise man in Proverbs 27:23. Jesus did not contradict that by His teaching on meekness. Turning the other cheek, or giving your cloak to the man who sued you for your coat, are not irresponsible actions concerning your possessions. Rather they are investments in God's economy of grace. "There is that scattereth, and yet increaseth; and there is that withholdeth more than is meet, but it tendeth to poverty" (Pr. 11:24). People who insist on keeping all that is theirs and who never want anyone to get an upper hand over them are often impoverished in spirit. Miserly people are miserable people, for the most part, and their reputations are not to be envied.

> *It is a good thing to look out for the things that are your responsibility.*

**Bible Reading:** Matthew 5:43-48

## Q132. In what way did Jesus say we are to be perfect?

### A. Jesus taught us to be perfect in love.

Many years ago a young couple in a Russian village faced persecution because they were Bible believing Christians.  Early one morning four young men went to the house of the couple, climbed onto the roof, and began throwing the thatch to the ground.  When the couple realized what was happening they went to prayer.  Then the husband told his wife to make a meal.  When she had it ready, her husband invited the four men to join them.  "You must be hot and tired from your hard work.  Come in for a drink of water and some food."

The young men thought it was a joke, and came into the house laughing and winking at each other.  Just before they ate, the Christian man got on his knees and prayed.  After he said "Amen," he stood up and invited the fellows to eat.  But during prayer they had lost their appetites.  Instead of eating, they left the table, went outside, and began to repair the roof.  In the days that followed all four of them began asking what it meant to really follow Jesus.  Soon they were all saved.  That couple loved their enemies, and they became their friends.  The teaching of Jesus is powerful.

*Instead of trying to steal someone else's disciples, John the Baptist encouraged his disciples to follow another.*

## ∿ Thinking Deeper ∿

Some people dismiss the idea of "being perfect" as impossible.  One writer in his commentary on this passage felt obligated to counter what he called "the false doctrine of entire sanctification."  In his answer he promoted not Christian perfection but the normalcy of sinning.  Why do many professing Christians continue to plead for sin?  Instead of hiding behind some theological argument, wouldn't it be more helpful and more honest to allow the teaching of Jesus to stand on its own?  Jesus taught us to yield our rights to God and in so doing relate to our enemies by turning the other cheek, praying for them, and giving to their needs.  That is part of being perfect as our heavenly Father is perfect.  The issue is not as much one of theology as one of obedience to God from the heart.

Theology, though, does have an influence on how people view this subject.  If one's theological bias obscures the teaching of Jesus to treat enemies a certain way, then that theology is negative.  When the first response to Jesus' directive for us to be perfect is a refutation of the possibility of perfection, there is a problem.  In this case, let God's Word be God's Word.  Love your enemies.

**Bible Reading:** Proverbs 6:20-29

**Questions in Review**

**Q129. How did Jesus explain the seventh commandment?**
   A. Jesus said that a look to lust is breaking the seventh commandment.
**Q130. Why is divorce wrong?**
   A. Jesus said that divorce was a cause of adultery.
**Q131. What did Jesus teach about standing up for yourself or for your rights?**
   A. Jesus gave examples of being meek in various ways.
**Q132. In what way did Jesus say we are to be perfect?**
   A. Jesus taught us to be perfect in love.

"Son, you just can't get into fights anymore." The boy's father was on the school board and let his son know that any more fighting would not be tolerated. The boy thought about it and then burst into tears. "Dad! I have six more years of school left. There's no way I can go that long without fighting." That boy knew his weakness. But his father knew there was a better way to live — the way Jesus taught. He helped his son make it through school and become a fine Christian man.

Jesus taught us how to live. His teaching is not easy. Many people have given up on being a Christian because they don't think they can live the Christian life. But God does not expect us to live as Jesus taught us on our own. He has also given us His power to live as He taught us. "But as many as received him, to them gave he power to become the sons of God, even to them that believe on his name" (John 1:12). You can follow Jesus if you give Him your heart. He will help you live the Christian life.

*You can follow Jesus if you give Him your heart. He will help you live the Christian life.*

## ∽ Thinking Deeper ∽

A young college student became a Christian by asking Jesus to forgive his sins and come into his heart. He joined a Bible study group and began learning what Jesus taught. After one Bible study session he said, "I want to be good ground." He understood that the Word of God needed an honest heart in which to grow. The student continued in the Word and became a serious follower of Jesus and a blessing to his church and community.

Following Jesus is much more than making a one time "decision for Christ." That decision is not ended by asking for forgiveness of sins. It is only the beginning of a new way to live – the Jesus way. Jesus spent three years with His disciples teaching them His way of living.

If we would follow Jesus, we must receive the Word with humble, honest hearts. Following Jesus is learning how He wants us to live and changing from our former way of living. Some things are much more difficult than others. It is not very hard to begin going to church and becoming part of a fellowship of believers. It is much harder to begin to love your enemies and to do good to those who make your life miserable. But that is the Jesus way.

**TEACHING OF JESUS III**

**Bible Reading:** Matthew 6:1-18

# Q133. When we pray, give, or fast, how are we to act?

### A. We are to do these spiritual activities in secret.

A little girl was riding her bicycle when her father drove by in his car. He turned around to make sure she would get home safely. When she saw him, she sped toward home, but instead of watching in front of her, she glanced at her father in the car. In that short moment of looking away, she came upon a parked car and veered into it. Bang! She and her bike hit the parked car, and she dropped to the ground. Her father watched the whole thing. He stopped and ran to her. Though she was slightly bruised, she was otherwise unhurt. It would have been better if she would have kept her eyes on where she was going.

Getting our eyes off of what we are doing, to see if someone is watching can cause problems, especially in things like prayer, fasting, and giving. We do those things not so people will see, but for God's glory. Some things are just between us and God.

## Thinking Deeper

Some politicians are very concerned about what are called photo-ops. They want to be sure the media records any special event that makes them look good. Hopefully, that will transfer into higher positive ratings and ultimately more votes in the next election. Even though that may be acceptable among politicians, the motivation is often questionable. Did the politician really do what he did out of a benevolent spirit, or was it to have a good picture to promote his popularity? Would he have done the same thing if there had been no camera or reporter present?

Giving to the needy, prayer, and fasting are activities that should never be done to play to a camera or to a reporter or to a church board member or to anyone else; except God. Those are private practices. The Lord sees and will reward acts of piety. If those same acts are done with an eye to the approval of men, there are no rewards except what man can give. God will reward the faithful who have an eye only to Him. He sees. Worship Him by almsgiving, prayers, and fasting.

*Giving to the needy, prayer and fasting are activities that should never be done to play to a camera, or to a reporter, or to a church board member, or to anyone else; except God.*

**Bible Reading:** Matthew 6:19-24

## Q134. Why should we lay up treasures in heaven?

### A. Because in heaven, thieves can't steal, and rust can't harm.

Jeffrey had been looking forward to getting a bicycle. He finally got a brand new one. It worked great, and he rode a lot with his buddies. But something started happening. The chain got rusty. The bike still worked, but some things didn't work as well as they used to. One day he rode his bike to school. Later, when he looked for his bicycle, it was gone. Someone had stolen his bike. Jeffrey experienced just what Jesus said happens on earth. Things get rusty and worn out, and sometimes they get stolen by thieves.

Jesus told us to lay up treasures in heaven. No thief will ever be in heaven. No one will ever take away those things that are there. Things don't get rusty or worn out in heaven, either. We can lay up treasure in heaven by doing things for God on earth. You can give money to God in offerings or to poor people. You can also give of yourself. Give some of your time to God. He will use it, and then you will have treasure in heaven. No one can take that away from you.

*We can lay up treasure in heaven by doing things for God on earth.*

### ⤳ Thinking Deeper ⤶

Howard Hughes was one of the wealthiest men of his time. He was rich, famous and exciting. He had numerous contacts with movie stars and people in politics and industry. He manipulated his wealth to his own great advantage. It is reported that when Hughes was a relatively young man, he contracted syphilis. Later in life he became a recluse, and it is thought that he had a form of mental illness due to his sexually transmitted disease. For years he was careful to be hidden from the public eye. When he died few people were close to him, but one report says that 1,000 people laid claim to his wealth. As for Hughes, he didn't take one penny with him.

Solomon had an interesting, though depressing view of amassing wealth. "Yea, I hated all my labour which I had taken under the sun: because I should leave it unto the man that shall be after me. And who knoweth whether he shall be a wise man or a fool? yet shall he have rule over all my labour wherein I have laboured, and wherein I have shewed myself wise under the sun. This is also vanity" (Pr. 2:18,19). In contrast, Jesus gave some more encouraging advice – lay up treasures in heaven. That way you'll reap the rewards yourself, and no one can take them from you.

**Bible Reading:** Matthew 6:31-33

# Q135. What advantage is there in seeking God's kingdom?

### A. If we seek God's kingdom first, He will supply our earthly needs.

Jenny was sitting on the floor of her log cabin home in Russia playing with her rag dolls when she overheard her mother talking. A cousin had come to their home with a problem. Jenny was too young to understand the problem, but she did understand her mother's advice to the cousin. "Seek first the kingdom of God and his righteousness, and all these things will be added unto you" (Matthew 6:33). Jenny remembered that verse as she grew older. She saw how God met her family's need time and time again. She came to strongly believe that God really did what He said He would do as their family put Him first. She saw it happen.

God watches how we live and then acts to help us as we obey Him. If we seek His kingdom first, God will supply our needs for food and clothing. It's a promise.

## ❧ Thinking Deeper ❧

Jenny's family lived in Soviet Russia under the iron fist of Joseph Stalin. Stalin implemented a five year plan to eliminate the name of God from Russia. To do that, he demanded that teachers teach their students that there is no God. Because Jenny's family believed in God, they prayed that God would help them even during Stalin's attack on faith. God helped them in a unique way. The government began to equalize all of the people, and to do that, taxed anyone who made money. Jenny's father was eventually put out of business because of government imposed taxes and then fines for not paying the heavy taxes. When he could not pay, he became disenfranchised (unable to vote). The children were then thrown out of school, and the family was deemed a drain on Soviet society. When Jenny's father went to the authorities to ask for permission to leave Russia, they saw the file on the family and without a word issued the papers.

Not long after, Jenny's family landed on the shores of America, under the shadow of the Statue of Liberty. They soon found jobs and had much more in the way of material things than they had ever dreamed of in Stalin's Russia. God was true to His word. They sought Him first, and He supplied their needs.

*God was true to His word.*

**Bible Reading:** Matthew 7:1-6

# Q136. Why are we not to judge others?

### A. If we judge others, we will be judged just as strictly ourselves.

"Mother, she's being a tattletale!" The girl glared at her sister. She couldn't stand it when her sister told on her. Why couldn't she just leave her alone. She wanted her mom to do something about it. She waited to see what her mother would do. But her mother just looked at her. "Didn't you hear me, Mom? She's being a tattletale!" Her mother stopped what she was doing.

"I think there is more than one tattletale." The mother looked from one girl to the other. "You just brought a tale to me about your sister's tales. If you think being a tattletale is wrong, you shouldn't come to me telling on your sister, should you?" The girl hung her head. Her mother was right. She had judged her sister, but found that she did the same thing. If her sister deserved a punishment, so did she. Jesus told us not to judge others. If we do, we will be judged by how we judge others. God is the judge. Leave the judging to Him.

## ❧ Thinking Deeper ❧

"What happens to the heathen?" This question is often asked by skeptics who think that God would not be fair to judge the "innocent heathen" by the Bible if they have never been exposed to it. However, those who ask the question often do so out of ignorance of what the Bible actually says about those "innocent" heathen. In Romans 2, we learn that "when the Gentiles, which have not the law, do by nature the things contained in the law, these, having not the law, are a law unto themselves: Which shew the work of the law written in their hearts, their conscience also bearing witness, and their thoughts the mean while accusing or else excusing one another."

If a man sees his neighbor stealing something, and says in his heart, "He shouldn't do that," he has set up a law. If next week this same man steals something, he will be condemned, not by the Bible, but by the law of his own conscience. He has judged himself in his own heart and will accuse himself on the day of judgment. So much for "innocent heathen."

Jesus said we will be judged by how we judge others. In Romans 2, Paul echoes that by saying the man is inexcusable who judges another, for he will be judged by that very judgment. God's ways are just.

*Jesus told us not to judge others. If we do, we will be judged by how we judge others.*

**Bible Reading:** Psalm 19:7-11

**Questions in Review**

Q133. When we pray, give, or fast, how are we to act?
   A. We are to do these spiritual activities in secret.
Q134. Why should we lay up treasures in heaven?
   A. Because in heaven, thieves can't steal, and rust can't harm.
Q135. What advantage is there in seeking God's kingdom?
   A. If we seek God's kingdom first, He will supply our earthly needs.
Q136. Why are we not to judge others?
   A. If we judge others, we will be judged just as strictly ourselves.

Some men took a few boys on a fishing trip. After they fished, they went to the cabin and ate. Then they sat down and talked about the Bible. "Do you think God knows what you are thinking?" asked one of the men. One of the boys didn't know much about the Bible or about God. "I hope not," he said. The men opened the Bible and showed him that God knows the very thoughts and intents of the heart. That boy learned something new about God.

Jesus taught us that the things that are spiritual are the most important things. It is more important to lay up treasures in heaven than on earth. It is more important to pray in secret than in the open. It is important to be careful how we think of others even in our hearts, because God judges our hearts. Jesus taught us to live like we really believe God is there.

*Jesus taught us that the things that are spiritual are the most important things.*

## ∽ Thinking Deeper ∽

A veterinarian who was a Christian talked to a lot of farmers who brought animals to him. Sometimes he would talk to them about God. One day he asked a man if he ever went to church. "I don't go to church," the man said, "because if I do, then I'll be responsible for what I hear."

"You already know too much," the vet answered. "You'll be responsible for what you could have known if you went."

Some people act as if God doesn't exist. They are called unbelievers. But even believers sometimes act as if God doesn't exist when they are too concerned about what others think, or they are too interested in money, or they only think about their earthly lives.

Jesus taught us not only to say we believe in God, but also to act on our belief by relying on Him to intervene in our lives. Real faith means we really trust God.

*TEACHING OF JESUS IV*

**Bible Reading: Matthew 7:7-12**

# Q137. How does God respond to our requests?

## A. God gives us good things when we ask.

A Christian man was shopping for shoes. The pair he was looking at was on a shelf near the floor. As he knelt down to look at the shoes a small girl walked up to him. "I got new shoes!" she said, and she skipped away. She was happy. Soon she came back. "I got new shoes," she said. And off she ran. When the man stood up and walked toward the checkout, he noticed the little girl again. This time she was on the shoulders of her father. The man was big and tough looking. But she was smiling. "I got new shoes!"

The Christian man was reminded that Jesus said, "If ye then, being evil, know how to give good gifts unto your children, how much more shall your Father which is in heaven give good things to them that ask him?" (Matthew 7:11). God loves His children more than any earthly father loves his kids. If you trust in Jesus, God will give you good things. Jesus taught us to ask God for the things that we need. God the Father loves you.

## ❧ Thinking Deeper ❧

Not all fathers show love to their children. In fact, as many as one-third of children in America are raised without both parents in the home, and often the single parent is the mother. Too many fathers are absent. Worse than that, when there is a man in the home who is not the father, the rate of child abuse soars. These children don't know the love of a father, and rather see adult males as sources of pain and fear. The results too often are devastating. Troubled children often come from homes without a dad. They are more likely to be involved in criminal activity, drug and alcohol abuse, promiscuity, suicide and death.

Not all children in fatherless homes go bad. Many mothers do a great job raising their children alone. Yet statistically children without fathers at home tend to have long range problems.

This causes some children to have a difficult time relating to God as the heavenly Father. They don't have a good father image. Yet there is great help. God cares deeply about the fatherless. Jesus taught us that God's love is great. He is listening for those who call out to Him. "Call unto me, and I will answer thee, and shew thee great and mighty things, which thou knowest not" (Jeremiah 33:3).

*God loves His children more than any earthly father loves his kids.*

**Bible Reading:** Matthew 7:13-20

## Q138. Does the broad way or the narrow way lead to life?

### A. The narrow way leads to life.

A hunter was in the Alaskan mountains on a goat hunt. He and his guide were coming down a very steep part of the mountain when they came to a very narrow passage with a rock wall on one side and a steep cliff on the other side. The guide went ahead and carefully walked on the slippery rock that took him to a wider place. The hunter froze in fear as he looked at the empty space just a half step away. The guide watched him for a moment, then said, "Here, give me your rifle." He put the rifle on the ground beyond the dangerous passage. Now the hunter had to either go on, or leave his rifle and go back. He took a deep breath and took several very careful steps on the steep rock. Soon he was past the danger zone and on his way down. It had been a very narrow place, but it was his way down the mountain.

Jesus taught his followers that the way to life was a narrow way. Only a few would find it, while many went on the broad way to destruction. The Jesus way is not the most popular way. But it is the way to heaven.

> *We follow the narrow way because that's how Jesus taught us to walk.*

## ～ Thinking Deeper ～

During the 1960s and 1970s there was a popular saying regarding things like the increase in recreational drug use and promiscuity among young people. "Everybody's doing it" was the excuse. The unsupervised college campus atmosphere and rock festivals like Woodstock seemed to prove the cliché. But there was a response that some wise parents picked up on. "No, everyone is not doing it." In fact, in conservative Christian homes there was an unwritten rule that went something like this: if everyone else is doing it it's probably wrong. And in the cases of drugs, promiscuity, cheating on tests, honoring evil men like Marx, Freud, and Nietzsche, and the Beatles, that advice has been largely proven correct. That stand of conservative Christian parents was based on the Bible truth from the Old Testament that said "thou shalt not follow a multitude to do evil" (Exodus 23:2).

We don't follow the narrow way just to be different. We don't follow it just to be confrontational. We follow the narrow way because that's how Jesus taught us to walk. He knows the best way to live. He knows the way to safety. He knows the way to life. It's a narrow way, but it's the only way to heaven.

**Bible Reading:** Matthew 7:21-23

## Q139. Who will enter the kingdom of heaven?

### A. Those who do the will of the Father will enter the kingdom of heaven.

It was at a kid's camp and the kids were divided into teams. Their team leader told them that on their next activity they were to follow the leader and not listen to anyone but him. "Just do what I say." If they did, they would get a reward. The leader began to walk through the camp with his team following. But some other adults at the camp came up to the kids and told them they needed their help with something. They sounded like they really did need help. Some of the kids followed them and left their teams, but when they rejoined their team, they were not given a reward. They hadn't listened to their leader. The team members who listened to their leaders were rewarded.

Jesus taught us that to enter the kingdom of heaven we must do the will of the Father. We can't go off on our own doing just what we want to do. We must do what God wants us to do. One thing God tells children to do is obey their parents. Disobedient children are not doing the will of the heavenly father. Do you obey your parents? If you do, you are doing what God said to do.

 **Thinking Deeper**

John was a college student who was learning about the claims of Christ. He had made some strides toward following Jesus, including getting baptized. However, in his heart he was not completely settled. Would he really do the will of the Father in heaven? As he continued his journey, he came to a conclusion that is significant: "When I begin to doubt that Jesus is true, my moral life begins to slide. There is a relationship between what I believe and how I act."

There are a multitude of beliefs and voices competing for our attention. Many of those voices lead people away from the truth. Secular psychology, sociology, scientism, humanism, Marxism all call for people to follow their precepts. Underlying assumptions to these beliefs contradict the Word of God. Many Christian young people have studied these ideas and have lost their faith. Is it because the Word of God does not stand up to these contrary beliefs? No. It is rather that these contrary belief systems allow for actions that are wrong. When secular beliefs assuage the conscience and give excuse for sins of the flesh, they are attractive. The flesh gravitates to that which will satisfy it. In all of this is the Word from God, calling us to follow the truth.

Jesus made it clear that the will of the Father is different than the popular systems of the world. He also made it clear that following God's Word is the only way to heaven. It's really rather simple. Follow the way of the world to destruction, or follow God's will to heaven.

*Jesus made it clear that the will of the Father is different than the popular systems of the world.*

**Bible Reading:** Matthew 7:24-29

## Q140. How does a wise man build his life?

### A. A man wise does the things that Jesus says he should do.

A house was built on the side of a mountain in a nice area. The family was happy to be living in their new home. What they didn't know was that the ground under the house was not solid. A storm came and it rained and rained. The ground on the mountainside became soaked with water. The water loosened the earth underneath the house. The more it rained, the more the ground was loosened. Then it started to move. The ground began slipping from beneath the house. Soon there was no ground under part of the house. The house began to tilt. Then it slid down the hill. When it stopped sliding it was ruined. The family was sad that they had lost their house. The ground it was built on was not solid.

Jesus taught us that living our lives is like building a house. If we build it on the solid rock of Jesus' teachings, then we will be able to stand the storms of life. But if we build on sand – the advice of the world – destruction will come with the storms of life. Build your life on the Word of God.

*Build your life on the Word of God.*

### ∽ **Thinking Deeper** ∽

In Boswell's *Life of Johnson*, Samuel Johnson responded to a skeptic's assertion that there is no difference between good and evil with this quote: "If he does really think that there is no distinction between virtue and vice, why, sir, when he leaves our houses let us count our spoons." Johnson understood that ideas have consequences. What we believe profoundly affects how we live. If we believe that Jesus is the Son of God and knows the truth about life, then we will take his word seriously.     People who ignore the teaching of Jesus and live their lives a different way will experience the consequences of their lifestyle choices. Despite the effort of their lobbying to change laws, and despite the media approval of their lifestyle, and despite their attempts to mainstream their lifestyle, the homosexual life expectancy, according to a study done in 2005 by Dr. Paul Cameron, is in the early forties.

Jesus taught us how to live, and when we violate His teachings we suffer. Worse than suffering in this life, will be the suffering in the next, where "the worm dieth not and the fire is not quenched" (Mark 9:44). On the other hand, there is eternal blessing for those who follow Jesus and live as he taught us to live.

**Bible Reading:** Psalm 1:1-6

**Questions in Review**

Q137. How does God respond to our requests?
A. God gives us good things when we ask.
Q138. Does the broad way or the narrow way lead to life?
A. The narrow way leads to life.
Q139. Who will enter the kingdom of heaven?
A. Those who do the will of the Father will enter the kingdom of heaven.
Q140. How does a wise man build his life?
A. A wise man does the things that Jesus says he should do.

Late one night a Christian young man went to a restaurant. He sat beside a man who had been drinking. Hoping to witness, the Christian started to talk about what happens when a person invites Jesus into his heart. "He'll change your life." The man looked at the Christian and responded, "You leave my wife out of this!"

Some people don't seem to understand plain words. There are people who call themselves Christians but who do not live according to the teaching of Jesus. Jesus asked some people a question: "Why call ye me, Lord, Lord, and do not the things which I say?" (Luke 6:46). Jesus taught us that following him was more than just saying we are a Christian. It is living like a Christian all the time. It is being a Christian every day of the week, when people are watching and when no one is around. It is living for God from the heart.

*Jesus taught us that following him was more than just saying we are a Christian.*

## ❧ Thinking Deeper ❧

Grace is a wonderful concept and is at the heart of the Christian life. We are saved by grace, and we are kept by grace. But there is an aspect of grace that is often overlooked in popular Christianity. That is that grace is the divine infusion into the believer of the desire and power to do what is right. By way of contrast, some theories of grace give theological cover to lawless living. They promote grace as a whitewash, where God overlooks the sins in a person's life. That is the basis of antinomianism, or life without law. That is not the kind of grace that marks the humble Christian who loves the Lord Jesus and loves His Word.

One pastor was frustrated because he preached grace and then found that his people were continuing in lives of sin. The failure may have been a faulty understanding of grace. If people are told that they are bound to sin every day in word, thought and deed, they will probably follow what they are taught. If, on the other hand, they are taught to follow holiness, they should be more prone to seek the grace that enables the holy life. Jesus taught us how to live. Anything short of following in his way is sin that needs the cleansing blood. Seek the grace that enables. That grace comes freely to those who believe.

## THE PREACHING OF JESUS

**Bible Reading:** Matthew 4:12-17

# Q141. What did Jesus preach to the people?

## A. Jesus preached that people should repent.

There is an old story about a dark and stormy night. A bridge was washed away by the high waters of a river. A man found out about the bridge and began stopping people. "Stop!" he shouted, as people came close to the river. "Turn around! The bridge is out!" The man was able to save many people from falling into the river.

When Jesus started preaching, He told people to repent. He knew that all are on their way to destruction. They need to stop and turn around. That's what it means to repent. All of us are born without God in our hearts. We all have sinned. Sin leads to death. Jesus doesn't want anybody to be destroyed. He came to turn people from their sins. He came to make us righteous. Jesus preached that people should repent so they would be saved. If you repent of your sins and believe in Jesus, you will be saved.

 **Thinking Deeper**

Repentance is not a very popular subject, even among Christians. One widely read conservative author had this to say about repentance as part of the Gospel presentation: "Since the Bible doesn't specify repentance as part of the gospel whereby sinners are saved, I dare not do so either."* The weakness in this statement is that Jesus began His Gospel preaching with repentance. He has been our model for preaching for two thousand years. "Repent and believe" has been the standard message of many evangelists. Yet in our day repentance has come to be viewed as an unnecessary distraction from the Gospel.

However, as one wrote years ago, the Gospel is not good news to people who don't know they are lost. Preaching repentance shows the need of a savior. Preaching repentance gives an opportunity for the listener to respond in humility. That is important. The Bible says that God resists the proud but gives grace to the humble. Jesus preached repentance. People must repent so that they are in a place to truly believe the Gospel.

*Dave Hunt, "Q&A," The Berean Call (January 2000): 4.

> *If you repent of your sins and believe in Jesus, you will be saved.*

**Bible Reading:** Matthew 4:18-25

# Q142. What Gospel was Jesus preaching?
## A. Jesus was preaching the Gospel of the kingdom.

In 1980, the tiny African country of Swaziland had a celebration. King Sabuza had been the ruler for sixty years. When you crossed the border into Swaziland you were greeted by a banner stretched across the road that said "Welcome to King Sabuza's Diamond Jubilee." Even the Coke cans in Swaziland had a special message written on them giving honor to the king's sixty year celebration. The celebration was only in Swaziland, though, because that was Sabuza's kingdom.

When Jesus preached the Gospel of the kingdom, He was preaching about God's kingdom. God's kingdom does not have boundaries like other countries. God rules in the hearts of people who believe in Him. The kingdom Jesus preached about is in the hearts of men. Does Jesus rule in your heart? If He does, you are part of His kingdom.

### ∼ Thinking Deeper ∼

Is it possible to have Jesus as Savior and not as Lord? This question was asked by John MacArthur in his book *The Gospel According to Jesus*. After studying the preaching of Jesus, MacArthur concluded that it is not possible. For a person to be part of the kingdom of God, God must rule in that person's heart.

*Does Jesus rule in your heart?*

There is a story about D. L. Moody walking on a city street and being stopped by an alcoholic. "Mr. Moody, I'm one of your converts," slurred the man. "I believe you are, Mister," answered Moody, "For it is obvious that you are not one of the Lord's converts."

How many false converts are there? Jesus said many will call him Lord who do not do God's will but work iniquity. How many will be truly in God's Kingdom? All those who have been washed in Christ's blood and who do God's will. One day these will come from the north and the south and the east and the west, from every kindred, tribe, tongue, and nation and enter the joys of the Lord. No wonder Jesus preached the Gospel (good news) of the kingdom. It is wonderful what God has prepared for those in His kingdom.

**Bible Reading:** Matthew 11:1-6

# Q143. Who did Jesus preach to that fulfilled prophecy?

### A. Jesus preached to the poor.

A family that didn't have a lot of money heard their preacher ask the congregation to give money for the poor. That family worked hard to save money, and when the Sunday came they were happy to put $70 in the offering for the poor. Later that day the preacher came by their house with an envelope. He told them that the church wanted to help a poor family. He gave them the envelope and then left. The children were somewhat upset. "We're not a poor family! We gave to help a poor family." But they opened the envelope. And then they were even more upset. The offering for the poor was $75. They had given $70 of that! It seemed that others in the church didn't really care about the poor.

Jesus cared about the poor. He preached the gospel to poor people. He wanted them to know that even if nobody else cared, God did. Jesus still cares about poor people. He wants us to care about those who are poor. He wants us to help them. Jesus wants the poor to get saved so that they will have treasure in heaven.

 **Thinking Deeper**

There has been a divide in Christian thinking about ministering to the poor. Some see it as a "social gospel" which is a compromise of the good news that Jesus saves from sin. What good does feeding the poor do if they eventually die and go to hell? They need the gospel of salvation. Others see it as the mandate for Christians to lift up the poor and fight for justice. If we allow injustice and poverty to go unaddressed, how are we fulfilling God's requirement to "do justly and to love mercy?" Some Christians seem to have a balance between the two. While some relief groups seldom if ever preach Jesus, others do good works of providing food, water, and clothing as well as proclaim the gospel. The early Methodist seemed to have had the two issues balanced.

The poor need to be fed and clothed – that is basic human compassion. But a poor man, fed and clothed and still a sinner, needs the Gospel. Otherwise he will lose his soul. Jesus asked, "What shall it profit a man if he gain the whole world and lose his own soul?" Jesus fed the hungry and preached the gospel. We should follow his example and do both.

> *Jesus wants the poor to get saved so that they will have treasure in heaven.*

**Bible Reading:** Luke 4:14-42

## Q144. What did Jesus preach that brought hope?

### A. Jesus preached that there was deliverance, freedom, and acceptance for sinners who repent.

In 1986, in the town of Midland, Texas, a little girl named Jessica fell into a well and was trapped. Rescue workers tried to get her out but she was hard to reach. For hours and hours they kept trying. While they were working, news reporters told people all over the United States and around the world about eighteen-month old Jessica. Finally, after fifty-eight hours, the team got her. A great cheer went up as she was brought out of the well. People all over the nation and the world were happy that Jessica was saved. While Jessica was trapped, the rescuers kept calling to her, letting her know that help was on its way. They wanted to give her hope that things would get better.

Jesus preached to people who were slaves to sin. He gave them hope. They could be delivered. God would accept them if they would repent and believe. The Gospel is a message of hope.

*Jesus' message is one of deliverance and freedom.*

## ❧ Thinking Deeper ❧

The young college professor was in bondage. He was not an alcoholic or a drug abuser. He had actually done quite well for himself—coming from a poor background but excelling academically and rising into the ranks of an honored profession. He was in bondage to a sense of worthlessness. He felt like a parasite on society. Was there deliverance from his inner dreariness? One day he heard the message of Jesus. It called him. If he could only meet Jesus! That day he did. In a moment of time he found Jesus as Lord and Savior. He was filled with hope. He was delivered from dreariness. He said that even the tree leaves looked greener and the sky looked brighter. From then on his life was marked by a special exuberance. Jesus gave him a bright hope and a cheerful witness to anyone who listen.

The Gospel is like that. Jesus' message is one of deliverance and freedom. Jesus came preaching the Gospel that people can be delivered from sin and have hope in this life and also in the life to come. It really is good news.

**Bible Reading:** Romans 10:9-15

**Questions in Review**

**Q141. What did Jesus preach to the people?**
   **A. Jesus preached that people should repent.**
**Q142. What Gospel was Jesus preaching?**
   **A. Jesus was preaching the Gospel of the kingdom.**
**Q143. Who did Jesus preach to that fulfilled prophecy?**
   **A. Jesus preached to the poor.**
**Q144. What did Jesus preach that brought hope?**
   **A. Jesus preached that there was deliverance, freedom, and acceptance for sinners who repent.**

Three young boys were hiking in the Pennsylvania mountains. Their hike took them beside a highway with a cliff on one side. The older boys began climbing the cliff but the youngest didn't want to. He was scared. But he didn't want to be left behind, so he tried to climb. He got part way up the cliff, but before he reached the top, he stopped. He just couldn't make it any farther. He was clinging to the rocks and wondering how long he could hold on. Just then he felt a hand on his. He looked up into the face of his older brother. "I'll help you up." How relieved he was when his big brother helped him get to the top.

Jesus came to give help to people who were too weak to make it on their own. "For when we were yet without strength, in due time Christ died for the ungodly"( Romans 5:6). If we call Him, He will answer us. He is a wonderful Savior.

*If we call Him, He will answer us. He is a wonderful Savior.*

## ∼ **Thinking Deeper** ∼

Jesus did not come to condemn the world. He came to save it. Yet He preached repentance. He preached about heaven and hell. These are convicting themes. How is it that Jesus preached in such a way that people would be convicted, yet He didn't come to condemn the world? Jesus gave the answer when He said that unbelievers "are condemned already."

Without God's forgiveness, men already stand condemned. Even if Jesus had never come into the world, the world would have stood condemned. Man is condemned as a lawbreaker, for all have sinned. Jesus' message convicted people because it showed them as sinners before a holy God. A conscience awakened by truth and convinced of lawbreaking will send out a guilty signal. That awakened sinner is in need of good news. He is in need of the Gospel. Jesus came into the world to save sinners. Christ died for our sins. There is hope. That is good news indeed.

*JESUS' HEALING MINISTRY*

**Bible Reading:** Matthew 4:23-25

# Q145. What kinds of people did Jesus heal?

### A. Jesus healed the sick and those who were possessed with devils.

In 1942, during World War II, a terrible thing happened. The Japanese captured 75,000 Americans and Filipinos. They made them march for 60 miles without food and sometimes only a sip of water. If people fell down or became sick, they would be killed. If someone tried to help one of the fallen, that person would also be killed. Thousands of prisoners were killed in that march. This was known as the Bataan Death March. Those Japanese soldiers didn't want to be bothered by prisoners who were sick or who couldn't walk right. Sometimes people do evil things to others.

Jesus did not harm people who were sick. He did not harm his enemies. He cared even about those who were actually possessed by devils. Jesus healed the sick and delivered the possessed. He came to help all people. If you are ever in trouble, remember that Jesus is kind and loving. If you call on Him, He will help you.

## ❧ Thinking Deeper ☙

In September 2008, a report came out of Russia that a Satanist group had killed four teens, stabbed them each 666 times, and then ate them. Commenting on the story, one writer claimed that most Satanists are kind people who only want to "put pleasure above penance." The writer went on to say that these Satanists must have had the Christian view of Satan and implied that it was the Christian view of Satan as evil that influenced these Satanists to be evil instead of kind and good. In other words, Christian teaching is at fault for what these Satanists did!

*If you call on Him, He will help you.*

When Jesus came, He came to deliver people from the clutches of Satan. He came to heal them of their diseases. And the followers of Jesus have done those same things throughout history. Christian charities have established clinics and hospitals around the world to help those who are sick. Also, a major part of prayers in Christian churches are for people who are sick or in trouble, asking God to heal the sick and deliver the oppressed. When someone does something truly evil, what do Christians do in church? They request prayer for the situation. They ask that God will bring deliverance. Even after Madelyn Murray was responsible for having prayer removed from schools in 1963, many churches prayed for her. [An interesting side note: her son William became a believer.]

Jesus came to heal and deliver. His followers continue in His footsteps.

**Bible Reading:** Matthew 8:14-18

## Q146. What special woman did Jesus heal?

### A. Jesus healed Peter's mother-in-law.

Martin Luther was a brave preacher who stood up for right beliefs. He is well known around the world. When he was a boy, his mother would often go hungry so that little Martin would have enough food to eat. She showed great love. Mothers are special people. Mothers-in-law are also special.

Peter's wife had a mother who was special. She was mentioned in the Bible because Jesus went to Peter's house and learned that she was sick. Jesus healed her. When she was healed, she fixed a meal for Jesus and the others in the house. Jesus cares about mothers and mothers-in-law. He cares when they are sick, and he has the power to heal them. The Lord said, "I am the LORD that healeth thee" (Exodus 15:26). We can always bring our needs to Him.

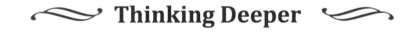

## Thinking Deeper

Peter was a married man who experienced the love of God and the power of God for his extended family. That included his mother-in-law. There is some controversy between Protestants and Roman Catholics about regulations for priests (one of whom will eventually become pope) and marriage. In 1139 A.D., the Roman Catholic Church officially decreed that priests should be celibate. Some Protestants say that Catholics contradict scripture by forbidding priests to marry. The Bible specifies that a church leader should be the husband of one wife. There is nothing in that which logically demands that the leader should be celibate. Also, Catholics admit in their literature that Peter had a wife.

Some say that requiring celibacy separates the clergy from the sinful world. The problem with that argument is that it equates non-celibacy as somehow sinful, or at least a lesser righteousness, when the Bible says that "marriage is honorable in all and the bed undefiled." Ultimately, the difference is that Protestants maintain that our rules of living come from only the scriptures, and Catholics see them coming from both scripture and church tradition. Peter's example of being married falls into the Protestant understanding of living out the scriptures without the burden of a man-made tradition to add to them.

*The Lord said, 'I am the LORD that healeth thee' (Exodus 15:26).*

**Bible Reading:** Matthew 9:27-31

## Q147. Why were the two blind men healed?

### A. They had faith to be healed.

A woman who lived in Kansas was diagnosed with cancer. Her family heard about her illness and began praying. A Christian woman in Ohio heard about her need. She helped the family pray. She told them not to be fearful but to bring their need to the Lord. The woman who was sick also prayed. She believed God's Word that she could be healed. It was not long until the cancer was gone. God heard her prayer, and the prayers of others, and healed her. That woman lived many years after that. She often testified about how God had healed her.

The two blind men called out to Jesus asking that He would heal them. They came to where He was. Jesus asked them if they believed He could heal them. They really did believe. Jesus said that what they believed would happen. They both received their sight.

We can learn from those blind men. Jesus answers us as we believe Him. "According to your faith will it be done to you."

## ～ Thinking Deeper ～

Does Jesus still heal? Of course He does. Do we understand why some people are healed and others are not? Of course we don't. Some people think they do, but they often cause trouble with their opinions.

A woman was in the hospital dealing with a serious illness. A couple men from her church came and told her to believe. They told her that the reason she was in the hospital was that she had not been exercising the right kind of faith. They didn't pray with her as much as they scolded her. When they left, she was in tears. A Christian who had overheard what they said came to the woman and told her to trust the Lord, not the words of men. Not all sickness is because of disobedience or lack of faith. Some people just get sick. That woman needed a kind word and an interceding prayer, not a scolding. Yet she could have hope that as she prayed and trusted the Lord, He would heal her according to His will. She dried her tears and prayed in faith. Her heart was at peace.

You can read how many godly men have pondered the questions about healing. You'll find that all the questions about it just can't be answered. Yet God has left us some instructions that we are to follow. If we're sick, call the elders to pray. The prayer of faith will save the sick and the Lord will raise him up. How God does that and in what measure is in His hands. It is ours to follow Him and believe. Trust and obey. Jesus has the power to heal in His hands.

> *Jesus answers us as we believe Him.*

**Bible Reading:** Matthew 15:21-28

## Q148. Why was the Canaanite woman's daughter delivered from the devil?

### A. Her mother had faith in the power of Jesus.

According to a Gospel for Asia report in February 2008, a man in India was acting in a strange manner. He was running around wildly, and people could not understand what he was saying. His family asked the missionary to come and pray for him. He started to get better. But they also asked a witch doctor to say a kind of spell over him. The spell actually made him worse. Finally, they brought him back to the missionary. The missionary prayed that God would deliver him. In answer to prayer, the man was delivered from the demonic influence through the power of Jesus Christ. When other people in their village saw what happened, they also became believers in Jesus.

The Canaanite woman had a daughter who was possessed by a devil. She came to Jesus and asked for help. She believed that the power of Jesus was so great, that just a crumb of it would be enough to deliver her daughter. Because she believed, Jesus delivered her daughter. Jesus has power to deliver people from Satan's grasp.

*Jesus has power to deliver people from Satan's grasp.*

## ～ Thinking Deeper ～

Who has more power, God or the devil? It is clear in the Bible that God has far greater power than Satan has. When someone is in the clutches of Satan, who can intervene? The person cannot help himself. Someone under Satan's power is deceived and powerless. He needs someone to step in on his behalf. When we see someone in that condition, what can we do? The story of the woman whose daughter was "grievously vexed with a devil" gives us an example.

The Canaanite woman realized that Jesus was God and that there is no power greater than his. Although Satan had intruded so deeply into her daughter's life that the daughter was unable to help herself, there was help. The woman realized that if she could have Jesus intervene, then her daughter could be delivered. So she cried out to Jesus. Jesus heard her cry. He had mercy on her. He delivered her daughter.

What did the woman do? She called on the Lord. What did the Lord do? He showed his mighty power and delivered the girl from the devil. What did the girl do? She merely received what another had done for her. There are times when a believer must act on behalf of someone who cannot act for himself or herself. Believing prayer and the power of God working together bring a great deliverance.

**Bible Reading:** Ecclesiastes 3:1-8

**Questions in Review**

**Q145 What kind of people did Jesus heal?**
   **A. Jesus healed the sick and those who were possessed with devils.**
**Q146 What special woman did Jesus heal?**
   **A. Jesus healed Peter's mother-in-law.**
**Q147 Why were the two blind men healed?**
   **A. They had faith to be healed.**
**Q148 Why was the Canaanite woman's daughter healed?**
   **A. Her mother had faith in the power of Jesus.**

Anna Warner wrote the words, "Jesus loves me this I know, for the Bible tells me so." Her song became very popular and was sung all over the world by Christians. They know that Jesus loves us. Jesus showed His love by helping people. He healed people who were sick and he delivered people who were possessed by devils. Devils do not like people, and people who are on the devil's side do not like God's people.

Rev. Ed Hird noted that when Mao was ruler, he wanted to destroy the church in China. The church was under great persecution from the communist government. However, in 1972, a word came out of China which said, "The this I know people are well." The communists didn't understand what it meant, but Christians around the world knew what it meant. They knew the song "Jesus Loves Me" and they knew that Jesus was helping His people in China.

*Jesus came to heal the sick and to deliver the oppressed.*

Jesus loves us today. If you are sick, call on Him. If the devil is giving you a hard time, call on Jesus. He loves you. He healed the sick and gave sight to the blind. He will help you when you call on Him.

 **Thinking Deeper**

Part of the message of the Gospel is that Jesus can deliver those who are in bondage. The Gospel doesn't stop with the forgiveness of sin, although that is a great part of it. It doesn't stop with giving freedom from the sinful life, although that is a major result of the Gospel when it is received. The message of the Gospel proclaims that there is deliverance. Jesus came to heal the sick and to deliver the oppressed.

When an army comes to liberate captives from an enemy, they first take the prison and tear down the bars. But they still must take the chains and handcuffs from the prisoners. Although it is good to be free of the general oppression of the enemy, it is better to have the shackles removed from each prisoner. Jesus came to remove us from the enemy's prison, and also to deliver us from the individual chains that bind our lives.

You have a great opportunity as a Christian to be free from the guilt of sin and also from the bondage of sinful habits and patterns. Jesus came to heal and deliver. What a wonderful Savior.

THE CLAIMS OF JESUS

**Bible Reading:** John 4; 6,7; 13-26

# Q149. When Jesus talked to the woman at the well who did He tell her He was?

### A. Jesus said He was the Messiah.

King Richard left England to lead his army in battle. While he was gone a wicked prince ruled the land and made it hard on the people. The people longed for their king but the prince did not want him to come back. He wanted to kill Richard and become king in his place. After a long time a strange knight came to England dressed in black. He became a hero of the people. But who was he? Just as the wicked prince was about to make himself king, the Black Knight appeared. He took off his helmet. The people saw that it was their beloved King Richard. They were happy to be freed from the wicked prince and have their true king back.

People who met Jesus didn't always know who He really was. The woman at the well knew He was some kind of a prophet. Jesus told her that He was more than a prophet. He told her that He was the Messiah – the Promised One. She was so happy that she told her whole town about Jesus.

## Thinking Deeper

When Jesus claimed to be the Messiah, He claimed that all the things prophesied about the Messiah either had been or would be fulfilled in Him. For the woman at the well that meant He would tell her what she needed to know about what was important: "He will tell us all things." The coming Messiah would tell her about herself and about her relationship with God. She already had religious tradition – "our fathers worshipped in this mountain" – but she needed the reality of the Messiah's message. It was not unimportant for her that He was born in Bethlehem, or that he had the proper lineage, or that He came at the promised time. She wanted to hear from the true Messiah. But the message for her was what she really needed.

When Jesus said "I that speak unto you am he," it suddenly dawned on her that He had been telling her exactly what she needed to know about herself and about her need for true worship. He really was the Messiah!

*He told her that he was the Messiah – the promised one.*

**Bible Reading:** John 5:5-19

# Q150. Who did Jesus tell the Jews that He was?

### A. Jesus said God was His Father, making Himself equal with God.

Two United States Presidents had sons who also became President. John Adams was the second President. His son, John Quincy Adams, was the sixth President of the United States. George H. W. Bush was the forty-first President. George W. Bush was elected as the forty-third President.

Sons will often follow in their fathers' footsteps and do the same kinds of jobs their fathers did. Farmers' sons tend to be farmers. Missionaries' sons tend to become missionaries. Carpenters' sons tend to become carpenters. When Jesus healed the sick man, He said He was doing what His Father was doing. Some people who heard Him say that became angry. They did not believe that God was Jesus' Father. Jesus knew who He was. God was His Father and He worked with God.

## ⟨ Thinking Deeper ⟩

*Some skeptics hold the view that Jesus never claimed to be God.*

In some criminal trials significant witnesses turn up dead. The witness knows enough that his testimony would be so convincing that the defendant's only hope is to kill the witness. When Jesus healed the man who had been sick for thirty-eight years, the Jews could not argue with the evidence that a mighty miracle had happened. What they did argue about was that the miracle was done on the Sabbath, violating their concept of the law of God. So they wanted to kill Jesus. Jesus made matters worse for them. He not only healed on the Sabbath, but also claimed that He was working with His Father on the Sabbath. The Jews understood exactly what Jesus meant – if God was His Father, then Jesus was deity.

Some skeptics hold the view that Jesus never claimed to be God. Their argument comes from willful ignorance. The Jews wanted to stone Jesus for that exact claim. Jesus claimed that God was His Father, "making himself equal with God."

**Bible Reading:** John 6:47-63

# Q151. Who did Jesus tell the disciples he was?

## A. Jesus said that He was the bread from heaven that if anyone ate, he would live forever.

Cannibals are uncivilized heathens who sometimes eat other people. When they hear about Jesus they realize how sinful they are. God's miracle of salvation has changed many cannibals. Some become loving Christians, completely different than they were before. When Jesus told His disciples that He was bread from heaven that they should eat, He did not mean they should become cannibals. He meant that they should invite Jesus into their hearts and lives and live for Him.

As we Christians eat the communion bread, we do not eat the literal body of Jesus. We are remembering what Jesus did for us. We remember that we've asked Jesus to come into our hearts. We remember that since He is in our hearts we have eternal life.

## ∼ Thinking Deeper ∼

C. S. Lewis came to faith partly as a result of logic regarding the claims of Christ. Lewis realized that Jesus really did claim to be the Son of God and man's way to heaven. His logic went like this: Jesus claimed to be the Son of God. That claim is either true or false. If it is false, there are only two options – either Jesus knew His claims were false and He was a liar, or He didn't know His claims were false and He was a lunatic. If the claims are true then Jesus is Lord. Lewis examined the three options. Jesus is either Lord, liar, or lunatic.*

When Lews studied the life of Jesus, he found no evidence that Jesus was a madman. Neither did he see that Jesus was a deliberate liar. He was forced by logic to conclude that Jesus is indeed the Lord of heaven and earth, the divine Son of God.

*This argument, known as the Trilemma, is developed in Josh McDowell's *Evidence That Demands a Verdict*.

*Jesus is either Lord, liar, or lunatic.*

**Bible Reading:** John 14:1-7

## Q152. When Jesus spoke to Thomas, who did he claim to be?

### A. Jesus said He was the only way to the Father.

Some young ladies were driving on Interstate 70 intending to go from the Indiana border to Columbus, Ohio. After they had driven a while, one of them noticed the road sign. "Oh, no! We've been going the wrong direction!" They had been going west instead of east. They had to turn around and go the other direction. If they hadn't, they would have never gotten to Columbus.

Jesus said that He was the only way to the Father. There are many other ways people live their lives, but no way will lead to God except one way. Jesus is that one way. There is good news for those who are on the wrong way. They can turn around and follow Jesus. When Jesus found people going the wrong way, He called them. "Follow me," said Jesus. Those who follow Jesus find the true way to God.

### ∼ Thinking Deeper ∼

Jesus not only claimed to be the way to God but also claimed that He was the <u>only</u> way to God. He is not one among several ways. He is the One Way.

*Jesus is not one among several ways.*

A Christian was talking with a proponent of the Bahai faith about the claims of Christ. The Bahai follower believed that each age had its prophet. Moses was God's man in his day, Jesus in His day, Mohammed in his day and Bahu-Allah most recently. The Christian said that Jesus had to be removed from the list. "Why?" asked the Bahai follower. "Because Jesus said He was the only way," answered the Christian. "If Jesus is only one among many who can get people to God, then Jesus was a liar. So He couldn't be part of that list."

The Bahai follower refused to believe that Jesus actually claimed to be the only way. He did so out of ignorance. The claims of Christ are clear. His disciples understood how exclusive His claims were. Peter proclaimed "Neither is there salvation in any other: for there is none other name under heaven given among men, whereby we must be saved" (Acts 4:12).

**Bible Reading:** John 6:28-35

**Questions in Review**

**Q149. When Jesus talked to the woman at the well who did He tell her He was?**
**A. Jesus said He was the Messiah.**

**Q150. Who did Jesus tell the Jews that He was?**
**A. Jesus said God was His Father, making Himself equal with God.**

**Q151. Who did Jesus tell the disciples He was?**
**A. Jesus said that He was the bread from heaven that if anyone ate, he would live forever.**

**Q152. When Jesus spoke to Thomas, who did He claim to be?**
**A. Jesus said He was the only way to the Father.**

Before airplanes were invented, a man decided to try to fly. He made some long wings that he figured would be large enough to help him fly. Then he climbed up a very high tower. He strapped the wings to his arms. He was ready. He jumped off the tower into the air and tried to flap the wings. It was too bad, because he couldn't make himself fly. He fell to his death.

When people try to find a way to God without Jesus, they always fail. No one else has the power to save us from our sins. The trouble with following other ways is that there are no other ways to salvation. Only Jesus died for our sins. Only Jesus can save us. When people follow other ways, they will find that they lead to death. "I, even I, am the LORD; and beside me there is no savior" (Isaiah 43:11).

*There are other beliefs, but no other salvation.*

## ∼ **Thinking Deeper** ∼

It has been popular among intellectuals who want to be inclusive in their beliefs to add Jesus in with other historical religious figures like Moses, Confucius, and Mohammed, and call Him a great teacher. C. S. Lewis said that Jesus has not left us with that option. He is either much more than a great teacher or he is much less. He is either Lord, or a liar, or a lunatic. There is no other possibility. Lewis was so convinced that it is illogical to call Jesus merely a "great teacher" that he made this classic statement: "A man who was merely a man and said the things Jesus said would not be a great moral teacher. He would either be a lunatic – on the level of a man who says he is a poached egg – or else he would be the Devil of Hell. You must make your choice. Either this man was and is the Son of God; or else a madman or something worse."

Why was Jesus so specific about His claims? He knew the consequences. He knew that there is no other salvation. There are other beliefs, but no other salvation. There are other religious leaders, but no other savior. Jesus is God's way for man to be saved.

THE MIRACLES OF JESUS

**Bible Reading:** John 2:1-11

# Q153. What was the first miracle Jesus performed?

### A. Jesus' first miracle was turning water into wine.

The older man was dressed in rumpled and stained clothes. He wore a knitted cap and an old pair of glasses. He seemed no different than any other homeless person. People entering the Trinity Methodist Church passed him without much thought to help him out. When it was time for service to start, the man got to his feet, and to the surprise of the congregation, walked to the front of the church. He took off his cap and removed a wig from his head. The people were surprised to see Derek Rigby, their pastor, standing in front of them. They had not recognized him until he revealed who he was.

When Jesus turned water into wine, He began to reveal who He was. His disciples began to see how great and wonderful He was. They saw that Jesus was different than they were. He did what none of them could do. He had power none of them had. His disciples believed that He really did come from God. "This beginning of miracles did Jesus in Cana of Galilee, and manifested forth his glory; and his disciples believed on him" (John 2:11).

 **Thinking Deeper**

In the wilderness, Satan had tempted Jesus to turn stones into bread. Jesus had refused. He maintained his mission to act only in accordance with the direction of His Father. Now Jesus had begun his ministry. He was revealing His identity to His disciples. He was beginning his works. He went about doing good. So when wine was needed at the wedding, Jesus furnished it through a miracle. He showed His glory. That is, He began to show who He was. His majesty and wonder began to be displayed.

A skeptic asked a Christian if Jesus did the miracles to prove He was God. The underlying assumption was that Jesus somehow needed miracles to authenticate Himself. The Christian answered that Jesus didn't need to do the miracles to prove to Himself that He was God. He was God by virtue of His own existence and where He had come from. At the age of twelve He knew who His Father was. But Jesus did the miracles to show others who He was. His disciples needed to see His power and majesty. When they did, they believed on Him.

> *Jesus didn't need to do the miracles to prove to himself that he was God.*

**Bible Reading:** Luke 8:22-25

# Q154. How did Jesus calm the storm?
### A. Jesus spoke and the storm was stilled.

A little boy lay in his bed in the dark night. Everyone else in the house was asleep. He was fearful. He wondered about God. And he wondered if he was saved. What could he do? He got out of bed and found his parent's room. "Mom?" he whispered. She woke up and asked him what was wrong. "Could you pray with me? I don't know if I'm saved." She got out of bed and they knelt at the couch. She told him that Jesus had died for his sins and he could trust Jesus to save him. She prayed with him. The storm of fear in his heart was stilled. He went back to his bed and slept peacefully.

The disciples were fearful that the storm would sink the ship and they would drown. They called on Jesus. He spoke to the storm and it became still. The disciples saw how powerful Jesus was. He could help them through anything. He can help us through anything, too.

## ⬳ Thinking Deeper ⬱

The great artist Rembrandt depicted this incident in his seascape, "Storm on the Sea of Galilee." There are several notable aspects of the painting. Sailors are frantically working with the wind-battered sails. One is mightily struggling with the tiller. A wave is sweeping furiously over the bow while overhead the clouds are menacing with blackness. Near the bottom of the boat a rather incongruous incident is taking place. Two disciples are waking a sleepy-looking Jesus. Despite the rush and tumble of activity by both nature and men, Jesus sleeps peacefully until awakened by his worried followers. For them, it seems like life and death. For Jesus it is another opportunity to get some rest. It is also another opportunity for Him to teach His disciples. Their trouble is no trouble to Him. Call on Him and He will help. Nothing is too mighty for His power.

We can learn from this lesson Jesus taught them. He is available to us in our storms. All we need do is call.

*He is available to us in our storms.*

**Bible Reading:** Luke 9:10-17

# Q155. How did Jesus feed the 5,000?

## A. He blessed five loaves and two fishes.

A mother saw that her daughter needed a coat. She prayed about it. The next day in church a woman asked, "Do you need a coat for your daughter? I bought one, but kept forgetting to bring it. This morning the Lord told me to take the coat to church today."

"Oh, thank you," said the mother. "I prayed for a coat for my daughter just yesterday." The coat fit the girl perfectly, and the mother's prayer was answered! In fact, for years after that when the girl needed a coat, it was provided without the mother having to buy it. God showed that He cared about them. He supplied their needs.

When Jesus saw the hungry multitude, He wanted to feed them. The disciples brought Him a boy's lunch. Jesus had the people sit down. Then He blessed the boy's food. Jesus fed all five thousand with just five small loaves and two fish. It was a miracle. Jesus showed that He cared about their needs. Jesus cares about people in need and He wants us to care, also.

## Thinking Deeper

In the fall of 2008, after tropical storm Hanna, thousands of people in Haiti were without food and water. In one city, aid groups set up a place where people could come and get supplies. People were pushing and shoving one another to get some water and food. One woman who had five children came away with five biscuits and some water. She was hoping to make the biscuits last. Later in the same season, Hurricane Ike made it worse for the people. Christian groups sent more food and water to help the people.

Followers of Jesus understand their duty to help people in need. Christian groups send food and clothing to people all over the world who have suffered disasters. Christians teams volunteer to go and work where relief is needed. Following the example of Jesus, Christians feed the hungry, clothe the naked, visit the sick and imprisoned, and preach the Gospel to the poor. It is Christianity in action to do what Jesus did.

*It is Christianity in action to do what Jesus did.*

**Bible Reading:** Matthew 17:24-27

## Q156. How did Jesus tell Peter to pay his taxes?

### A. Jesus told Peter to cast a line into the water, catch a fish, and find money in the fish's mouth.

Tiger sharks will eat almost anything. Here are some of the things found in the stomachs of tiger sharks: aluminum cans, nails, roll of tar paper, empty wallet, shoes, pants, can of peas, bag of potatoes. They seem to eat anything. One tiger shark had even eaten a bag of money.

The fish that Peter caught was not a tiger shark, but it did have something unusual in its mouth. It had a gold coin. Jesus had told Peter to go fishing and look in the mouth of the first fish he caught. When Peter caught the fish, he found the gold in its mouth. He took it and paid taxes for both himself and Jesus.

How did Jesus know Peter would catch a fish? How did He know which fish Peter would catch? How did He know it had gold in its mouth? Jesus knew because He is the Son of God.

## ∿ **Thinking Deeper** ∿

*How did Jesus know Peter would catch a fish?*

He had seen the fish one time. It had drifted out from beneath the grass-covered bank when the fisherman had dropped his bait upstream. The current swept the bait in front of the trout. But something spooked the trout and that was that. The fisherman was patient. He waited for several days for the conditions to be right. Now he was back. Carefully, he laid his plans and cautiously approached. He knew the fish would be there. Quietly he eased the bait into the stream. There was a flash of fish, and then it was gone. Fail! How had it seen him? The fisherman left the stream with an empty stringer. Sometimes it's tough catching that special fish.

It's amazing that Jesus knew there was one particular fish near the water's edge. It's amazing He knew Peter would go to the right spot. It's amazing that He knew there was a coin in its mouth. It's amazing He knew the fish would bite and Peter would catch it. Why is this account in the Bible? Because the Holy Spirit intended that we see just "what manner of man this is."

**Bible Reading:** Luke 11:16-20

**Questions in Review**

**Q153. What was the first miracle Jesus performed?**
   **A. Jesus' first miracle was turning water into wine.**
**Q154. How did Jesus calm the storm?**
   **A. Jesus spoke and the storm was stilled.**
**Q155. How did Jesus feed the 5,000?**
   **A. He blessed five loaves and two fishes.**
**Q156. How did Jesus tell Peter to pay his taxes?**
   **A. Jesus told Peter to cast a line into the water, catch a fish and find money in the fish's mouth.**

A missionary lady was traveling with some natives in a motor boat. They were a long way from home when the engine sputtered. They had run out of gas! She asked her group to pray for God to intervene. After they prayed they pulled the rope on the engine. It started! They were able to go a long way and make it home. They praised God for the miracle.

The Bible tells us that God works miracles. He can do anything. He sometimes does miracles for people today. One of the greatest miracles He does is to change people. He takes sinners and makes them into saints. Many Christians are walking miracles because Jesus saved them. They have been changed from the inside out. God still works miracles.

## ◁∿▷ Thinking Deeper ∿

Jesus told his disciples that "the Son of man is Lord also of the Sabbath." From his miracles we see that He is Lord of matter (turning water into wine), He is Lord of nature (calming the storm), He is Lord a of increase (multiplying the loaves and fishes) and He is Lord of circumstance (money in fish's mouth). We who believe Jesus is the divine Son of God have no trouble believing that He could do all of these things. He who created all things has power over all things. He can do it!

Skeptics struggle with the issue of miracles. Miracles don't fit the "scientific" paradigm. If there is no natural explanation, naturalists naturally reject them. So Jesus couldn't have done miracles since miracles are not natural, and "science" only deals with natural things. Because of their prior *assumptions*, they cannot allow the concept of miracles to be seriously discussed. But their argument is really mental sleight of hand. Since the definitions they impose eliminate any supernatural possibility, the miraculous is rejected. "We don't allow any miraculous explanations, therefore miracles are impossible." It is the ultimate in being closed minded.

Believers have a much richer realm of possibilities to draw from than naturalists. Since God is Creator, He can work in nature, through nature, or suspend natural limitations and work above nature. Our God is an awesome God!

> *God can work in nature, through nature, or suspend natural limitations.*

*THE PASSION OF CHRIST*

**Bible Reading:** Matthew 6:5-15

# Q157. What did Jesus teach us to pray?
### A. Jesus taught us to pray The Lord's Prayer.

A small child was asked by her mother to pray before eating lunch. She bowed her head and prayed, "Dear Lord, don't let us ever get too much that we forget about You, and don't let us ever have so little that we have to steal." She paused a moment and then said to her mother, "That's in the Bible." The little girl had been listening to the words from the Bible and made them part of her prayer.

The disciples listened to what Jesus said about prayer. The prayer He taught them is what is called The Lord's Prayer. For two thousand years people who follow Jesus have been praying that prayer. It can help you pray, just like it helped the disciples to pray.

## ～ Thinking Deeper ～

On at least two occasions Jesus taught His disciples to pray these words. One was while He preached the Sermon on the Mount. The other is when the disciples heard Jesus pray and asked Him to teach them to pray. It has been the practice of Christians since the time of the early church to pray this prayer. What we have called The Lord's Prayer is actually the prayer the Lord taught us to pray. Some shrink from praying this prayer because it can become ritual. However, just because some have sunk below the level of reality does not invalidate the prayer for those who have a warm heart. In the Sermon on the Mount, Jesus told His disciples to pray "after this manner." The prayer can be used as a pattern for our prayers. But that is not all it is, for when they asked Him to teach them to pray, He said, "When ye pray, say, Our Father..." We ought not abandon what Jesus clearly taught. It is in keeping with the teaching of Christ and with the practice of the historic Christian church to pray the prayer we call The Lord's Prayer.

*Some shrink from praying this prayer because it can become ritual.*

## Q158. Why did Jesus pray out loud before Lazarus was raised from the dead?

### A. Jesus prayed out loud so that the people who heard Him would believe.

Charlie Wireman was an outlaw who lived in the mountains of Kentucky. He was mean and tough. On evenings when Charlie was in town, he would see the lawman and say, "It's your bedtime. You need to go home now." The lawman was afraid of Charlie. He would go home, leaving the town unprotected from the outlaw. Charlie drank a lot, and became weak from drinking liquor. One day he was walking along a street and passed the house where a Christian lady lived. Charlie was so weak that he had to lean against her gate. Her window was opened and she was praying. He heard her pray for various people. Then she raised her hands heavenward and pled with God, "And oh Lord, I pray for that wicked Charlie Wireman. Get a hold of his heart! Save him for Jesus' sake." Charlie couldn't get away from that prayer. Finally, he realized he needed to get saved. He was delivered from his meanness and his drinking. Charlie heard a prayer that helped him to faith.

When Jesus prayed for Lazarus, he prayed out loud so that the people who heard would believe. When Lazarus came out of the grave, they knew that God the Father had answered Jesus' prayer.

> *Our prayers can be answered as we stay close to Jesus.*

## ∼ Thinking Deeper ∼

Jesus lived His life on earth in a unique way. He had a constant relationship with the Father in heaven. Jesus often went by Himself and prayed. Sometimes the disciples overheard His prayers. They wanted Jesus to teach them to pray. In this case, they heard Jesus pray, and then watched as Lazarus, who had been dead for four days, emerged alive from the grave. This dramatic prayer and answer was a great boost to the disciples' faith.

Jesus did not need a boost to faith. Of all people who have lived on earth, Jesus lived the closest to the Father in heaven. Jesus had ongoing communion with Him. Jesus was one with the Father. So Jesus said, "I knew that thou hearest me always." Jesus did not pray with distance between himself and the Father. He did not live with the need of a "mediator between God and man" since He was the mediator.

Our prayers can be answered as we stay close to Jesus. He is our mediator. He is at the right hand of the Father in heaven. The closer we stay to Jesus, the clearer will be the answers to our prayers.

**Bible Reading:** John 17:13-20

## Q159. What did Jesus pray for His own disciples?

### A. Jesus prayed that the Father would sanctify His disciples.

A family installed a hot tub on the deck beside their home. The family made some rules about the hot tub. They were to keep it covered, except when they used it. The water was to be clean and hot. Also, it was to be used only by that family. No one else was to get into that water—not even other close relatives. The hot tub was special to that family. It was just for them.

When Jesus prayed that His disciples would be sanctified, He was praying for something that was only for believers in Jesus. His prayer included all believers, because He prayed for those who would believe. People who don't believe in Jesus can't be sanctified. Jesus said clearly that His prayer was for "His own" and "not for the world." Sanctification is a special cleansing only for people who already believe in Jesus.

 **Thinking Deeper**

A young man was working on his car. The longer he worked, the greasier his hands became. He tried to wipe the grease off his hands with a cloth, but his hands were still greasy. Grease was in his skin and under his fingernails. To get the grease off his hands, the mechanic had to use detergent. The detergent applied to the skin, along with water, released the chemical bonds that imbedded the grease into the skin. The detergent freed the skin from the grease.

Humans are flawed creatures. They were not flawed at creation, but because of sin fell into a state of depravity. When people are saved, God forgives their sins and lives in their hearts. But there is still "something lacking in their faith." The apostle, including himself with the believers he addressed, said, "let us cleanse ourselves from all filthiness of the flesh and spirit" (2 Corinthians 7:1). But we cannot cleanse ourselves without Christ's blood anymore than the mechanic can wash the grease from his hands without detergent. God has made provision for our cleansing. "Jesus also, that he might sanctify the people with his own blood, suffered without the gate" (Hebrews 13:12). We "cleanse ourselves" by going to Christ by faith and appropriating His blood, which sanctifies us.

> *We "cleanse ourselves" by going to Christ by faith and appropriating his blood.*

**Bible Reading:** Luke 23:33-38

## Q160. What did Jesus pray for those who crucified him?

### A. Jesus prayed that his Father would forgive them.

There is an old story about a soldier who kept getting in trouble. The judge ordered him to have extra duty. He was made to work very hard. He was lectured. He was put in prison. But he kept getting in trouble and was sent to the judge again. The judge looked at his record. Then he decided to do something different. "Young man," said the judge, "you have been in trouble too many times to remember. You have a very bad record. But nothing we do seems to make any difference. I'm going to do something we haven't tried before. I'm going to forgive you. I'm taking your bad record and throwing it away. You can start over." The young soldier was so amazed that he changed his ways. He didn't get in trouble anymore. Forgiveness changed him.

Jesus showed us how to forgive when he was on the cross. He asked God to forgive the soldiers that crucified him. If we follow Jesus, we will show forgiveness to people who wrong us.

## ～ Thinking Deeper ～

A New York pastor preached a message called "One Way Forgiveness." He spoke of how Jesus gave forgiveness from the cross. Jesus didn't wait for the soldiers to ask for forgiveness. He offered them forgiveness one way—from His standpoint. That is how God offers forgiveness. "If we confess our sins, he is faithful and just to forgive..." The forgiveness is there for the asking. God has it offered to those who will confess. It is there for the taking. It is not forced. It is not coerced. But it is available, anytime.

A minister received some very negative words from a parishioner. The words were hurtful and accusatory. Later, the parishioner sought the Lord, came back to church and was welcomed into the fellowship. Several years went by. One day the parishioner came to the minister and asked for forgiveness for those hurtful words. "I've forgiven you a long time ago," said the pastor.

Jesus gave us the pattern for forgiveness. We are to have it available, anytime.

*I've forgiven you a long time ago.*

**Bible Reading:** Psalm 91:9-15

**Questions in Review**

Q157. **What did Jesus teach us to pray?**
 A. **Jesus taught us to pray The Lord's Prayer.**
Q158. **Why did Jesus pray out loud before Lazarus was raised from the dead?**
 A. **Jesus prayed out loud so that the people who heard Him would believe.**
Q159. **What did Jesus pray for His own disciples?**
 A. **Jesus prayed that the Father would sanctify His disciples.**
Q160. **What did Jesus pray for those who crucified him?**
 A. **Jesus prayed that God would forgive them.**

David Brainerd was a missionary to the American Indians. He had a secret that helped him reach them. He prayed for God's power. George Washington was General of the American Army when it was so poor as to not have shoes for the soldiers. He had a secret that helped him win anyway. He prayed for God's help. John Wesley was a great preacher in England. He was not allowed to preach in many churches. He had a secret that helped him preach to thousands of people anyway. He prayed for God to help his preaching.

Jesus knew the secret of prayer. He knew how to talk to His Father in heaven. Jesus did great things because He knew what His Father wanted Him to do. Jesus taught us to pray also. We can use the secret of prayer to do great things for God.

*Powerful prayer is often secret prayer.*

## ◡ Thinking Deeper ◡

There is something about praying in secret that God responds to. Jesus often went to pray alone. The Bible says He withdrew Himself. Jesus told the disciples if they prayed in private, God, "which seeth in secret," would reward them openly. Powerful prayer is often not public prayer. Powerful prayer is often not loud prayer. Sometimes Jesus prayed out loud in public, but more often Jesus prayed alone. Powerful prayer is often secret prayer.

The stories about George Washington praying are found not because Washington prayed to be seen, but because people came upon him by accident. Many great men of God prayed in secret, often early in the morning before the rush of the day was upon them. Among those who prayed secretly and to great effect were Monica (mother of St. Augustine), John Wesley (founder of Methodism), John Fletcher (great Methodist theologian), Praying Hyde (who saw many answers to prayer).

There is nothing to stop any of us from doing great things for God. The door to our prayer closet is open. Just go in and shut the door.

THE PASSION OF CHRIST II

**Bible Reading:** Luke 22:14-23

# Q161. What was the Last Supper?

### A. The Last Supper was the Passover meal Jesus ate with His disciples before He was crucified.

A little boy sat in a church pew. The ushers were doing something different. Usually they passed a plate and took up a collection. This time they were passing a plate with little pieces of bread and a tray with little cups of grape juice. The boy didn't understand why he couldn't get any of the bread or juice. When he grew older, he understood what the bread and juice stood for. They were a reminder of the last supper Jesus ate with His disciples.

Jesus took bread and told the disciples to remember how His body was broken for them when they ate it. He took a cup and passed it to the disciples to drink. He told them they were to remember how He shed His blood for their sins. This Passover meal was a time for Israel to remember how a lamb was killed and its blood put on the doorposts during the tenth plague of Egypt. The Lord would pass over that house and not kill the firstborn, making a difference between Israel and Egypt. Jesus showed His disciples that in His death, He would keep them from dying for their sins.

When Christians take communion, this is what they remember.

## ❦ **Thinking Deeper** ❦

One of the major church scandals of the last several years had to do with priests who abused people in their parishes. The disgrace that the priests were immoral was compounded by what they did every week—serve communion to the people. Like Judas, who ate the last supper with Jesus and then went out and betrayed Him, their actions betrayed the Christ they were supposed to be serving. Jesus said of Judas, "good were it for that man if he had never been born." Serving communion with a wicked heart is evil. But so is partaking in communion with unconfessed sin. Paul the Apostle gave a warning to those who take communion unworthily. They eat and drink damnation to themselves.

Remembering The Last Supper and the suffering of Christ in communion is a time of blessing, worship, and reception of grace to those with faithful, honest hearts. But it is also a time of betrayal and tragedy for those who take communion unworthily. Make sure your heart is right with God when you take communion.

*Paul the Apostle gave a warning to those who take communion unworthily.*

**Bible Reading:** Luke 22:39-48

## Q162. What did Jesus pray just before He was betrayed?

### A. Jesus asked his Father if the cup could be removed from Him.

Once there was a beautiful queen in a kingdom where the king was very stern. No one, not even the queen, could visit the king unless he gave an invitation. But the queen's family was in great danger. Her cousin asked her to visit the king. "But I could die if he doesn't welcome me," answered the queen. Her cousin told her it was her place to go to the king. No one else had a chance. "Who knows," he said. "You may have been brought to the kingdom for such a time as this." The queen agreed to go see the king. He welcomed her, and she convinced him to save her family.

Jesus came to earth to be the savior of mankind. But it was going to cost Him His life. He prayed, if it was possible, that the Father would remove the cup from Him. Could mankind be saved if He didn't die? Then He said, "Not my will, but thine be done." Even though it was hard, Jesus was willing to do the Father's will and save mankind.

*The Second Adam came to fix the problem the first Adam had caused.*

## ∼ Thinking Deeper ∼

The Bible speaks of Jesus as the Son of God and also as the Son of Man. The ancient Christian creeds decreed that Jesus is wholly God and wholly man. Here we see the human side of Jesus facing the prospect of dying for man – taking on the sin of the world, becoming sin for us. The Second Adam came to fix the problem the first Adam had caused. In his humanity, the prospect of receiving the penalty of sin seemed to Jesus to be almost overwhelming. "If it be possible, let this cup pass…" Jesus saw the great difficulty of the work that must be done. He saw the agony that awaited him. Indeed, he already agonized. He sweat drops of blood. "Nevertheless." What a word in such a time! "Nevertheless." What a statement of submission to his Father! "Nevertheless." What a model for all of us who face difficulty in following in his steps! "Nevertheless, not my will, but thine be done."

"Yet it pleased the LORD to bruise him; he hath put him to grief: when thou shalt make his soul an offering for sin, he shall see his seed, he shall prolong his days, and the pleasure of the LORD shall prosper in his hand" ( Isaiah 53:10).

Thank you Jesus, for doing the Father's will.

**Bible Reading:** Luke 22:63-71

## Q163. What two questions did the council leaders ask Jesus?

### A. The council asked Jesus if He was the Christ and if He was the Son of God.

It was a quiet night and the family was asleep in their house. Suddenly there came a loud knock on the door. The father woke up and went to the window. Below at his doorstep he saw a man. He opened the window. "Who are you, and what do you want?" The figure at the door answered. "I'm your neighbor and I need your help. A visitor came to my house and I don't have any bread to serve him. Please give me some bread." To be safe, the father needed the answers to his questions before he opened the door. It took some convincing, but the man finally gave his neighbor some bread.

The council asked Jesus two questions. When Jesus answered, they should have believed him. They missed their chance to know who Jesus was and find salvation.

 **Thinking Deeper**

Hearings on political scandals often have two questions: What did you know? And when did you know it? Cover-ups are often revealed when it comes to light that a politician knew about unethical dealings beforehand and did nothing about fixing them.

The two questions the council asked Jesus are revealing in that they are the questions upon which the claims of Christ rested. When Jesus came, John called Him the lamb of God. Jesus Himself stated that the prophets spoke of Him and His day, and He referred to God as His Father, making Himself equal with God. The whole controversy about Jesus was not about what He did, but was about who He was.

The questions are two-edged swords. If Jesus was not Christ nor the Son of God, then the council was right in condemning Him. But if He was in fact the Christ, the Son of the living God, then they condemned themselves.

So the questions the council asked were the right questions. Sadly, they got the answers wrong.

> *The controversy about Jesus was not about what he did, but was about who he was.*

## Q164. At the trial of Jesus, who did Pilate send Jesus to?

### A. Pilate sent Jesus to Herod.

President Truman had a special sign on his desk in the White House. The sign said, "The Buck Stops Here." When people didn't want to make a decision about something, they would pass the decision on to someone else. That was called "passing the buck." Harry Truman knew that as President he had to make the final decisions. There was no one else to whom he could pass the decision.

When Pilate sent Jesus to Herod, he was "passing the buck." He hoped that Herod would put Jesus on trial. But Herod sent Jesus back to Pilate. Pilate had to decide what to do with Jesus. Each of us must decide what we will do with Jesus. We must either accept Him and follow Him, or follow the ways of sin. Will you follow Him?

## ∼ Thinking Deeper ∼

The record states that Pilate sent Jesus to Herod. Many things about the crucifixion of Christ are ironic – this one particularly so. That Pilate, a self-absorbed, political opportunist whose large concern was keeping his post in this Roman outpost, could actually send Jesus, the omnipotent creator and sustainer of the universe who speaks and it is done and has all power in heaven and earth, is ironic. But the Bible says, "He sent him." In a world that was right, Jesus would have sent Pilate, who like the centurion that knew about an authority that "says go and he goeth," would have certainly followed the command. But the world was upside down. Pilate sent Jesus.

The world hasn't come right yet. People still "send Jesus." Unbelievers send Him away when He knocks at the doors of their hearts. Liberals "send Jesus" on their missions of government suppression. Liberation theologians and Black Theology proponents "send Jesus" into violent missions, claiming Him as a leader of the purveyors of hatred. And professing Christians send Jesus to do their bidding as they "name it, and claim it."

On the other hand, true followers of the resurrected Christ repeat with heartfelt devotion Isaiah's humble offering, "Here am I, send me."

*Each of us must decide what we will do with Jesus.*

**Bible Reading:** I Peter 2:19-25

**Questions in Review**

Q161. What was The Last Supper?
A. The Last Supper was the Passover meal Jesus ate with His disciples before He was crucified.
Q162. What did Jesus pray just before He was betrayed?
A. Jesus asked His Father if the cup could be removed from Him.
Q163. What two questions did the council leaders ask Jesus?
A. The council asked Jesus if He was the Christ and if He was the Son of God.
Q164. At the trial of Jesus, who did Pilate send Jesus to?
A. Pilate sent Jesus to Herod.

Church was over. The people who were visiting began walking outside. A small boy was in the church basement. He didn't know everyone else had gone. Suddenly the lights went out. The little boy was alone in the darkness. He began to scream. People heard him from outside. They opened the door. He ran to his family. He didn't like being left alone.

When Judas betrayed Jesus, the guards took Jesus from the garden to the council. His disciples didn't go with Him. They followed afar off to see what would happen, but Jesus was alone. He had to face His trial by Himself. Part of the suffering of Jesus was that He was alone.

Maybe that's why Jesus says to His followers, "I will never leave thee nor forsake thee" (Hebrews 13:5). He assures us that we are never really alone.

*Putting God on trial is not novel to modern skepticism.*

##  Thinking Deeper

C. S. Lewis wrote an essay entitled "God in the Dock." Being "in the dock" means being on trial. "Man is on the Bench and God in the Dock." Lewis understood that modern man has lost the fear of God and would be God's judge. Consider the questions that often come as objections to Christianity. "What happens to the heathen?" The assumption of the question is that heathen cannot be rightly judged if they have never heard the Gospel, so God is not just in condemning them. Or consider the question, "How can a God of love allow suffering and evil in the world?" It is an assault on either the power of God (since he cannot control evil), or the goodness of God (since He does not stop evil). In both cases, as in other objections to Christianity, God is on trial.

There are good answers to these questions that cannot be answered in this small space. What can be said is that putting God on trial is not novel to modern skepticism. It was done openly when the Jews took Jesus to their council and then sent Him to Pilate. Consider the end, though, before you join those on the bench. Jesus arose and is now at the right hand of the Father in heaven, and will come again to judge the world.

THE PASSION OF CHRIST III

**Bible Reading:** Luke 23:13-25

## Q165. When Pilate asked the people who should go free, Jesus or Barabbas, who did they choose?

### A. The people chose Barabbas to go free and called for Jesus to be crucified.

There was a very sad boy who climbed a high building. He was so sad that he decided to jump off the building. As he stood on the edge, he stopped. Should he jump or not? That's when people on the ground saw him. Instead of helping him, they started to yell at him. "Jump!" they said. He listened for a while, then he jumped. The story was on the news. It was a sad story about the boy, but a bad story about a group of people. How could a crowd be so cruel?

The crowd that watched at the trial of Jesus was cruel. Jesus had done nothing wrong. Barabbas was a murderer. Still the crowd decided, "Give us Barabbas!" Pilate asked them what to do with Jesus. "Crucify him!" they yelled. Pilate listened to the crowd and sent Jesus to the cross. Crowds can do wicked things. That's why the Bible says, "thou shalt not follow a multitude to do evil." Follow Jesus. He will help you say no to a crowd that is evil.

## ⤜ Thinking Deeper ⤛

Jerry Falwell was a high profile Baptist preacher who made a mark on America. He was instrumental in launching crisis pregnancy centers all around the country. He founded an association called Moral Majority which informed churches throughout the nation about moral issues and the need to get involved. He was a significant factor in the election of Ronald Reagan as President of the United States.

Falwell was not loved by everybody. When he died, people from the abortion movement and those who promoted same-sex lifestyles rejoiced. In the mainstream media, reports of Falwell's death were accompanied by statements of glee from these elements as well as people from Hollywood. Why was there so much hatred? The answer can be found in John's discussion of why Cain killed Abel. "And wherefore slew he him? Because his own works were evil, and his brother's righteous."

Why did the people choose Barabbas? Why did they crucify Jesus? Why did people rejoice at Falwell's death? Why did Cain kill Abel? Because wicked men do not want to be confronted by their sin.

*Wicked men do not want to be confronted by their sin.*

**Bible Reading:** Luke 23:32-38

## Q166. Where was Jesus crucified?

### A. Jesus was crucified at Calvary.

Ford's Theatre in Washington, D. C., is a historic place. It was there that in 1865, President Abraham Lincoln was shot by John Wilkes Booth. Many people visit Ford's Theatre every year. They go to see where Mr. Lincoln was sitting when it happened. They see the stage where the assassin jumped after the shot. It is a very interesting and very sad experience to go to this place of history.

There is another place of history where many people visit each year. It is outside of the walls of Old Jerusalem in Israel. It is a place that was called Calvary, which means the place of the skull. The soldiers led Jesus there. They then took spikes and nailed Jesus' hands and feet to a cross. Then they stood the cross up. Jesus hung there on the cross until he died. People visit that historic place to remember how Jesus was crucified.

 **Thinking Deeper**

Is the crucifixion of Christ a historical fact? Does it really matter whether or not Jesus was literally crucified on a cross that was made of wood? Some argue that what matters is not whether the story of Jesus is factual, but that there is a "deeper meaning" behind the story. That "deeper meaning" is where truth can be found for each individual. Each person must find that deeper meaning for himself. This view of the Biblical record is called liberalism. It is a belief that the Bible is a not necessarily true but there is somehow a truth to be learned through the Bible on a deeper level. In fact, liberals get offended by the suggestion that the Bible is a true record of actual happenings, and that the Bible is truly the authoritative Word of God.

In contrast to liberalism's empty leap of faith, St. Luke described the crucifixion as a real historical event. Jesus of Nazareth died on a cross at Calvary on a specific day in history. He really died for us. We can have real faith in him.

*People visit that historic place to remember how Jesus was crucified.*

**Bible Reading:** Luke 23:39-43

## Q167. What did Jesus tell the thief on the cross?

### A. Jesus told him that they would be together that day in paradise.

The great preacher John Wesley lay dying. Friends had come to be at his side. He tried to talk but it was hard. His friends could not understand what he was trying to say. He paused a moment, and gathered his strength. Then Mr. Wesley clearly spoke. "The best of all is, God is with us." He left a clear testimony of his faith and trust in the Lord.

Jesus was dying on a cross between two thieves. They were also dying. One of them wanted to find forgiveness for his sins. He asked Jesus to remember him. Some of the last words Jesus spoke before he died were to this thief. "Today shalt thou be with me in paradise." Jesus gave him hope and comfort. Anyone who comes to Jesus with a humble heart may also find hope and comfort. Just ask Him.

 **Thinking Deeper**

Does a soul that dies go to sleep until the last judgment? Some argue that when a person dies, he goes into "soul sleep" and will not wake up until the great day of judgment. What Jesus said to the thief on the cross contradicts the theory of soul sleep. Jesus told the repentant thief that they would be together in paradise that very day. This very new Christian who would die in moments would be ushered into the holy presence of God. He would not have to wait for the thousands of years to come before the resurrection of the last day. His spirit would go that very day to God who gave it.

When Christians die, they go to heaven. They are with the Lord. Their body is in the grave on earth, but they are together with all the other "spirits of just men made perfect." They are part of that "cloud of witnesses" who have made an abundant entrance "into the everlasting kingdom of our Lord." Just as Lazarus was accepted into Abraham's bosom, so are believers welcomed into heaven. Praise God for the blessed hope of those who follow the Lord Jesus Christ.

*Jesus told the repentant thief that they would be together in Paradise that very day.*

**Bible Reading:** Luke 23:47-56

## Q168. When Jesus died, where was he buried?

### A. Jesus was buried in the tomb of Joseph of Arimathaea.

In east central Kansas there is a small cemetery north of the small town of Melvern.  There are some graves from the 1800's in that graveyard.  At the back of the cemetery is an Indian grave.  It is evidently the burying place of a little child.  It is not marked by a gravestone.  Instead, there is an outline of small stones pressed into the ground surrounding the grave.  The outline is about four feet long and three feet wide.  Not many people ever see that grave, but a few find it and wonder what kind of story is behind it.

There is a very important story behind an empty tomb in Jerusalem.  It is the story of how Jesus died and was put in that tomb.  The tomb belonged to a rich man named Joseph of Arimathaea.  When Jesus died, Joseph took his body and put it in his own tomb.  Then a large stone was rolled in front of the tomb.  That's how Jesus was buried.

> *The Bible prophesied that Jesus would make His grave with the rich.*

### ❧ Thinking Deeper ☙

There is a rather strange report out of India.  In 2007, a rich man died and was buried in his car.  He had bought the car in 1958 and requested to be buried with it when he died.  His wish was granted.*  There is another rather amusing anecdote told of a man who requested to be buried in his Cadillac, with its plush interior, shiny paint job, and flashy hub caps.  As one of the workers at the site watched the car being lowered into the ground, he commented, "Now that's livin'!"  The trouble is, the one in the car was not really around to enjoy it.

Jesus was buried in a tomb belonging to a rich man.  Jesus of Nazareth was not a rich man.  Yet the Bible prophesied that He would make his grave with the rich.  Just as the Bible foretold, a rich man took the body of Jesus and buried it in his own tomb.  The death and burial of Jesus is part of the Gospel—"I declare unto you the gospel...how that Christ died for our sins according to the scriptures; And that he was buried..." (1 Cor. 15:3,4).

* www.freerepublic.com/focus/f-news/1811895/posts

**Bible Reading:** Psalm 22:11-19

**Questions in Review**

**Q165. When Pilate asked the people who should go free, Jesus or Barabbas,who did they choose?**
 A. The people chose Barabbas to go free and called for Jesus to be crucified.
**Q166. Where was Jesus crucified?**
 A. Jesus was crucified at Calvary.
**Q167. What did Jesus tell the thief on the cross?**
 A. Jesus told him that they would be together that day in Paradise.
**Q168. When Jesus died, where was he buried?**
 A. Jesus was buried in the tomb of Joseph of Arimathaea.

In September 2008, in Prince William County, Virginia, the son of Thomas Vander Woude fell into a septic tank. He was in danger of drowning. Thomas saw his son in danger and jumped in to save him. Rescue workers arrived and pulled them both out of the tank. The son was saved, but Mr. Vander Woude died. He died saving his son.*

God saw that mankind was lost. Man's sin separated him from God. How could man be saved? God sent Jesus to earth to save man. "God so loved the world that he gave his only begotten son." But the only way to save him was to die for him. Jesus died on the cross for our sins. He died to save us. If we believe on Him, we can be saved. "That whosoever believeth on him should not perish, but have everlasting life."

*Justice demands that the penalty of sin be paid.*

* www.catholicnewsagency.com/new.php

## ❦ Thinking Deeper ❧

Why did Jesus have to die? Was there no other way for mankind to be saved? There is some help in answering this question in the scripture which states that "if we confess our sins, he is faithful and just to forgive us our sins." God is just to forgive us our sins. Justice demands that the penalty of sin be paid. "The wages of sin is death." So because sin must be answered by death, one must die for sin. In our case, we all have sinned. That means we must all die. How then can God, who is perfect in justice, justly forgive us? The answer is that Christ died for all, the just for the unjust, that he might bring us to God. Because of what Jesus has done through his passion and death, we can be freely forgiven of our sins. So God maintains His integrity in forgiving repentant sinners. He is faithful and just to forgive us our sins.

There is no other sacrifice for sin. No other savior has ever been found that can satisfy God's just requirement of death for sin and yet forgive men. That is at the foundation of the reason Christians say there is only one way to heaven. Jesus, the perfect Son of God, has died for our sins. There is simply no other way.

*THE RESURRECTION OF CHRIST*

**Bible Reading:** Luke 24:1-7

# Q169. Early Sunday morning, what did the women find at the tomb?

### A. The stone was rolled away and the body of Jesus was gone.

Two boys got up very early one Easter Sunday morning. They were sure that their mother had some Easter baskets somewhere. No one else was awake, so they tiptoed through the house as they searched. When they looked in the extra bedroom, their eyes grew wide as they saw two baskets in the dim light. Their eyes grew even wider as they saw a brand new baseball bat lying on the stand beside the baskets. The boys crept back into their beds for a little more sleep with a warm feeling in their hearts about the surprise they had found. They could hardly wait until Monday to try out the new bat.

When the women went to the tomb very early in the morning, they wondered how they would move the stone that covered the entrance. What they saw when they got there was a great surprise. The stone was rolled away and the tomb was empty! Then they saw two angels who told them that Jesus had risen from the dead. They could hardly wait to tell the disciples what they had seen.

## Thinking Deeper

Before his death, Jesus very clearly told his disciples that he would rise from the grave. "For he taught his disciples, and said unto them, The Son of man is delivered into the hands of men, and they shall kill him; and after that he is killed, he shall rise the third day" ( Mark 9:31, see also Mark 10:34). However, they didn't understand. When the first day of the week arrived, the women went to the tomb with spices for the body. What they found amazed them. The stone was rolled away and the tomb was empty. Jesus was gone. Mary Magdalene's initial response was "they have taken away the Lord out of the sepulchre, and we know not where they have laid him." Why didn't they connect the absent body of Jesus with the resurrection?

Jesus had already told them he would rise on the third day. The evidence was right before them that something extraordinary had happened. The angels at the tomb told them that "he is risen." Yet they didn't understand.

Believing something so fantastic as the resurrection was hard, even for those who had the most reason to believe. No wonder Jesus said "blessed are they that have not seen, and yet have believed."

> *The evidence was right before them that something extraordinary had happened.*

**Bible Reading:** John 20:1-10

# Q170. What did Peter and John find in the tomb?

### A. Peter and John found the grave clothes and the face cloth.

Some boys in Israel were chasing goats in the hills. They saw a cave in the hillside and threw a rock into the cave. Crack! They heard the sound of pottery breaking. What could be in the cave? The next day they climbed up to the cave and explored. The found pottery, some with the lids still on, that had been there for two thousand years. Inside the jars were scrolls. They didn't know it, but they had discovered very old copies of the Old Testament. These are called the Dead Sea Scrolls. The world was amazed by what the boys found in the cave.

Many years before those boys found the treasure in the cave, some ladies went to Jesus' tomb on Easter morning and found something that amazed the world. They found the tomb of Jesus empty and his grave clothes still there. People have been talking about the resurrection of Jesus Christ ever since.

 **Thinking Deeper**

*The notable thing was that the clothes were undisturbed.*

When Peter and John went into the tomb of Jesus, they saw something that made at least John believe. What did he believe? Evidently he believed that Jesus had indeed risen from the dead. What made him a believer? The only two notable items in the tomb were the clothes that had been wrapped around Jesus' body and the head cloth. That's what they saw. What they didn't see was a body. Jesus was gone! The notable thing was that the clothes were undisturbed. In other words, they were lying there just as they had been when Jesus was laid in the tomb. And the head cloth was still wrapped together as it had been when it was wrapped abound Jesus' head. But the clothes were empty. Imagine the grave clothes with up to a hundred pounds of spices sprinkled in them making a sort of soft body cast. Peter and John saw them collapsed but neatly in place. For John, that was enough. The only explanation of those clothes lying there was that Jesus had actually risen from the dead and passed through the grave clothes, much like he later did when he exited the room of the disciples by passing through the wall.

Everything about the resurrection is miraculous. God intended it that way.

**Bible Reading:** Mark 16:9-14

## Q171. How did the disciples know that Jesus was risen?

### A. Jesus appeared to the disciples after he arose from the dead.

During a war, a mother got word that her son had been killed. She was very sad. Some time later an official from the government came to her house. "We have good news for you," said the man. "We have found out that we were mistaken. Your son was not killed. He is alive and is on his way home." The mother was very happy to hear the good news.

The disciples were very sad when Jesus died on the cross. Before he died, Jesus told them that their sorrow would be turned to joy. When they saw Jesus alive, they were very glad. We still rejoice that Jesus is alive. He is our savior and friend. Thank God he's alive.

## Thinking Deeper

There is an old story about a hunter who was shaken early in the morning by his Indian guide. It had snowed the night before, and the crisp morning in the Rocky Mountains greeted the hunter along with a whisper from his guide, "Elk tracks in the back of camp." The hunter was wide awake. "Are they fresh?" the hunter asked excitedly. "Elk still in 'em," answered the guide. The hunter was convinced by an eyewitness account.

When Jesus appeared to the disciples, their doubts about his resurrection were over. It appears that there were mixed reactions to the events on early Easter morning. The women went to the tomb and found it empty. They came with the amazing report to the disciples. Peter and John went to look. John believed, but Peter seemed to still have doubts. The other disciples had mixed reactions. They were "slow of heart to believe." But when they saw Jesus, their doubts vanished. They were convinced of the truth.

At the heart of preaching the gospel in those early days was the claim that Jesus had risen from the dead. The gospel message is still not complete without the preaching of the resurrection. Christ is risen!

> *When Jesus appeared to the disciples their doubts about His resurrection were over.*

**Bible Reading:** I Corinthians 15:3-8, 13-20

## Q172. Why is the resurrection so important?

### A. If there is no resurrection, we have no hope.

A man named Voltaire was a famous atheist. He didn't believe in God. When he was dying, he spoke to his doctor. "I will give you half of what I am worth if you will give me six months' life." The doctor told him he couldn't give him more time to live. "Then I shall go to hell," said Voltaire. He had no hope when he was dying.

Christians have hope when they are dying because of the resurrection. Because Jesus arose, those who trust him will also rise from the dead to be with him forever. People who don't trust in Jesus don't have that hope. If there is no resurrection, no one has hope.

## ～ **Thinking Deeper** ～

Theologian Lloyd Greening has stated that the resurrection of Jesus "has to do with faith rather than objective fact."* For Greening, there is no compelling historical evidence that Jesus ever rose from the dead. For Presbyterian minister Greening, that does not mean abandonment of the hope of the resurrection. The hope of the resurrection means "not the endless prolongation of a conscious self." Rather, it means there is some hope for meaning "in the lives of men who follow." If you follow Greening's thinking and compare it to Hinduism where the individual completely loses self awareness and becomes one with the universe, you find no difference. Ravi Zacharias calls it a religion of death to the individual.

In contrast to these systems that see death to the individual as ultimate, the Biblical message of hope presupposes eternal life. Jesus said that the God of Abraham, Isaac, and Jacob "is not the God of the dead, but of the living." The resurrected Christ will raise us up also, and so shall we ever be with the Lord. Christ is risen!

*www.religion-online.org/showbook.asp?title=2734

> *If there is no resurrection, no one has hope.*

**Bible Reading:**  Psalm 16:6-11

**Questions in Review**

**Q169. Early Sunday morning, what did the women find at the tomb?**
   **A. The stone was rolled away and the body of Jesus was gone.**
**Q170. What did Peter and John find in the tomb?**
   **A. Peter and John found the grave clothes and the face cloth.**
**Q171. How did the disciples know that Jesus was risen?**
   **A. Jesus appeared to the disciples after he was risen from the dead**
**Q172. Why is the resurrection so important?**
   **A. If there is no resurrection, we have no hope.**

Do you believe in angels?  A family in Africa did.  Their little girl was lost in the wild.  For a whole night she stayed by herself.  In the morning her father found her.  He asked his daughter if she had been afraid.  The girl told him that some nice yellow dogs stayed with her all night.  The father looked around and saw lion tracks all around where the girl had stayed.  That family believes that God's protecting angels stayed with the little girl through the night.

Angels were important in the story of the resurrection.  An angel rolled the stone away from the tomb.  Angels told the women that Jesus had risen. They told the women to take the message of the resurrection to the disciples. God still uses angels.  They are "ministering spirits, sent forth to minister for them who shall be heirs of salvation."

## Thinking Deeper

Historic Christianity is a supernatural religion based on significant activity of God in the world.  God created the world from nothing.  God killed animals and made clothes to cover Adam and Eve after they sinned.  God called Abraham.  God spoke to Moses from a burning bush.  God parted the Red Sea and the Jordan River.  God spoke to prophets.  God's Son came to earth in the form of a man, died, and then rose from the dead. God confronted Saul of Tarsus on the road to Damascus, spoke to him and changed his life.  God continues to call men to follow Him and does miracles in the lives of people who believe Him.

The humanists/naturalists/materialists can't allow for any of these miracles.  By definition they can't admit to anything supernatural.  However, they can neither refute miracles not stop them.  Sinners still get saved and God still provides for His people.  Christ is risen! Believers trust him who said "I am the Lord, the God of all flesh: is there anything too hard for me?"

*Naturalists can neither refute miracles nor stop them.*

---

**BIRTH OF THE EARLY CHURCH**

**Bible Reading:** Acts 1:1-8

## Q173. What promise did Jesus give the disciples?

### A. Jesus promised that the Holy Ghost would give them power to be witnesses of him.

Every Sunday, a small girl went to the community center where there was a church service. She learned the songs and memory verses. She listened carefully to the Bible story. When she would go home, she would try to remember everything she learned and tell her family what she had heard. She wanted them to know what the Bible said and how Jesus loved them, too.

Jesus told his disciples that the Holy Spirit would give them power to be witnesses. God would use them to tell others about Him. God's Spirit would live in their hearts. He would give them power to show others that Jesus loved them. You can be a witness also. Ask God to fill you with the Holy Spirit and make you His witness.

## ∽ Thinking Deeper ∽

Lee was a milkman who made home deliveries. One of his stops was to a house in the country on a twenty-three acre parcel of land. Lee didn't mind making that stop except on Saturdays when the father of the family was home. That man kept talking to him about Jesus. It made Lee nervous. He couldn't get away from what he had heard. That man was persistent and persuasive. Months went by and the milkman became miserable. He recognized that he was a sinner and needed a savior. Finally, Lee gave in to the work of the Holy Spirit in his heart. He repented of his sins and trusted Jesus Christ as his Lord and Savior. It was because of that man who kept telling him about Jesus. That's what Lee said at the man's funeral.

After Jesus rose from the dead, he was with his disciples. They were excited that he would now bring back Israel to its proper place. Would he overthrow Rome and re-establish Israel as a sovereign nation with its own king? "Lord, wilt thou at this time restore again the kingdom to Israel?" Jesus turned the question. They wanted to know what Jesus would do. Jesus was about to tell them what they would do. "Ye shall be witnesses unto me."

We often pray that God will send a revival of His Spirit and do great things. He turns it to us. When we are filled with his Spirit He will make us His witnesses. His plan is to work through us to do His will. Who is the Lee in your life?

*Jesus told His disciples the Holy Spirit would give them power to be witnesses.*

**Bible Reading:** Acts 1:9-11

## Q174. How did Jesus return to heaven?

### A. Jesus was taken up into a cloud.

A lawyer from Pennsylvania was traveling. He stopped at a shop for a short break. He parked his car in the parking lot. But the lawyer disappeared. No one knew where he went. The police looked for clues, but could not find out anything about him. To this day no one knows where he went. Did someone kidnap him? Did he disappear on purpose? No one knows. It is a mystery that has not been solved.

Jesus was with his disciples on a mountain. He talked with them. Then he was taken up into a cloud. He disappeared. This event is called the Ascension. The disciples watched this happen. As they kept staring up at the cloud, two men in white stood beside them and told them that Jesus was taken up into heaven. They said that Jesus would come again in the clouds the same way that he was taken. Some day Jesus is coming back again. Be sure to be ready when he comes.

## ∼ Thinking Deeper ∼

Miracles make some people nervous. In this culture that is so fixated on naturalism, the supernatural is often looked upon with suspicion and spoken of with derision. Speak about the Bible as the Word of God and people call you an ignorant relic of some bygone era. Believe in creation and you are on par with people who believed in a flat earth. Promote personal, heart-felt relationship with the Lord Jesus Christ and you are a fanatic. So there are Christians who shy away from overtly emphasizing anything miraculous. The supposed "quest for the historical Jesus" was an attempt by nervous theologians trying to "demythologize" the story of Jesus.

The story of Jesus is full, from womb to the empty tomb, of the miraculous. It is just there. If it is a made up story, it should be shelved with the tales and abandoned as irrelevant. However, there is power in this story , and the power is good. There is force in its righteous claims, and the force is positive. There is transformation in its promises, and the transformation is virtuous. There is truth in the story, and the truth has not been contradicted. There is light in the story, and the darkness has not extinguished it. Jesus ascended into heaven. Jesus is coming again.

*There is light in the story, and the darkness has not extinguished it.*

**Bible Reading:** Acts 1:12-14; Acts 2:1-4

## Q175. What happened to the disciples on the day of Pentecost?

### A. They were all filled with the Holy Spirit.

In 1872, D.L. Moody was a great preacher. But he was working too hard. Some ladies told him they were praying that he would get his strength from God's Holy Spirit, and not from his own hard work. Mr. Moody began praying for that strength, too. One day while walking on a busy New York street, he suddenly became overcome with a sense of God's Spirit. He found a room where he could pray. He was filled with the Spirit. From that day on, his work for God was different.* He was a mighty preacher. Many people found God when they heard him preach. He had the power of God's Spirit on him like the disciples did on the day of Pentecost.

God has not changed. He wants us to be filled with His Spirit also. Jesus told us to ask for the Holy Spirit. "If ye then, being evil, know how to give good gifts unto your children: how much more shall your heavenly Father give the Holy Spirit to them that ask him?" (Luke 11:13).

*Nathan Oates, in Introduction to *I Believe in the Holy Ghost* by D.L. Moody, Billy Graham Center, Wheaton, 1997.

## ❧ Thinking Deeper ❧

Is speaking in unknown tongues "the evidence of the Holy Ghost?" Some people point to Pentecost as their proof that it is. One man who attended a Pentecostal church was denied membership because he didn't speak in tongues. He said he felt he had divine love in his heart and that was more important than tongues. That would reflect the sense of I Cor. 13:1. "Though I speak with the tongues of men and of angels, and have not charity, I am become as sounding brass, or a tinkling cymbal." The word tongues can be translated as languages. Sanctified speech is important, but the Bible points to a greater issue than even angelic language. It is love. "The love of God is shed abroad in our hearts by the Holy Ghost which is given unto us" (Rom. 5:5).

What is the purpose of tongues, as given at Pentecost? It was to convince unbelievers that the believers in Jesus had something real. Here is how the people from fifteen different language groups present responded. "And they were all amazed and marvelled, saying one to another... how hear we every man in our own tongue, wherein we were born?"

"Wherefore tongues are for a sign, not to them that believe, but to them that believe not" (1 Corinthians 14:22).

> *The Bible points to a greater issue than even angelic language.*

**Bible Reading:** Acts 2:12-17, 22-24, 32-38

## Q176. What did Peter preach at Pentecost that caused so many people to believe?

### A. Peter preached that since Jesus fulfilled the prophesies of the Messiah, was crucified by the wicked hands of the people, and rose again, they should repent.

A missionary went to an island where people had never heard about Jesus. He was able to preach to them. As he talked about man's sins and told what sin was, the chief of the tribe listened carefully. The more the preacher preached, the more angry the chief became. Finally he asked one of his men, "Who told that man about me?" Nobody had told the missionary about the chief. The word of God showed the chief what his sins were. He saw how sinful he was.

Peter's message at Pentecost made people see how wicked they were to have crucified Jesus. When they listened to Peter they realized that they had killed the Son of God. Many people were sorry for their sins. Many of them believed in Jesus as their savior and were baptized. This was the beginning of the Christian church.

### ∽ Thinking Deeper ∽

Charles Finney, the great nineteenth century evangelist, gave some advice about how to preach to be effective in bringing people to Christ. He emphasized the need to speak to the conscience. There are times when an appeal must be made to the intellect, but the intellect can often argue against the message. It is more difficult to argue with one's own conscience. What was so effective about Peter's Pentecostal message was how it pointedly spoke to the people's sense of right and wrong. The crucifixion of Jesus had been less than two months before, and was still fresh on the minds of his audience. When he showed how Jesus had fulfilled the O.T. prophecies of the Messiah, including that he would not see corruption, but that he was raised from the dead, they were convinced that they had killed God's Son. They had committed deicide. "When they heard this they were pricked in their hearts." Their consciences were smitten. Peter's message brought them to repentance and faith.

It is doubtful that Peter's approach would be welcomed in contemporary seeker friendly churches. He actually said they killed Jesus with "wicked hands." But Peter was effective. Three thousand people came to Christ and the church was born.

*It is doubtful that Peter's approach would be welcomed in contemporary seeker friendly churches.*

**Bible Reading:** Joel 2:27-32

## Questions in Review

**Q173. What promise did Jesus give the disciples?**
    A. Jesus promised that the Holy Ghost would give them power to be witnesses of him.

**Q174. How did Jesus return to heaven?**
    A. Jesus was taken up into a cloud.

**Q175. What happened to the disciples on the day of Pentecost?**
    A. They were all filled with the Holy Spirit.

**Q176. What did Peter preach at Pentecost that caused so many people to believe?**
    A. Peter preached that since Jesus fulfilled the prophecies of the Messiah, was crucified by the wicked hands of the Jews, and rose again, they should repent.

One of the most important events in American history happened in what is called New England. The Pilgrims landed at Plymouth Rock in December of 1620. They started a new community in a new country. The new colony was started with 102 people. It took several years before the people understood how to live in the new world. The first Thanksgiving was held in the Fall of 1621. The Pilgrims gave thanks to God for their harvest and for His help in starting their life in the new world. These Pilgrims were part of the church. They were followers of Jesus. The church started many years before they ever came to America.

*What Christians call the church began when the Holy Spirit came upon the disciples at Pentecost.*

What Christians call the church began when the Holy Spirit came upon the disciples at Pentecost. When Peter and the apostles preached, 3000 people believed in Jesus and were baptized. The church began to grow. If you are a follower of Jesus, you are part of that church.

## ❧ Thinking Deeper ☙

The church has emerged in many different forms. Some congregations are small, some are large, some are wealthy, others are poor, some are highly organized, others are very simple. But all have the same beginning, and all come into the true church the same way. Jesus said, "Ye must be born again." People are not part of the church by natural birth, but by spiritual birth.

When the disciples were filled with the Holy Spirit, they preached Jesus and people were added to the church. When Peter and the disciples preached at Pentecost and in the days that followed, people would believe and be baptized. The Bible says, "And the Lord added to the church daily such as should be saved." From then on the church has added people the same way as in the early days. It is through the preaching of Christ that God has chosen to bring people into the church. We must keep preaching Christ.

**MINISTRY OF THE EARLY CHURCH**

**Bible Reading:** Acts 3:1-10

# Q177. How was the lame man at the gate healed?

## A. The lame man was healed in the name of Jesus.

A young evangelist was preaching in a country church in Kansas. He heard that a lady in the church had cancer. He became very concerned. As he prayed, he felt that he needed to go to pray for the lady. He asked the pastor of the church to go with him. They went to the lady's house. The evangelist prayed earnestly that the Lord would heal the woman. He prayed in the name of Jesus. It was not long after that the lady was well. She lived for many years after she was healed. She often thanked the Lord for healing her.

Peter and John saw the lame man at the gate of the temple. They told the man to rise in the name of Jesus. The lame man was healed. The man was so happy that he shouted and leaped as he praised the Lord.

## ～ Thinking Deeper ～

Rip Engle had been the head football coach at Penn State University for years. When he retired, the coach that followed him was a slight young man who had been quarterback for Brown University and then part of the Penn State staff. There were questions about the new coach. Could he motivate the players? Did he have a good philosophy for winning? Would he be as good as Rip Engle? Would he be able to recruit star players? Those questions have been more than answered. The year 2008, was the coach's forty-third season and as of then he had won 75% of his games. He learned well from old coach Engle and proved he was ready to coach.

Jesus had taught his disciples to minister to people. They had seen Jesus' ministry for three years. But Jesus had ascended to heaven leaving them to continue the ministry. Jesus told them His Spirit would be with them and fill them. When Peter and John saw the man at the gate, they did what Jesus would have done had he been there. They reached out and touched him in the name of Jesus. The man was healed! Because they had been prepared and empowered, they were able to continue the ministry of Jesus. He is still with the church today, and we are to continue the ministry to needy people.

> *The man was so happy that he shouted and leaped as he praised the Lord.*

**Bible Reading:** Acts 4:1-22

## Q178. What did the leaders tell Peter and John after the lame man was healed?

### A. The leaders told Peter and John to stop preaching in the name of Jesus.

A boy in elementary school liked to read his Bible during breaks. His teacher saw him and told him he was not allowed to read it. She said he was doing something against the law. The boy told his mother that his teacher wouldn't let him read his Bible. The boy's mother told her pastor. The pastor visited the school superintendent. He told him that it was legal for the boy to read his Bible if it was free time. The superintendant realized that in a free country the boy should be able to read the Bible on his free time. So the boy was allowed to take his Bible to school.

Ever since the days of the disciples, people have tried to keep Christians quiet about their faith. When Peter was told to keep quiet about Jesus, he realized that he still needed to tell the truth. "We ought to obey God rather than men," he said. Christians should tell others about Jesus.

*Ever since the days of the disciples people have tried to keep Christians quiet about their faith.*

## ～ Thinking Deeper ～

A Christian veterinarian at a major American university used his contacts with farmers to drop a word here and there about his faith in Jesus Christ. Periodically, a farmer would not appreciate the witness. One complained to the department head who came to the laboratory with a letter. The letter stated that he, the veterinarian, would not speak about his faith while he was on the job at the university. The pressure was put on the Christian to sign the paper. He objected. "I have a Constitutionally guaranteed freedom of speech," said the Christian. "I will not sign the paper." The department head took the letter with him, unsigned, and the veterinarian continued to witness as the doors opened. That Christian knew about, and was inspired by, Peter's run-in with the religious leaders who tried to suppress his witness for Jesus.

Peter and John were bold in calling on the name of Jesus as they ministered to people in need. They knew that the only truth that would help people was in Jesus, for "there is none other name under heaven given among men, whereby we must be saved."

**Bible Reading:** Matthew 28:16-20

**Questions in Review**

**Q177. How was the lame man at the gate healed?**
   **A. The lame man was healed in the name of Jesus.**
**Q178. What did the leaders tell Peter and John after the lame man was healed.**
   **A. The leaders told Peter and John to stop preaching in the name of Jesus.**
**Q179. Why did Ananias and Sapphira die?**
   **A. Ananias and Sapphira died because they lied to the Holy Ghost.**
**Q180. Why was Stephen stoned to death?**
   **A. Stephen was stoned to death because he preached that the people had crucified Jesus.**

A boy was asked what "faith" meant. He answered, "Faith is believing what you know ain't so." That boy was wrong about faith. Faith is believing in things that are true even when you can't see them. Peter and John had faith and they told the lame man to walk. He walked. The leaders told Peter to stop preaching in Jesus' name. Peter kept preaching because he knew that Jesus was real. Ananias and Sapphira had the wrong kind of faith. They thought they could lie and get away with it, but they didn't. Stephen had the right kind of faith. He told the truth even when it cost him his life. Real faith is in things that are real, even when you don't see them.

You can believe in Jesus even though you haven't seen him. Many people have found out that Jesus is very real. He saves sinful people, and he helps Christians to be strong believers. He will help your faith.

> *Real faith is in things that are real, even when you don't see them.*

## ⟨⟨ Thinking Deeper ⟩⟩

There is a story about a liberal theologian who did not believe the Christian creeds. Yet he would go to church services and join in with the singing. It was during the speaking of the creeds that he refused to join in. What was the difference? In his mind, singing words somehow insulated him from their meanings. Since he sang them he felt he really didn't mean them. He may not be the only one who takes a compartmentalized view of proclamation. Another liberal preacher felt like he spoke the word of God when he preached, but when he left the pulpit there was nothing to it. No wonder children get the idea that faith is "believing what you know ain't so."

The account of the early church is filled with the reality of faith that is truly alive. Things happened. People were changed. The enemy was stirred up. Persecution came to the church. But in it all they were triumphant in faith. Stephen showed it well. From his shining face to his final words ("Lord Jesus, receive my spirit."), he showed that faith alive is faith victorious. Keep the faith. It is real.

**EARLY CHURCH MINISTRY**

**Bible Reading:** Acts 8:22-40

# Q181. What did Philip preach to the Ethiopian?

## A. Philip preached about Jesus from the writings of the prophet Isaiah.

David Denton was a preacher who wrote a book about a spy. The book was called *The Reverend Spy*. The spy was a young preacher who was able to help the government fight communist spies. Some things in the book caused people to wonder if David Denton himself was really the spy or was he writing about someone else. Who was the spy? It was a mystery.

Philip found the Ethiopian reading the book of Isaiah. The Ethiopian didn't know if Isaiah was writing about himself or about someone else. Philip told him that Isaiah was writing about Jesus. He showed how what Isaiah wrote about a lamb being led to the slaughter and not making any noise was what happened to Jesus when he was taken to be crucified. When the Ethiopian heard the Bible explained, he was convinced that Jesus was the savior of all men. He was baptized and became a happy follower of Jesus.

## ∼ Thinking Deeper ∼

A Christian worker was having a Bible study with a man from a sect-like denomination. When he brought up some of Jesus' teachings from the Sermon on the Mount, the man objected. He only accepted the Bible's instructions from the New Testament which were written after the Gospels. According to him, all pre-Calvary scriptures were no longer in force. The time that Jesus completed the work of redemption on the cross marked the beginning of the dispensation of grace. The teaching before that is not to be applied. Was the man in the Bible study right?

Philip preached to the Ethiopian about Jesus from the Scriptures. Those scriptures were from the Old Testament. During the early days of the Christian church the New Testament had not yet been written. Philip depended on the prophetic passages that described the Messiah as the foundation for his message. Later, when the New Testament writers mentioned the scriptures, they were talking about the Old Testament. The Old Testament is foundational to the New Testament. When Paul said "all scripture...is profitable for doctrine, for reproof..." he was speaking about the Old Testament. Of course, that applies to the New Testament as well. What we can be assured of is that the Biblical account of Philip shows that all scripture is to be used and applied. We are to study so that we can "rightly divide the word of truth," not reject it. The man in the Bible study was wrong.

*When the New Testament writers mentioned the Scriptures, they were talking about the Old Testament.*

**Bible Reading:** Acts 9:1-20

## Q182. Who convinced Saul of Tarsus that Jesus was the Lord?

### A. Jesus himself appeared to Saul and spoke to him.

Johnny Depp is an actor who played a character named Jack Sparrow. Some boys saw a flier posted that announced that Jack Sparrow would be coming a local store. They really wanted to go and see Jack Sparrow, so they got someone to take them. They were excited when they got to see Jack Sparrow. They got their picture taken with him. But something wasn't quite right. When they got home they looked at the picture of Jack Sparrow and the picture they had on a poster, and it wasn't the same person. They had been tricked by a look-alike.

Saul didn't want to follow someone who wasn't true. He didn't think Jesus was the Messiah. But Jesus appeared to Saul. Saul realized that Jesus was alive. That meant he was the Son of God. Saul was convinced. So Saul decided to follow Jesus.

> *The encounter with the living, resurrected Christ convinced Saul of the truth.*

### ❧ Thinking Deeper ❧

A college student was sitting on a wall just ready to light up a cigarette, when a youth worker approached, pointed at him, and asked, "Are you a Christian?" The student slowly dropped the cigarette to his side and said, "Sit down." During the conversation, the student indicated that he was searching and was ready to try a cult. "If that doesn't work, maybe I'll try Jesus." That student illustrates a problem that Christians face in telling others about Jesus. The problem is the diversity of truth claims. There are many claiming to have the truth. When one says "I am the way" and another says "No, I am the way" and that is repeated by numerous voices, it certainly creates confusion for any seeker for truth. How is one to know?

Saul of Tarsus thought he knew the truth. He was so convinced that he punished those who didn't agree with his traditional views. But Saul was changed. He had an encounter with Jesus, whom he thought was dead. The encounter with the living, resurrected Christ convinced Saul of the truth. People today need to have that same kind of encounter. We can trust that God, who is no respecter of persons, offers all men an opportunity to respond to the truth.

**Bible Reading:** Acts 10:1-6, 25-28, 34-36, 43-44

## Q183. What did Peter learn at the conversion of Cornelius?

### A. Peter learned that the Gospel was for Gentiles as well as Jews.

Places where people play golf are often owned by clubs. Some of these clubs only let certain people play. Even if you have a lot of money, you cannot play unless you are invited by a club member. Of all places to play, Augusta, Georgia, may be the hardest to get into. It is a very exclusive club. Most people can never play golf at Augusta. That's how the first followers of Jesus thought about the Gospel.

The first followers of Jesus were Jewish people. They thought the Gospel was only for them. People who were not Jews were called Gentiles. The Jewish believers in Jesus didn't think much about the Gentiles. But God thought about them. In fact, the Old Testament writers talked about how the Messiah would be a light to the Gentiles. God gave Peter a vision about how the Gentiles needed the Gospel, too. Because of the vision, Peter went to a Gentile home. It was the house of Cornelius. When the gospel was preached to Cornelius, his household and their friends believed. Peter saw that God cared for all people, both Jews and Gentiles.

## Thinking Deeper

During the latter days of apartheid in South Africa a farmer was hosting some Americans. As they traveled around his farm looking for game animals, they were discussing the rights of American blacks to vote. The Americans indicated that it seemed only right for blacks as well as whites to vote. Suddenly a baboon darted across the pathway in front of them. "I suppose you'll want to give that the right to vote next," commented the farmer. The Americans dismissed the idea. Animals are not human.

The problem of discrimination often has a component of evolution imbedded in it. If evolution has occurred, it could be that some humans are less evolved than others. The South African farmer, though he may not have admitted it openly, viewed blacks as lower on the evolutionary scale than whites. And to be fair, if evolution is true, then why not view different races on different evolutionary planes. But with no history to identify which race is most evolved, who is to tell? Hitler used the concept of survival of the fittest and wiped out those less evolved.

The Gospel is for all people. God made it very clear to Peter that he was to go to the Gentiles with the message of salvation. The Christian Gospel is for people of all "kindreds, tribes and nations."

*Why not view different races on different evolutionary planes? But with no history to identify which race is most evolved, who is to tell?*

**Bible Reading:** Acts 11:19-26

## Q184. Where were the disciples first called Christians?

### A. The disciples were first called Christians at Antioch.

The word *dinosaur* was never in use until 1841. A man named Sir Richard Owens put two Greek words together which meant "terrible lizard." Before 1841, if someone had used the word *dinosaur* no one would have known what that person was talking about. Before the word was used, other words described what we now call dinosaurs. People talked about dragons and monsters. The Bible used the words behemoth and leviathan. Now we just call them dinosaurs.

When Jesus called his followers to him, they were called disciples. In the first days of the early church, people who followed Jesus were called believers. After a while, the church was in Antioch. That is where they were first called Christians. Christians are believers who follow Jesus. If you are a believer in Jesus as your savior, and if you follow him every day, then you also can be called a Christian.

*If a Christian is a disciple of Jesus who follows Him every day, how can that person also be a disciple of the Beatles, who mocked Jesus Christ both by word and deed?*

## ∼ Thinking Deeper ∼

The 1960s were years of dramatic change in American culture. Traditions of long standing were questioned, then mocked, then discarded. Music changed drastically. The Beatles brought "rock" to the USA, and teens and college students quickly adopted the new style of music. With it came an acceptance of alternative lifestyles, including sexual liberalism, drugs, and rebellion against traditional American culture. At the heart of it was a rejection of the Judeo-Christian ethic.

Not to be outdone was a popular form of Christianity that accepted much of the new culture. "Christian rock" followed a few years behind secular rock, adopting not only the music, but also the rebellion against the established Christian way of life. Dancing in the sanctuary and heavy metal were part of the new Christian scene, as well as statistics that showed that Christian teens were little different in almost every way from their non-Christian contemporaries. There is a problem, though. What is a Christian? If a Christian is a disciple of Jesus who follows him every day, how can that person also be a disciple of the Beatles, who mocked Jesus Christ both by word and deed?

Just because people use the word Christian does not make them a Christian. A turkey can pin a sign on itself that reads "eagle" but that doesn't change it into an eagle.

If the word Christian means anything, then some people are walking lies. Be true. Follow Jesus. Really.

**Bible Reading:** 2 Corinthians 5:14-21

Questions in Review

**Q181. What did Philip preach to the Ethiopian?**
    **A. Philip preached about Jesus from the writings of the prophet Isaiah.**
**Q182. Who convinced Saul of Tarsus that Jesus was the Lord?**
    **A. Jesus himself appeared to Saul and spoke to him.**
**Q183. What did Peter learn at the conversion of Cornelius?**
    **A. Peter learned that the Gospel was for Gentiles as well as Jews.**
**Q184. Where were the disciples first called Christians?**
    **A. The disciples were first called Christians at Antioch.**

Tim was often grumpy. Things did not suit him. One day his brother John noticed that he was different. He was happy. He didn't complain nearly as much as he did before. He said he had gotten saved and now he was a follower of Jesus. John thought about the difference in Tim. "Maybe there is something to this being a Christian," he thought. Some time passed, and John gave his heart to Jesus. His life changed too. John told about the change in his life years after it happened. He was happy to be a Christian.

*The inside as well as the outside of a Christian is crafted by God.*

The Ethiopian became a Christian and was happy. Saul of Tarsus became a Christian and was joyful in following Jesus. His name was changed to Paul and he became a great apostle. Cornelius the Roman became a Christian and was happy. He was among the first Gentile believers. The disciples were so happy about following Jesus that people who saw them called them Christians. Being a follower of Jesus is a wonderful thing.

## ∽ **Thinking Deeper** ∽

Rolex watches are among the most expensive and most sought after watches on the market. They are worth thousands of dollars. They are also some of the most copied watches. A genuine Rolex is worth a lot. Copies are not worth very much. There are ways to tell if a watch is a genuine Rolex. Certain tiny marks on the band are a clue if the watch is genuine. Another difference is a very tiny etching of a coronet (crown) below the 6 on the face. Counterfeiters usually get it wrong if they put it on at all. Another major difference is often the weight of the watch. Genuine Rolex watches can include gold and other valuable metals that are heavier than the lighter metals used in cheap imitations. A trained jeweler can spot a fake with not much difficulty. Usually the inner workings of a fake watch are a dead give-away. The workmanship is so cheap and inferior that it is easily discerned. The genuine Rolex has superior craftsmanship on the outside and the inside.

Some religious people want to pawn themselves off as Christians. But the real thing is hard to duplicate. The inside as well as the outside of a Christian is crafted by God. "By their fruits ye shall know them," said the Lord himself. Don't settle for fake Christianity.

INSTRUCTIONS TO THE CHURCH

**Bible Reading:** 1 Tim. 1:1-5

## Q185. What was Paul's assignment to Timothy at Ephesus?

### A. Timothy was to be sure that the church taught sound doctrine.

A missionary came upon a village in the South American jungle. As he was visiting in one of the homes, he found various gods placed on a shelf. Among the gods was a picture of Jesus. "Where did you get this?" he asked. They told him that years before someone had come to the village and told them about Jesus. They put his picture among the other gods. No one stayed in the village to help them understand the truth that there is only one God. They needed more teaching.

Paul wanted to make sure that the church in Ephesus understood the truth about God. He told Timothy to stay there and teach right doctrine. They needed to know what was true. They also needed to know what was false. It is very important that churches teach the truth and keep false teachings out. Be sure you follow the truth.

## Thinking Deeper

There is a church denomination that professes to be Christian that openly celebrates homosexuality. It is their identification. Another so called Christian church has ministers who proclaim their worship to "Mother God," instead of Father God. Some who claim to be Christian openly support Marxist rebel forces in South America which take credit for killing people to promote their agenda. The religious landscape is littered by almost every conceivable belief. In every case, the leaders of these churches have, in the words of Peter, "wrested the scriptures."

By contrast, there are churches that are valiant for truth. Some have left their denominations to maintain their integrity. Others are under fierce attack by radical Hindus, Buddhists, and Muslims. Multiplied thousands of Christians each year are regularly attacked, displaced, harassed, or otherwise persecuted because they stand for Biblical Christianity. Their leaders have been careful to teach sound doctrine. Paul assigned Timothy to stay at Ephesus so that the church would be strong in sound doctrine. Every minister of Christ has the same task. Those that allow false doctrine unchallenged in the church are miserable failures as ministers of the Gospel.

*The religious landscape is littered by almost every conceivable belief.*

**Bible Reading:** 1Timothy 2:1-10

## Q186. What is very important for people who are part of the church to do?

### A. They are to pray and live holy lives.

Somebody told a joke about a not very smart girl. She went to the library and in a loud voice said, "I'd like a hamburger, coke and fries." The librarian answered, "Shhh. This is a library." "Oh, I'm sorry," whispered the girl, and in a very quiet voice said, "I'd like a hamburger, coke and fries." The story is funny because we don't expect to order food from a librarian. The library is a place to find books.

The church is for prayer and being holy. When Paul wrote to Timothy, he wanted him to help the church be what it is supposed to be. The church is not a building but is made up of people. Men who are part of the church are to pray everywhere and live holy lives. Women who are part of the church are to be modest in appearance and show godliness in all they do. It is very important that those who are part of the church pray and live holy lives. Otherwise the church is not what it is supposed to be. Take care to pray, and take time to be holy.

*The church is not a building but is made up of people.*

 **Thinking Deeper**

John Calvin was a leader in the Reformation. His *Institutes of the Christian Religion* were important in formulating the Calvinist, or Reformed, doctrines. A significant element in the Calvinist system is the doctrine of limited atonement. That is, Christ's atonement is only for those who are elected to be saved. And the elect are chosen by God with no preconditions. In very basic language, God only wills to save the ones He elects, and when Christ died, his death was only for the elect.

Part of Paul's exhortation to pray for all men tells us that prayer is a good thing in God's eyes. There is a connection between men's praying for people and God's desire to save people. Two truths stand out here. One, it is important to pray for people. The Holy Spirit inspired Paul to write "first of all" about this kind of prayer. Second, God really desires to save all men. Calvin's "limited atonement" must be rejected because the Holy Spirit's inspired message is that God "will have all men to be saved." Despite the twists and turns Calvin's defenders take to hold on to their scheme, there are too many "all's" that relate to God's salvation to limit it. Look at it again: "God our Savior...will have all men to be saved." Thank the Lord, "all" means that no one is left out. God wants you to be saved.

**Bible Reading:** 1Timothy 3:1-10

## Q187. What is required of those who are church leaders?

### A. Church leaders are to live blameless lives.

Benedict Arnold was an American general during the Revolutionary War. He was a good general and a hero at the battle of Saratoga, where he was wounded. But as the war went on, he thought the Americans would lose. He decided to help the British. He planned to surrender the fort of West Point to the British, but a British spy carrying a secret message with the plans was caught by the Americans. When Benedict Arnold heard that the spy had been caught, he escaped to the British side. After the war ended, he had to live in England. He was not welcome in America. Monuments that were made to remember his efforts in battle on the American side don't mention his name. He was a traitor.

Some leaders of churches do not live like a Christian should live. They are like traitors because they really help the enemies of God. True church leaders follow Jesus as closely as they can. They want to please God, not the world. Church leaders are to be blameless.

## Thinking Deeper

In September 2003, the Roman Catholic Archdiocese of Boston agreed to pay as much as $85 million to victims of child sex abuse by priests. In June 2005, San Francisco's Archdiocese paid $21 million, in 2006, the Kentucky Archdiocese of Covington paid S85 million, and in 2007, the Archdiocese of Los Angeles announced it would pay $660 million dollars for settlements of child abuse victims, some who were abused as long ago as 1946. A big part of the story of these abuse cases was that when the church leaders found out that a priest had abused someone, they would assign him to a different parish without telling the new parish about the former abuse. The church leaders were accused of covering up for the priests.

Catholics were not alone in their abuses. Several high profile televangelists were found to have been involved in immorality or financial corruption. In a major scandal, the head of the National Association of Evangelicals in 2006 was found out to have a homosexual relationship and also a drug problem.

The fallout from these ministers who harmed the name of Christ is continuing. Some people left the churches, others left their faith entirely. When King David sinned, the prophet told him he had given "A great occasion for the enemies of the Lord to blaspheme." It is important that we heed God's word which makes it very clear that church leaders are to be blameless.

> *Some leaders of churches do not live like a Christian should live. They are like traitors because they really help the enemies of God.*

**Bible Reading:** 1Timothy 4:1-6, 16

## Q188. Why is teaching right doctrine so important?

### A. Teaching right doctrine is important because living according to right doctrine has promise of salvation.

Many years ago on an "Unshackled" radio program was the true story of a preacher named Joe. He had a nice church with a nice congregation. He preached nice messages about living and getting along with others. But Preacher Joe did not preach the gospel. One day he was called to visit a man who was dying. As the preacher stood beside the bedside, the dying man looked into his face. "Why didn't you tell me, Joe? Why didn't you tell me?" The man was not ready to die, and his preacher hadn't told him the truth. That was a sad story. The good part of the story was that Preacher Joe later found the truth and was saved by putting his own faith in Jesus. Then he began to preach the gospel.

Church leaders are to teach the truth. The Bible is the truth. That is what leaders are to teach. If they teach people to live according to the Bible, they will keep themselves and their people from destruction.

## Thinking Deeper

*What good is religion that does not have a practical benefit? Not much.*

John Wesley helped people to order their spiritual lives. He helped them put their faith into practice. He was methodical in his own application of Christianity and helped others to carefully apply Biblical principles. It is an understatement to say that not all of his contemporaries were favorably impressed. Wesley's followers were called "Methodists" in derision, but Wesley was not deterred. He continued in his efforts at spiritual formation, and his efforts paid off. Wesley noted, after watching some of his elder saints pass from this life, that "our people die well." He saw the benefit of teaching Christians to "take heed to the doctrine."

What good is religion that does not have a practical benefit? Not much. When religious instruction allows for "sin every day in word, thought and deed," how is that a "doctrine according to godliness?" Instruction that gives more weight to the weakness of humanity than to the power of God's enabling grace fails to encourage people to believe they can live a victorious Christian life. Paul's instruction to Timothy was to promote the great doctrines that gave confidence in God's transforming and keeping grace in this present world. It is a saving message.

**Questions in Review**

**Q185. What was Paul's assignment to Timothy at Ephesus?**
  A. Timothy was to be sure that the church taught sound doctrine.
**Q186. What is very important for people in the church to do?**
  A. They are to pray and live holy lives.
**Q187. What is required of those who are church leaders?**
  A. Church leaders are to live blameless lives.
**Q188. Why is teaching right doctrine so important?**
  A. Teaching right doctrine is important because living according to right doctrine has promise of salvation.

"Pastor," complained an elderly lady one Sunday, "some young people are chewing gum in the church." The pastor answered, "Sister, the church is chewing the gum." The pastor did not mean that chewing gum is a good thing when God's people get together to worship. What he meant was that the church is not a building. The church is the people who are following God. On Sunday, the church is often gathered in a building. On Monday, though, the church is scattered throughout the community. In some countries where Christians are persecuted, the church must gather secretly. They are still the church even though they don't have a building.

The church is made up of the people of God. When Paul wrote to Timothy, he gave him instructions for the church. He did not write about a building. He wrote about the people who were saved from their sins and believed in Jesus as their Lord. If you are a believer in Jesus who follows him daily, you are part of the church.

*If you are a believer in Jesus who follows him daily, you are part of the church.*

## ∼ Thinking Deeper ∼

Firefighters were called to a church which was burning. The pastor found the fire chief. "Chief, this is the first time I've ever seen you at church, and we've been here for forty years." "Well, preacher," said the chief, "this is the first time I've ever seen this church on fire!"

It is true that some churches are rather lifeless, and many people have no attraction to a dull church. Churches are to be places that are alive. The church, after all, is "the body of Christ" and Jesus said, "I am come that they might have life." An alive church is a church that is living as God calls it to live.

The Apostle Paul, inspired by the Holy Spirit, was concerned that the New Testament churches demonstrated what God had in mind for His people, the ecclesia, "the called out ones." He encouraged them to pray, to be faithful to the Word of God, to live holy lives, to reach the lost, and to "earnestly contend for the faith which was once delivered unto the saints." We are to be part of that church which through the centuries has lived as God's special people. The world needs to see the church be what it ought to be.

# ENTIRE SANCTIFICATION

**Bible Reading:** 1 Thessalonians 1:1-10

## Q189. Why did Paul believe the Holy Spirit was at work in the Thessalonians?

### A. Paul knew about their faith and joy, and that they followed the true God.

Ivan had gone to war in World War I for the Russian army. He had been captured by the Germans and was in prison. A Christian lady came by the prison and gave him a gospel tract. When he read it, he realized he was a sinner. He asked God to forgive him of his sins and trusted in Jesus as his savior. The lady came back and gave him a New Testament. He read it and grew in his faith. After the war he went home to his Russian village. His family watched his life. "He's different," they said. "Maybe he's lost his mind. Maybe the war was too much for him." They saw that he didn't live like he used to live. As time passed, they listened to what he said about Jesus. They believed he was a true Christian. Ivan was able to lead his family to Jesus because his life had been changed by God.

Paul was encouraged about the Thessalonians. After they heard the gospel their lives were changed. They followed God instead of idols. They were joyful in serving Jesus. Paul was convinced that the Holy Spirit was at work in their lives. They were true Christians.

### ∽ Thinking Deeper ∽

Jenny, a teen aged girl, came with her family from Russia to America in 1929. Theirs was a Christian family. One by one she and her sisters had given their hearts to the Lord. When they came to America they looked for a church to attend. Their priority in the land of opportunity was to find a place to worship God in spirit and in truth. They did not want to become part of the world, which was so alluring. They chose to find God's people, where God was working, and where they felt his Spirit moving. When they visited the large city churches, they were disappointed. These people did not remind them of the Russian Christians, who were separated from the world. They searched for two years before they found a group of Christians that reminded them of the earnest Christians back in Russia. How happy they were to find sincere believers!

Paul was happy that the Thessalonians were sincere followers of Christ. Yet Paul was somewhat unsettled about the Christians. He was concerned that they might give up their faith, or that something would cause them to lose their love for Christ and for other believers. This letter was written out of concern that these Christians needed more than they had. Paul knew what it was. They needed to have their hearts made pure.

*This letter was written out of concern that these Christians needed more than they had.*

## Q190. What was lacking in the faith of the Thessalonian Christians?

### A. They needed their hearts to be established unblameable in holiness.

After a message at church, a boy went to the altar to pray to be saved. He went home from church and sometime later his younger brother talked to their parents. "I know he went to the altar, but it didn't work," he commented. The younger brother didn't see what he expected to see in a Christian. Sometimes children do not understand what it means to be a Christian. Sometimes they do. They see when someone doesn't act like a Christian. And they know that Christians should live in a way that pleases God.

When Paul wrote to the Christians at the church in the city of Thessalonica, he wrote that he was praying for them. He was praying that they would have holy hearts. If someone has a holy heart he will live a holy life. The Bible says "keep your heart with all diligence for out of it are the issues of life." Good things come from a good heart, and evil things come from an evil heart. Ask God to give you a holy heart so that you will life a holy life.

> *If someone has a holy heart he will live a holy life.*

### ❧ **Thinking Deeper** ❧

Jenny and her sisters from Russia were Christians who had come to America to find religious freedom. They diligently searched for likeminded followers of Christ. Eventually they became part of the Free Methodists where they heard about entire sanctification. When the girls heard the message about heart purity they came to the altar, seeking God's best. After praying in faith, they trusted God for His great work of giving them pure hearts. The minister, on hearing their testimonies, was grateful for the grace working in them. "These young ladies are spoiled for the world," he said. He was right. The long lives of those sisters were marked by dedication and service to God.

Paul's prayer was that the Christians at the city of Thessalonica would have their hearts made "unblameable in holiness." He knew that the establishing grace that comes from a heart made pure by God's gracious work was important for them. God's purpose for His people is that their hearts are made perfect in love. That is the heart of entire sanctification. When a person "loves God with his whole heart, soul and mind, and loves his neighbor as himself," he is exhibiting the character of the sanctified life. Paul prayed for that kind of life for the Thessalonian Christians.

**Bible Reading:** 1 Thessalonians 4:1-8

# Q191. To what did God call His people?
## A. God called his people to holiness.

It had rained in Kansas for several days. A girl and her younger brother saw a small pool of water. It looked like fun. First they waded in it. Then they started splashing. Before long, they were both lying down in the water. But they stirred up the muddy bottom of the pool. The water was dirty brown, and their clothes, which had been clean and nice, became muddy. In fact, both of them were caked in mud, even on their faces. When they came home, they had to be hosed off. It took a lot of scrubbing to make them clean again.

When God calls people to follow Him, he calls them not to be dirty with sin, but to keep themselves clean. He is not talking about clean clothes but about clean hearts. God has not called us unto uncleanness. He has called us to be holy. If you follow Jesus, you will follow a clean and holy life. Jesus came "to cleanse us in his own blood." When you know you have some uncleanness in your heart, go to God in prayer. Ask Him to make you clean. "Create in me a clean heart, Oh God" (Ps. 51:10).

## ~ Thinking Deeper ~

Pietism was a movement that began among Lutherans in the seventeenth century. It gained popularity because the church seemed to be focused on liturgy but lacking in practical Christian graces. Later, John Wesley was influenced by pietistic thinking in his formulation of the doctrine of Christian perfection, commonly known as "holiness" in our day. Some people are nervous about pietism, even considering it to be heresy. Calling for Christian graces to be lived out in one's practical life is seen by some as diminishing grace. This fits nicely with the current emphasis on Reformed Theology, but, as Wesley said in dealing with similar objections to holiness in his day, "What shall we do with our Bibles?"

There is no question that the Bible demands holiness. "Be ye holy," wrote the inspired Peter. "Follow peace with all men and holiness, without which no man shall see the Lord," affirmed the writer of Hebrews. And Paul wrote, "God has called us...unto holiness." It is probably true that some proponents of pietism got it wrong and emphasized human efforts instead of God's grace. But it is also true that the grace described in the Bible teaches us that we should "deny ungodliness and worldly lusts and live soberly, righteously and godly in this present world." The church today needs less profanity and more piety.

*God has not called us unto uncleanness. He has called us to be holy.*

**Bible Reading:** 1 Thessalonians 5:14-24

## Q192. To what extent will God sanctify His people?

### A. God will sanctify them wholly, their whole spirit, soul and body.

Amanda Smith wanted God to make her holy. She was praying to be sanctified. She was a wash woman, so she got her cleaning supplies and brought them to church. She put her brushes and cleaning rags on the altar. Then she put her soap supplies on the altar. Then she put her wash tub on the altar. "What else do you want, Lord?" she prayed. She felt like the Lord answered, "Now, Amanda, crawl into the tub." God wanted all of her. Not just her things, but her whole self.

God wants all of you. Not just your spirit, or just your body. He wants to sanctify every part – your "whole spirit, soul and body." God wants to make us His through and through. Some people want to give God everything except one special thing they want for themselves. But God wants everything. When He has everything, then He can bless everything. Give God everything so you can have God's blessing in every part of your life.

*God wants all of you. Not just your spirit, or just your body.*

### ∿ **Thinking Deeper** ∿

A deep division has happened among some Christian groups over the issue of Lordship Salvation. Some who hold that Jesus will not be savior if he is not Lord have been banned from certain popular venues. Interestingly, these groups have a Baptist/Reformed theological framework which has historically downplayed the doctrine of entire sanctification. At heart of the division is the eternal security position that allows for people who have been saved to live in open sin and still be on their way to heaven. The Lordship salvation side says that if they live that way they were never saved.

The Wesleyan position on sanctification answers this issue before it comes up. When a person is saved, he is initially sanctified. That in itself excludes a life of sin. The further work of inner cleansing, called entire sanctification, comes when the earnest Christian sees the self-principle reasserting claim to rights. Entire sanctification deals not with open sin or rebellion. That was done at the cross at salvation. It deals with the inner struggle of self being yielded completely to God. At the point of crisis, an eternal "Yes" to God is settled. The process of continual sanctification follows as that "Yes" is daily applied to the issues of life. Have you said that eternal "Yes"?

**Bible Reading:** Hebrews 12:6-14

**Questions in Review**

**Q189. Why did Paul believe the Holy Spirit was at work in the Thessalonians?**
   A. Paul knew about their faith and joy, and that they followed the true God.

**Q190. What was lacking in the faith of the Thessalonian Christians?**
   A. They needed their hearts to be established unblameable in holiness.

**Q191. To what did God call His people?**
   A. God called his people to holiness.

**Q192. To what extent will God sanctify His people?**
   A. God will sanctify them wholly, their whole spirit, soul, and body.

Duncan Campbell was wounded in a war. He was lying on a field when a Canadian soldier rode by on his horse. When the battle was over, the Canadian came back and put Duncan on his horse. As they were riding, Mr. Campbell was praying. He had been saved, but somehow felt unfit for heaven. He remembered a prayer he had heard his father pray. "Lord, make me as holy as a saved sinner can be." God answered that prayer. Though wounded and bumping along on the horse, he felt clean in his heart. He felt like God had filled him with the Holy Spirit. God can make his people holy. He can make you holy. Whether you are young or old, you can have a holy heart. Jesus said, "Ask and ye shall receive, seek and ye shall find, knock and it shall be opened unto you" (Matthew 7:7). Ask. He will give you a holy heart.

*There must be a cleansing agent.*

## ∽ **Thinking Deeper** ∽

In the Old Testament, vessels that were to be used in the temple were set apart for temple use. They could not be defiled by other uses. They were to be clean. We who are His vessels for Christian service are to "cleanse ourselves from all filthiness of the flesh and spirit, perfecting holiness in the fear of God" (2 Corinthians 7:1). When someone is sanctified, he is set apart (consecrated) specifically to God. He is also made pure.

How are we made pure? "Jesus also, that he might sanctify the people with his own blood, suffered without the gate" (Heb. 13:12). It is true that we are to "cleanse ourselves," but that is not by our own means. There must be a cleansing agent. When you have grease on your hands, it does no good to rub your hands together. You must apply detergent, which chemically releases the bonds that holds the grease to your skin. Similarly, we are to bring ourselves to the "cleansing stream" where we find that "the blood of Jesus Christ, God's son cleanseth us from all sin." Come to God in faith for cleansing. "Faithful is he who calleth you who also will do it."

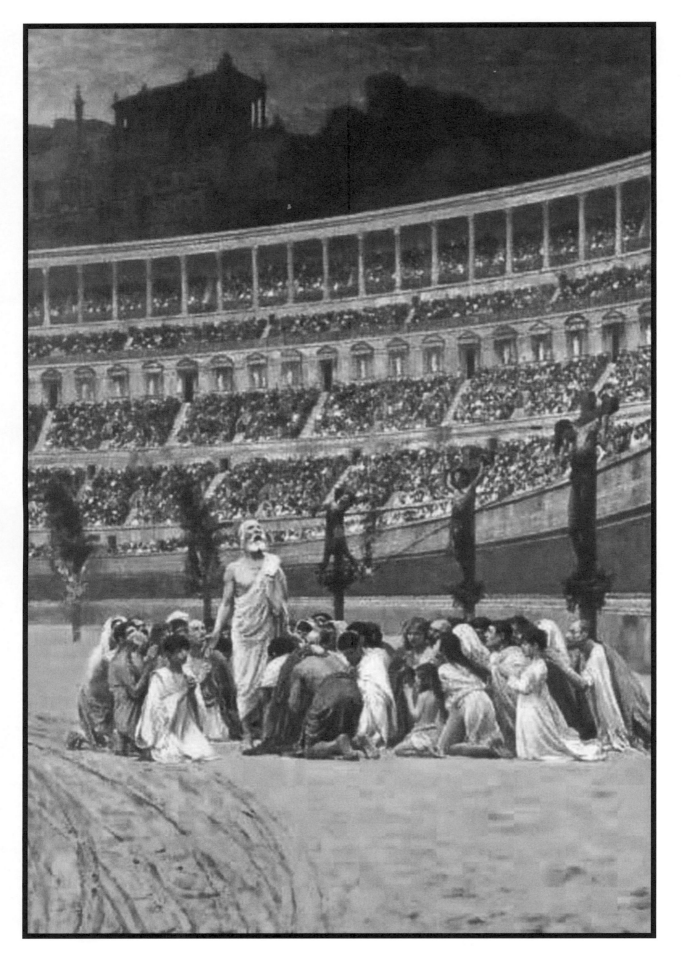

*FACING TRIALS*

**Bible Reading:** 1 Peter 1:3-9

# Q193. What is the benefit of having your faith tested?

## A. Faith that is tested brings glory to God.

A fisherman tied a bright orange lure to his line. He was beside a cool creek in Kodiak, Alaska. He cast his line into a deep pool of water. A fish grabbed the lure. The fisherman pulled back on his rod to set the hook. But suddenly the line went slack. The lure had come off the line. The fisherman realized that he had not tested his knot. He didn't have his lure tied on well. After that, the fisherman tested his knots when he tied a lure to his line. Later, a large salmon bit his lure. Because he had tested his knot, it held, and he caught the fish.

God will allow your faith to be tested. He will allow trials to come into your life. Maybe you have a problem getting along with someone. That is a trial. Ask God to help you. Trust Him to make you friendly and kind even to that person who is hard to get along with. God will bless your faith as you trust Him.

##  Thinking Deeper

A patient lying in a hospital bed was questioning where God was. He had been involved in ministry, but now was undergoing cancer treatment. Had God abandoned him? He asked God to help him. "Lord, I have been telling people that You can help them in their trouble. Where are You today?" The patient thought about Job, who couldn't find God when he needed him most. Job looked all around him, in front, in back, to each side, and couldn't discern God. But Job said, "He knoweth the way that I take. When He hath tried me, I shall come forth as gold." That morning some Christians came to visit the patient and encouraged him. Before the day was over, he realized that God had been with him. He hadn't abandoned him, even when he felt alone.

What kind of faith is it that quits when God doesn't seem to be there? What kind of faith is it that has to see or feel, or it gives up? That kind of faith certainly is not Christian faith. Faith goes on believing God's word despite the circumstances. How does God strengthen our faith? He does it by sending us trials. The trial of our faith is necessary if it is ever to grow. So Peter, inspired by the Holy Spirit, told us that the trial of our faith is "much more precious than of gold that perisheth." The trial of your faith is designed to strengthen your faith and to bring glory to God. God is working. Rejoice.

*If your faith is never tested, how do you know it will stand?*

> **Bible Reading:** 1 Peter 2:13-21

## Q194. When does God get the most glory from Christians suffering?

### A. When Christians suffer well for doing good, God gets glory.

Kalu Singh, a Christian college student, was traveling from village to village with a mission. He was showing a film about the life of Jesus. One day his bus was stopped at a check point. Some policemen came onto the bus. They beat Kalu, and took his papers. Later, when he and other Christian workers went to the police station to complain about the beating, they found the police were different. They apologized to Kalu for beating him and they asked him to show the film about Jesus at the police station. Kalu asked people to pray for the policemen. God used a bad thing to open a door for the gospel to be presented. Because Kalu suffered well, God was able to use him. (from www.persecution. org, Dec. 9, 2008, India)

Remember to walk like a Christian even when you suffer for doing the right thing. God will get glory through your life.

## Thinking Deeper

In 2004, approximately 75 million speeding tickets were issued to drivers in the United States, according to one estimate. Some of those speeders were Christians, who sheepishly pulled over to face the fact that they had broken the law. But some were likely not sheepish, but peeved, or even angry. Others may have been angry and kept their anger hidden. "At least I kept my temper when the cop pulled me over." But what good is that? The policeman was doing his job, and any heathen knows that if you get caught breaking the law, you pay the fine. It is no badge of honor to keep your temper when you are caught for doing wrong. There is little redeeming value in having a meek spirit when you've done wrong. You just plain deserve what you get. Take your medicine.

What counts as pleasing to God is when you've done a good thing and suffer for it, yet keep a good attitude. "For if, when ye do well, and suffer for it, ye take it patiently, this is acceptable to God" (1 Peter 2:20) .

*What counts as pleasing to God is when you've done a good thing and suffer for it, yet keep a good attitude.*

**Bible Reading:** 1 Peter 3:8-18

## Q195. What kind of witness is it to the world when Christians suffer well?

### A. Christian suffering brings shame on their accusers.

A mechanic became a Christian. The other mechanics in the shop watched his life. Was he a real Christian? As they watched him, they saw that he lived like a Christian every day. He trusted God. The workers noticed that he did things differently than before he was saved. After some time, one of the workers said, "If I ever get religion, I want the kind Merle has." The workers saw that Merle really tried to live the Christian life, even when it was difficult. They were convinced that he was a real Christian.

Have you noticed that the most interesting stories about Christians are about how they came through very hard places and still trusted God? Don't give up when you face a trial. It may be that God wants to show the world through you that Christian faith is real. Your faith can help you in your trials. Keep trusting. God will use you to be a blessing.

## Thinking Deeper

A man was preaching on a college campus. He was speaking in a loud voice outside of a classroom building. The campus police came and told him that he was disturbing the classes, and he should quiet down. The preacher became very agitated. He ran to his briefcase and pulled out some papers which he said showed his Constitutional right to preach in public. He yelled at the policemen that he could keep preaching. They tried to calm him down. A Christian who witnessed the encounter was ashamed of the preacher, not because he was preaching, but because of the attitude of the preacher when he was being confronted by the police. He did not exhibit a meek spirit. Any message the preacher had tried to preach was obscured by the angry spirit he showed during the encounter.

One of the best witnesses of a Christian is to exhibit a Christ-like spirit. When people see the quality of Christian grace in a person's reaction to difficulty, it is much easier for them to have confidence in that Christian.

> *Have you noticed that the most interesting stories about Christians are about how they came through very hard places and still trusted God?*

**Bible Reading:** 1 Peter 4:12-19; 5:10

# Q196. How is a Christian to respond who suffers for Christ?

## A. A Christian who suffers for Christ is to give glory to God.

The fifth grade class was learning how to dance. One of the boys in the class was not comfortable being part of the dancing lesson. His family values didn't allow dancing. He went to his teacher and told her his problem. He didn't feel clear about dancing. She understood and excused him, but the other students in the class did not understand. They thought he should be forced to dance. They began calling the boy names. "You're the teacher's pet," they said. The boy didn't think he was the teacher's pet. He only wanted to follow Jesus. He let the students talk. He was happy to be able to try to keep pleasing Jesus in school.

Sometimes you have to take a stand for Jesus. Other people may not understand and some of them may become angry. What is most important is to have God's blessing in your life. Then you can rejoice even if things get difficult. Stand for God. He will bless you.

## Thinking Deeper

A man had been a Christian for only a few months. Another Christian wondered how he was doing in his Christian life. "Are you suffering any persecution for being a Christian?" asked the interested man. The new Christian answered, "A little." "That's good," said his friend. He knew that everyone who follows Jesus would have some hard times. If it is very easy being a Christian, then it is hard for the Christian's faith to grow. Years went by, and the Christian kept following Jesus. At work one day, one of his fellow workers made an attempt to make fun of the Christian's walk with Christ. "You're all wrapped up in your Lord!" he sneered. The Christian listened to the words, not the tone. He felt good inside. He was all wrapped up in Jesus. His life was "hid in Christ." For years after that he remembered those words "all wrapped up in your Lord" and rejoiced.

You can rejoice when you are called on to suffer for Jesus. He will smile on you.

> *Sometimes you have to take a stand for Jesus.*

**Bible Reading:** Psalm 27:1-14

**Questions in Review**

**Q193. What is the benefit of having your faith tested?**
   **A. Faith that is tested brings glory to God.**
**Q194. When does God get the most glory from Christians suffering?**
   **A. When Christians suffer well for doing good, God gets glory.**
**Q195. What kind of witness is it to the world when Christians suffer well?**
   **A. Christian suffering brings shame on their accusers.**
**Q196. How is a Christian to respond who is called to suffer for Christ?**
   **A. A Christian who suffers for Christ is to give glory to God.**

"Can you drive a truck?" the foreman asked a young man who was looking for a job. "Yes," he answered. "Then be here in the morning," said the foreman. The young man reported for work. Part of his job was to mix concrete into the truck. He had to break open forty bags of concrete weighing ninety-four pounds per bag for each load of concrete. That first day he was worn out. The work was really hard. But at the end of the summer, he could easily lift the bags and break them open. He had gotten stronger and bigger. The hard work made him strong.

Just as hard work builds strength, so testing can build faith. Faith only grows when it is tested. At first, it seems hard to walk by faith. But as you keep doing things by faith and learn to trust God, you will find that your faith develops. It is good to have your faith grow.

*Just as hard work builds strength, so testing can build faith.*

## Thinking Deeper

Preparing for the 2008 Christmas season, the Creation Museum worked for months with the Cincinnati Zoo on a promotion that would allow people to visit both facilities and view their spectacular Christmas displays. When the promotion was made public, some atheists began a campaign against the partnership. They said some very ugly things about the Creation Museum and organized a major e-mail campaign to the zoo that resulted in the promotion being cancelled after 2 ½ days. "It's a pity that intolerant people have pushed for our expulsion simply because of our Christian faith. Some of their comments on blogs reveal great intolerance for anything having to do with Christianity," responded Ken Ham, the director of the Creation Museum.

Mr. Ham did not react in anger, and the results probably weren't what the opponents of the museum expected. The museum leaders were glorifying God for how he used the incident. There were so many reports in the press that Ham stated, "The media has promoted us far more than we could have imagined." Rejoicing in persecution gives glory to God and confuses the enemy.

## *LAST DAY WARNINGS*

**Bible Reading:** 2 Peter 3:3-10

# Q197. What will mark scoffers in the last days?

## A. Scoffers will make fun of Christ's return.

The sixth grade teacher in a Russian village asked each student in the class a question. "Do you believe in God?" Jenny listened as each of the students in her class said "No." When it was her turn to answer, Jenny answered in a quiet yet firm voice. "Yes, we believe in God." The teacher asked, "Do you believe that God is a spirit, and they that worship him must worship him in spirit and in truth?" Jenny answered clearly, "That's what the Bible says, and that's what we believe." Then the teacher turned to the rest of the class and told them how stupid it was to believe the Bible, since science had proved that the Bible was nothing but a fairy tale. But Jenny didn't let that harm her faith. She knew that God was present in their home and in her heart. She felt sorry for the teacher and for the other students who didn't know God.

The Bible warns us that in the last days scoffers will make fun of those who believe in Jesus. Don't be surprised if people make fun of your faith. Stay true to Jesus.

 **Thinking Deeper**

Those of us who believe in the Second Coming are looked upon with disdain by popular culture. It is similar disdain that is shown to those who believe in creation or intelligent design. The vitriol is unprecedented. We are considered stupid or retarded, and our beliefs are described as nonsense, wholly-owned subsidiary of the fundamentalist religious right, sectarian, threat to freedom, pseudo-science, flat earth thinking, substituting mythology for reason, un-American, fictitious garbage, and fairy tales. On reading the scoffer's views, one surely doesn't "feel the love."

On the other hand, there is seldom if ever any scientific discussion of the creation scientists' arguments for intelligent design or creationism. In fact, most of the animosity comes from people who are not scientists themselves, and most scientists who weigh in on the matter don't have the credentials to make the statements they make.

The whole issue comes down to presuppositions. Peter's inspired predictions of the last days indicate that the presupposition of uniformitarianism – "all things continue as they were from the beginning of creation" – will cause skeptics, "willingly ignorant" of the flood, to scoff at God's promises. The presupposition that God's word is truth opens the door to another view of the past – one that includes God's involvement. So it's belief versus unbelief. Theism versus atheism.

Keep the faith!

> *Don't be surprised if people make fun of your faith. Stay true to Jesus.*

## Q198. Who did Jesus warn would deceive many in the last days?

### A. Jesus warned that false prophets would deceive many.

A man walked up to a small boy and asked, "Could you help me? I've just lost my dog." The little boy's parents had told him never to go with strangers. So he said, "I'll go get my dad and he can help you." Then he ran home. The man really hadn't lost his dog. He was trying to trick the boy. He may have been a kidnapper. The boy did a wise thing by going to get his dad. Some people are very bad. They may try to trick you. Always be careful to obey what your parents tell you. Think about this; no adult needs the help of a child. Always check with your parents if a stranger approaches you.

Jesus said that we should watch out for false prophets. Some people will act as if they belong to God, but will lead people the wrong way. Many people will be tricked who listen to them. Always follow Jesus. He will lead you right.

## ∼ Thinking Deeper ∼

A preacher named Jim Jones was in a meeting with some of his staff when he said that too many people were following the Bible and not following him. Jones became a cult leader with as many as 8,000 followers. Eventually he led many of them to South America where they formed a community called Jonestown. People sensed that things were not right in Jonestown, and Congressman Leo Ryan traveled there to investigate. As he was leaving, some people tried to leave with him. On November 17, 1978, gunmen from Jonestown ambushed the group and Congressman Ryan was killed. The next day, Jim Jones declared a state of emergency, and everyone was either to kill himself or be killed. 912 people died that day because they had followed a false prophet.

Jesus said that in the last days many people would be deceived by false prophets. It is important to know the Bible for yourself so you will not be deceived. False prophets will teach other things than the Bible. Don't be deceived. Jesus said, "Heaven and earth shall pass away, but my words shall not pass away." Stay with the Bible.

*It is important to know the Bible for yourself so you will not be deceived.*

**Bible Reading:** 1Timothy 4:1; 2 Tim. 4:1-5

## Q199. What will be a major compromise in the last days?

### A. People will turn away from the truth and listen to fables.

According to a Greek legend, the Isle of the Sirens was an island in the sea where beautiful ladies would sing to ships that passed by. As the sailors heard the singing, they were so captivated that they would turn their ship toward the island. But the ships never made it because of the rocks. Many ships were lost. One captain named Orpheus decided how to keep the sailors from the rocks. When they came near the island, Orpheus began to play his lyre and sang so that he drowned out the other voices. The sailors listened to the musician and didn't hear the music from the island. They made it safely passed the danger.

Just as the Bible warned, there are many voices in these days saying things that seem nice to hear. But these voices often tell things that are not true. If you follow them, you will lose your faith and be destroyed. It is important to keep the truth in your heart and mind. That way you will save yourself from destruction.

 **Thinking Deeper**

An article on a web site was written by a man who said he'd "grown" beyond believing that the Bible was true. He scorned people who hold to the fundamentals of the Christian faith. He encouraged others to leave the "outmoded" ideas of Christianity. On the same website was an article promoting crystals as a way to find meaning and direction in life. Crystals! The contrast was notable. The Bible is scorned while crystals are exalted. It's Romans 1 coming to life. They serve the creature above the Creator.

People will believe in something. If they reject God, they will turn to something else. Post-modern man has tried scientism which has failed, and now turns to fables – the earth has a supernatural power of its own (Gaia), or life on earth was planted years ago by aliens, or life spontaneously generated out of nothing. Standing firm in the faith in these evil times is not stupid or foolish. It is the mark of wisdom. Fight the good fight!

> *People will believe in something. If they reject God, they will turn to something else.*

**Bible Reading:** Jude 1-4; 17-21

## Q200. What are Christians to do in the last days?

### A. Christians are to earnestly contend for the true faith.

A fifth grader listened to his teacher give a lesson on evolution. After a while he raised his hand. "I don't believe that evolution is true," he said.

The teacher looked at the boy and said, a little sternly, "I am older than you and I have a college education. I believe in evolution, and so should you."

The boy did not back down. "My father is older than you, and he has a doctor's degree. He doesn't believe in evolution, so you shouldn't believe in it either."

The Bible teaches us to be strong in our belief in God. Jude wrote that we should "earnestly contend for the faith." Don't let someone talk you out of your belief in Jesus. Be strong in the faith. God said, "Fear thou not; for I am with thee: be not dismayed; for I am thy God: I will strengthen thee; yea, I will help thee" (Isa. 41:10).

*This is no time for weak Christians. It will take earnest hearted believers to stand in these evil days.*

## ⤳ Thinking Deeper ⤳

Anti-Christian sentiment is growing in these times. Television, talk radio, print media, the internet, government schools, higher education, business giants, and political organizations are mostly controlled by people who have non-Christian philosophies. Books by atheists mocking Christianity are given prominent shelf space in book stores. This is no time for weak Christians. It will take earnest hearted believers to stand in these evil days. Yet we are not without resources.

Jesus said, "In the world ye shall have tribulation, but be of good cheer; I have overcome the world" (John 16:33). The inspired apostle wrote, "If God be for us, who can be against us?" (Romans 8:31). These are days that demand courage and boldness. Our Lord said, "I will never leave you, nor forsake you" (Hebrews 13:5). Take heart and take heed to Jude's admonition: "Keep yourselves in the love of God, looking for the mercy of our Lord Jesus Christ unto eternal life" (Jude 1:21).

**Bible Reading:** Luke 17:22-30

**Questions in Review**

**Q197. What will mark scoffers in the last days?**
     **A.  Scoffers will make fun of Christ's return.**
**Q198. Who did Jesus warn would deceive many in the last days?**
     **A. Jesus warned that false prophets would deceive many.**
**Q199. What will be a major compromise in the last days?**
     **A. People will turn away from the truth and listen to fables.**
**Q200. What are Christians to do in the last days?**
     **A. Christians are to earnestly contend for the true faith.**

A group of lions is called a pride.  Usually one male lion is the pride leader.  Sometimes a strange lion will come and fight with the leader.  If the leader loses he will run away, and the new lion will take his place.  This is the most dangerous time in the life of little lion cubs.  The new leader will often kill them. For the cubs, those are perilous times.  Their lives are in great danger.

The Bible tells us that in the last days there will be perilous times. Christians will be made fun of.  Evil powers will try to destroy their faith.  Many people will be deceived.  God's people must be aware of the plan of the enemy. We know that the devil goes around "like a roaring lion" seeing who he can eat up.  The words of Jesus give us encouragement for these times.  "In the world ye shall have tribulation: but be of good cheer; I have overcome the world" (John 16:33).

*These are perilous times for Christians.*

 ## Thinking Deeper

In many parts of the world, these are perilous times for Christians. Iraqi Christians have fled to safe places and remain in hiding.  Christians are overtly persecuted in many Arab nations.  In one part of India, Christians suspended their Christmas celebrations because of violence.  Chinese Christians continue to face government sanctioned oppression in a major crackdown on house churches.  In November 2008, thousands of Egyptian Muslims attacked a Coptic church.  In southern Mexico, traditionalist Catholics have stepped up oppression against evangelicals.  And as a throwback to Soviet policy, legislation in Russia has targeted evangelical Christian groups with the goal of making them illegal, forcing them to stop their Russian work.

These are perilous times for Christians.  In addition to the overt persecution, there is the continuing denigration of faith in the main institutions of society.  What is a Christian to do? Daniel's prophecy tells us what faithful Christians will do in these days.  "But the people that do know their God shall be strong, and do exploits" (Daniel 11:32).

## END TIMES CONFLICT

**Bible Reading:** Revelation 1:1-11

# Q201. What is the book of Revelation about?

## A. The book of Revelation is about future things.

A boy was mowing the lawn. He was thinking about how great God is. "If God knows everything, He knows if I will be saved or lost. If He knows I will be lost, then I'm doomed." He felt hopeless. But then another thought came into his mind. "What if I decide to trust God and follow Jesus? Wouldn't that change what God knew? If I decide to ask Jesus into my heart, then that's what God knew I would do. I will decide to trust Jesus." The boy went on mowing the yard, but his heart was lighter. He didn't feel hopeless just because God knows the future.

The book of Revelation is about future things. Some of those things are scary. Some are very wonderful. If you trust God, He will keep you through hard times. He will also give you wonderful blessings. Your future is in His hands.

 **Thinking Deeper**

Proponents of open theology deny that God knows what people will do in the future. He knows all possible decisions everyone can make and the consequences of those decisions, but He doesn't know what way people will take. The book of Revelation poses a problem for open theology. It includes major events that are definitely going to happen, and it also includes prophesies of people and their decision about accepting or rejecting God. Revelation is about "things which must shortly come to pass." Included in those things is that "the rest of the men which were not killed...repented not of the works of their hands" (Revelation 9:20. Not one of them will repent. God knows the future of these people. Did God determine that they wouldn't repent? No, because God "is not willing that any should perish, but that all should come to repentance" (2 Peter 3:9). So here God foreknows something that is not His will, yet He declares that it will happen. God doesn't make it happen, yet He knows it will happen. God sees the future. He "inhabiteth eternity."

*God sees the future.*

---

# Q202. What is the war that Revelation describes?

## A. Revelation describes a war between Satan and God's people.

Ruth, from the country of Uzbekistan, told her teacher that there is only one God. The teacher told Ruth, "Quit telling fairy tales or I will take you to the principal and you will be expelled."

Eight students in Eritrea brought Bibles to a camp their school required them to attend. They talked about Jesus to other students. They were punished by being locked up in metal shipping containers.

In India, about 60 children were attending VBS when radical Hindus disrupted their meeting, tore up Bibles, and chased the children away.

*The truth is that there is a spiritual battle going on for the hearts and minds of men, and on the dark side of this battle is Satan himself.*

These are examples* of how Satan is fighting a war against God's people. Satan hates God and God's people. Pray for those who are being persecuted. Pray that you will be a strong witness for Jesus. Don't let Satan defeat you. Trust in Jesus every day.

*from Kid's of Courage Archives on Voice of the Martyr's web site.

## Thinking Deeper

Nero was a ruthless Roman ruler who blamed Christians for the burning of Rome. He then had many of them killed in the arena. During the communist rule of Russia, Christians were called "sick" members of society who should be destroyed so that they would not contaminate the rest of society. In contemporary western culture, Christians are often blamed for being the cause of most of the wars of history. Christians are branded as intolerant, ignorant people who are actually dangerous to the rest of progressive society. Christians who believe in creation as an act of God, in marriage as between one man and one woman, and in the sanctity of human life from conception to natural death, are a hated minority.

Where does this visceral animosity against Christians come from? The truth is that there is a spiritual battle going on for the hearts and minds of men, and on the dark side of this battle is Satan himself. Jesus battled with Satan during his temptation in the wilderness, and we are in a battle with him every day. Be encouraged because Jesus has overcome the wicked one by his victory on the cross. That victory is ours "by the blood of the lamb and the word of our testimony."

**Bible Reading:** Revelation 13:11-18

# Q203. What is the mark of the beast?

## A. The mark of the beast is a mark that every one must have to be able to buy or sell.

A truck driver decided to play a trick on his friend who was riding along. When they came to a toll plaza he said, "I'm tired of paying tolls. I'm not paying this one." He stepped on the pedal and drove right through the plaza without even slowing down. His friend thought they were in trouble. Finally the driver told him that he had a pre-paid pass. Inside his truck was a special radio that sent out a signal and paid automatically. To go through the plaza without stopping, you had to have the special radio.

Revelation says that a time will come when everyone will be required to have a special mark. It may allow buying or selling automatically. But it will be identified with a very wicked being who will demand that everyone has his mark. People without the mark will have a very hard time on earth. The anti-Christ will be very wicked.

 **Thinking Deeper**

During the Nazi domination and occupation of most of Europe, Jewish people were required to wear an identifying mark. It was a prominent yellow star. They were singled out for "special treatment."

In the Soviet Union, a youth organization called the Young Pioneers educated youth to be good communist citizens on the community level. They wore identifying red scarves.

Gang members in the inner city usually have identifying marks that allow them special privileges on their turf.

Coercive societies often have a very visible means to distinguish those who are accepted and those who are not. The ultimate coercive society is yet to come. A leader will arise who will have society organized from the top to the bottom. He will be a great community organizer. He will require all people to receive a visible mark which the Bible calls the mark of the beast. This mark will be an open identification with the leader and his agenda. It will be a decision between Christ and the anti-Christ. That is a decision we must all make. Who will you choose?

*Revelation says that a time will come when everyone will be required to have a special mark.*

## Q204. What will happen to those who receive the mark of the beast?

### A. Those who take the mark of the beast will experience the wrath of God.

"If you're going to be part of our club you have to prove that you are brave. That means you have to steal something and bring it to the next meeting." Joey listened as the club leader gave instructions to become a member. Some really cool kids were in the club. He wanted to be part of them. But should he steal? "I can be tough," thought Joey. At the next meeting Joey was there with the expensive radio he had stolen. He was going to be part of the group! Suddenly, the door burst open and in rushed several policemen. "We're going to search everybody for stolen goods!" they said. Joey was found out. He had to go with the police and face what he had done. How he wished he hadn't joined the gang.

People who take the mark of the beast will be able to buy and sell. They will be accepted by the powers of earth. But that is not the end. God will come and destroy the kingdom of the anti-Christ. Everyone who has the mark of the beast will suffer the wrath of God. Don't ever side with evil. It is not worth it.

### ∽ Thinking Deeper ∽

After World War II, officials from the now deposed Nazi regime appeared in court at the famous Nuremburg Trials. They were accused for crimes against humanity and war crimes. The world had been shocked by the discovery of the holocaust, where millions of Jews had been brutally slaughtered by the Nazis. What was the defense of those who were involved in these atrocities? "We were just obeying orders." After all, resisting the powers over them could have been fatal. The world court at Nuremburg rejected the defense. Evil actions, even if they are ordered by higher authorities, are still evil. The war crimes perpetuators were convicted and executed.

The ruling authorities will demand that people take the mark of the beast. It will be a requirement to show support of the world order. However, that is not the ultimate authority. Anyone who takes the mark will be guilty of violating God's commandments. "Thou shalt have no other gods before me" (Exodus 20:3). Those who take the mark will have no defense. They will experience the wrath of God. God always has the last word.

*Those who take the mark will have no defense. They will experience the wrath of God.*

**Bible Reading:** John 5:25-29

**Questions in Review**

**Q201. What is the book of Revelation about?**
   **A. The book of Revelation is about future things.**
**Q202. What is the war that Revelation describes?**
   **A. Revelation describes a war between Satan and God's people.**
**Q203. What is the mark of the beast?**
   **A. The mark of the best is a mark that everyone must have to be able to buy or sell.**
**Q204. What will happen to those who receive the mark of the beast?**
   **A. Those who take the mark of the beast will experience the wrath of God.**

Davy Crockett was an American hero. He was one of the freedom fighters at the Alamo, a fort in Texas. They were greatly outnumbered. Colonel Travis was their leader. He called the men together and told them they could choose to stay and fight, or they could flee. He drew his sword and made a line in the sand. "Cross the line if you choose to fight." Davy Crockett stepped across the line. So did many others. This small group of men fought bravely, but they were all killed. Later, in an important battle, the Texas army thought about their bravery. They shouted, "Remember the Alamo!" They won, and Texas became independent.

*You will either fight on God's side or on Satan's side.*

You are called to make a choice about which side you are on. You will either fight on God's side or on Satan's side. You will be on one side or the other. You must decide. "Choose you this day whom you will serve" (Joshua 24:15).

## ⟿ Thinking Deeper ⟿

"Who's to say what's right and wrong?" That question marked many college debates on American campuses during the 1960's and 1970's. Truth was out and "experience" was in. Each person decided what was true for himself. There was no ultimate truth or morality. Tolerance of others, regardless of how deviant, became a mark of enlightenment. But that wasn't the only thing happening in the world. Islam was on the move, and fundamentalist Muslims had no qualms about what was right or wrong. They were right, and everyone else was wrong. Now the truth has come home to the West, but the West isn't prepared to fight. The West still doesn't know right from wrong, truth from falsehood. So many intellectuals endeavor to see a kind of moral equivalence among all the diverse beliefs of our day.

That will not last. There will be a clear line between God's people and those who follow the anti-Christ. Revelation is written partly to prepare us for the battles to come. Be ready.

*FINAL THINGS*

**Bible Reading:** Revelation 20:10-12

# Q205. What will happen at the great judgment?

## A. The dead will be judged by their works at the great judgment.

"Hey, Buddy. Can you come and play?" Danny and Davy wanted their neighbor boy to come and play with them. "Just wait a minute. I have to finish the lawn. I only need to clip around the edges. And I know where my dad checks, so I don't have to do it all." Buddy clipped the edges of a few places on the lawn, and then the boys ran off to play.

Maybe Buddy got away without clipping all the edges. Maybe he didn't. He thought his dad only checked a few places. It won't be like that at the great judgment. When everyone stands before God, every work will be judged. The Bible tells us that all things are "opened unto the eyes of him." In fact, everything is written in God's books, and at the judgment "the books are opened." God won't miss anything. Make sure you are living so that you won't be ashamed at the judgment.

## Thinking Deeper

The concept of man giving account of his works to God is one that is completely unacceptable to the secular, naturalist mind. The following quote illustrates it well.

"It is not that the methods and institutions of science somehow compel us to accept a material explanation of the phenomenal world, but, on the contrary, that we are forced by our a priori adherence to material causes to create an apparatus of investigation and a set of concepts that produce material explanations, no matter how counter-intuitive, no matter how mystifying to the uninitiated. Moreover, that materialism is absolute, for we cannot allow a Divine Foot in the door."*

Also hoping for a life without accountability to God, Carl Sagan said, "The cosmos is all that is or ever was or ever will be." He claimed that man is "lost in the cosmos." In contrast, the Bible declares that one day every man will stand before God and give account. Despite the wishful thinking and vain words of the naturalists, God has not ceased to exist. And not one word of God will fall to the ground. There will be a great judgment.

*Lewontin, R.C, "Billions and Billions of Demons", Review of "The Demon-Haunted World: Science as a Candle in the Dark," by Carl Sagan, New York Review, January 9, 1997.

> *Despite the wishful thinking and vain words of the naturalists, God has not ceased to exist.*

**Bible Reading:** Revelation 20:13-15

## Q206. What happens to people whose names are not in the Book of Life?

### A. Those whose names are not in the Book of Life will be cast into the lake of fire.

"Have you ever burned your hand on a hot stove?" Woody asked. He was the teacher of a class of boys. He paused as the boys thought about how much that hurt. Burns are awful. Woody continued. "Hell will be ten times hotter than that!"

We don't really know how hot hell will be. But we do know what the Bible says about the rich man in hell. He said he "was tormented in this flame" (Luke 16:24). It also says that hell is a place where "the worm dieth not and the fire is not quenched" (Mark 9:44). People in hell are in the worst possible place. God warns us about hell so that we will make preparation to escape. Only Jesus can save us. Trust in Jesus as your savior from sin and hell. "Whosoever believeth in him should not perish but have eternal life" (John 3:15).

### ∾ Thinking Deeper ∾

Fourteen-year old Jenny had come from Russia to America with her family in 1929. They had come across the ocean and were in New York on Ellis Island where the papers of immigrants were processed before they were allowed to be free in the society. While they were there, they noticed a man whose papers were not in order. On the other side of the fence were the man's wife and child. How they wanted their father to be with them in America as a free man! But that was not to be. Some agents in Russia had put together papers for him, but they were forged. The officials discovered the forgery and sent the man back across the ocean to Russia. For many, many years Jenny remembered how that man and his family were devastated. She often told that sad story.

Imagine how much more devastating it will be when people stand before God and find that their names are not in the Book of Life. No wonder there will be weeping and wailing. Now is the time to prepare for that day. Put your faith in Christ and commit yourself to Him. He is your salvation, sanctification and redemption.

*We don't really know how hot hell will be.*

**Bible Reading:** Revelation 21:1-7

# Q207. What will heaven be like?

## A. Heaven will be where all things are new and God dwells with his people.

Jenny and her family had arrived in America after escaping from repression in Stalin's Russia. As they rode through the streets of New York City for the first time, they were greeted by sights they had never even imagined. In Russia, they lived in a small village. Now they were surrounded by stores that were filled with things to sell. Neon lights lit up the city as though it was daytime. Jenny thought she was in a fairy land.

Compared to this world, heaven will seem like a fairy land. Everything will be magnificent. There will not be any sickness. There will not be any kind of suffering. Everybody will be happy. There will not be any sin. There will not be any temptation. No evil thing will be in heaven. No evil people will be there. Everything will be made new, and God will be with His people. Don't miss heaven. It's going to be wonderful.

## ➤ Thinking Deeper ➤

Joe Hill was a labor activist and a songwriter who wrote an anti-Christian song mocking preaching about heaven that included this phrase: "You'll get pie in the sky when you die -- that's a lie." Hill had a particular antagonism to the Salvation Army and "holy rollers" who "jump and shout." He went on to ridicule the concept of living for the next world and called the idea of a reward in heaven a "dirty lie." Factions of the labor movement have idolized Hill, who was tried and convicted for murder in Utah. He was executed in 1915.

Not all of the "struggling masses" have accepted Hill's earthly vision of what is important. One black minister reacted by defending the idea of heaven as something to look forward to. "Don't take that hope away from my people," he said. That hope is more important than any other hope. Rich people who "have it all" are going to leave it all behind. The "workers of the world" who deny anything but having their pie now, will find their pie is rather unappealing when they step into the next world. Christians have hope of heaven. That hope will not be a disappointment. "Eye hath not seen, nor ear heard, neither have entered into the heart of man, the things which God hath prepared for them that love him" (1Cor.2:9).

*Compared to this world, heaven will seem like a fairy land.*

**Bible Reading:** Revelation 22:8-17

# Q208. What is God's final invitation?

## A. God invites people who will to come to Him.

Jeffrey was excited. One of his friends had given him an envelope. In it was an invitation to a party. A lot of his friends were going to be there. There was going to be food and some games. The whole party was going to be a great time. Jeffrey was glad to get the invitation. He let the family know that he was going to go to the party. They were prepared for him when he got there. It really was a lot of fun.

At the end of the Bible, God gives an invitation for people to come to Him. "And the Spirit and the Bride say, Come" (Revelation 22:17). Have you accepted God's invitation? Have you given your heart to Jesus, to believe in Him and to serve Him? If not, give Him your heart today. He wants you to be with Him forever.

## Thinking Deeper

There is probably no greater contrast between Calvinism and Wesleyanism than their interpretations of the great invitation at the end of Revelation which says, "Whosoever will, let him take the water of life freely" (Revelation 22:17). Adam Clarke wrote that "no soul is excluded." In contrast, Herman Hoeksema wrote that any sinner's "will to come is a sure manifestation of God's eternal purpose of salvation concerning him." That is, if someone will come, it is because God made him willing, and he would come because that purpose of God in him is "irresistible." So, there is really no will of man involved except as God places it in him. Furthermore, man can't resist it. The contrast is that in Calvin's scheme everyone is excluded from the invitation except the elect, whereas in the Wesleyan view no one at all is excluded from the invitation.

The verse is clear. Do you have a desire to come to Christ? Do you have a longing for God's forgiveness? Will you come? Then you may.

*At the end of the Bible God gives an invitation for people to come to Him.*

**Bible Reading:** I Thessalonians 4:13-18

Questions in Review

**Q205. What will happen at the great judgment?**
    **A. The dead will be judged by their works at the great judgment.**
**Q206. What happens to people whose names are not in the Book of Life?**
    **A. Those whose names are not in the Book of Life will be cast into the lake of fire.**
**Q207. What will heaven be like?**
    **A. Heaven will be where all things are new and God dwells with his people.**
**Q208. What is God's final invitation?**
    **A. God invites people who will to come to Him.**

A small boy looked up into the starry sky. He saw the wonderful creation that God had made. He sensed the great expanse of space. He felt very small. Then he made a wish. "I wish I wouldn't have to die. I wish I could live forever." That boy grew up. Maybe he forgot his wish or maybe he didn't. But when he was a man he heard about Jesus. He heard how Jesus could forgive him of his sins and be his Lord and savior. That man opened his heart to Jesus. He found what his heart had longed for as a boy. He found eternal life in Jesus.

You can find eternal life by trusting in Jesus as your savior. You can open your heart to Him. If you do, He will cleanse you from your sins and come into your heart. "Behold, I stand at the door, and knock: if any man hear my voice, and open the door, I will come in to him, and will sup with him, and he with me" (Rev. 3:20).

> *You can find eternal life by trusting in Jesus as your savior.*

## Thinking Deeper

If the Bible is true, we are in the midst of a great battle between truth and lies, between right and wrong, between heaven and hell. That battle rages in the spiritual realm and greatly affects the world we live in. At the end will be the great judgment. There all those who are involved in the battle will be separated. Some will be cast into the lake of fire; some will be welcomed into heaven to ever be with the Lord.

You are involved in that battle on one side or the other. It is important that you are on God's side, "earnestly contending for the faith which was once delivered unto the saints." How you live and what you believe are closely connected. If you are walking in obedient faith which worketh by love, your life will be marked by holiness. If you are doubtful and self-assertive, your life will be stained with sin. How you live is an outgrowth of what you believe, and that will determine your eternal destiny. Jesus said, "Verily, verily, I say unto you, if a man keep my saying, he shall never see death" (John 8:51). Walk in faith and obedience with Jesus and you win.

GoLive Publications

## Resources by David Gordeuk:

David Gordeuk began his fourteen year ministry on college campuses with the Overcomers in 1970. Following that, he pastored in Kansas for 20 years. He is currently serving as Pastor for Spiritual Life with Hobe Sound Bible Church and as part of the Hobe Sound Bible College faculty. He and his wife Janice reside in Florida. They have four children.

### By the Book: A One Year Devotional Through the Bible

A devotional book that hits the high points of God's revelation to man from Creation through the beginnings of the nation of Israel to the life, ministry and redemption of Jesus Christ, and on to Revelation. Each lesson has an easy to understand section appropriate for children and a Thinking Deeper section that deals with worldview issues, doctrine, theology, and apologetics.

Hardcover
**$25 (includes shipping)**

### Discipleship By the Book: Anchoring Your Faith in the Word

This Bible based study can help even the newest Christian understand the basics of how a Christian is to relate to family, to church, to the community, and to himself. This book is a tool for individuals, families, classes, small groups, or for the whole church to understand the essentials of following Jesus.

Softcover
**$10 (includes shipping); 2 or more $7.50 each (includes shipping)**
**10 or more $5.00 each (plus shipping)**

### New Life By the Book: 21 Days of Personal Spiritual Formation

Even the newest Christian can establish a routine to build an ongoing relationship with Christ. These carefully chosen Bible passages and reflective prayers are designed to strengthen faith and encourage an individual's personal spiritual formation.

Softcover
**$4 (includes shipping); 2 or more $3 each (plus shipping)**

### Living for Christ

You can give this small book to new Christians to show them how to grow in their faith, develop Christian character and morality, build positive relationships, speak with grace, and be a Christian influence.

Softcover
**$5 (includes shipping); 2 or more $3 each (plus shipping)**

### Getting Ready for the Next Step

This little booklet can be given to people who are not sure they are prepared to meet God after they die. Written with the elderly in mind, this is appropriate to leave with them after a visit, or to send as a gift by mail.

Laminated Pamphlet
**10-19 $7.50 (includes shipping); 20 or more $12.50 (includes shipping)**

Available from GoLive Publications, P. O. Box 1065 Hobe Sound, FL 33475
or contact Hobe Sound Bible Church 772-546-5696 officestaff@hobesoundbiblechurch.com